The Experience of Samādhi

THE EXPERIENCE OF SAMĀDHI

An In-depth Exploration of Buddhist Meditation

Richard Shankman

SHAMBHALA
Boston & London
2008

Shambhala Publications, Inc.
Horticultural Hall
300 Massachusetts Avenue
Boston, Massachusetts 02115
www.shambhala.com

9 8 7 6 5 4 3 2 1
First Edition
Printed in Canada
♾ This edition is printed on acid-free paper that meets the American National Standards Institute z39.48 Standard.
♻ This book was printed on 100% postconsumer recycled paper.
For more information please visit us at www.shambhala.com.
Distributed in the United States by Random House, Inc., and in Canada by Random House of Canada Ltd
Interior design and composition: Greta D. Sibley & Associates

Library of Congress Cataloging-in-Publication Data
Shankman, Richard.
The experience of samadhi: an in-depth exploration of Buddhist meditation / Richard Shankman.—1st ed.
p. cm.
Includes bibliographical references and index.
ISBN 978-1-59030-521-8 (pbk.: alk. paper)
1. Samadhi. 2. Buddhist literature, Pali—History and criticism.
3. Buddhists—Interviews. I. Title.
BQ5630.S16S43 2008
294.3'4435 DC22
2008017613

CONTENTS

■

PART TWO
INTERVIEWS WITH CONTEMPORARY
MEDITATION TEACHERS

PREFACE

THE IDEA AND MOTIVATION FOR WRITING THIS BOOK HAS EVOLVED ever since first beginning meditation in 1970. Since then I have been fortunate to have studied and practiced with a number of teachers, each of them offering their own understanding and perspective of the Dharma and of meditation practice. Dharma practice comprises a wide range of wise instructions and skillful means, and each teacher will offer guidance based on his or her own understanding and experience. The resulting diversity of approaches to conveying the core teachings and the meditative path can be confusing, and there seemed a need to try to unravel the mix of conflicting views and styles of meditation.

Much of what is written and taught by contemporary meditation teachers is heavily influenced by the Pāli commentaries, which represent the understanding and interpretation of the Pāli suttas that existed sometime around the first century C.E. The commentaries evolved in the early centuries after the Buddha's passing and may not necessarily reflect how the teachings were understood in the early years. This is an area of great disagreement and debate.

Samādhi holds an important place in many Buddhist traditions. In order to understand the range of views and opinions on the subject, which exist even within individual Buddhist traditions, one currently has to study many sources, including the Pāli suttas and other foundational sources such as the Visuddhimagga, an extremely influential treatise written in the commentarial tradition.

This book differs from most books on samādhi in that it is not presenting teachings from only one teacher or perspective. Rather, the intent is to provide an in-depth, broad, and thorough examination of various foundational texts, interpretations of the texts, and teachings on samādhi, and then discuss some of the controversies, disagreements, and views on the topic. Clearly, there are plenty of areas in the suttas that can be interpreted in more than one way. Anyone engaging in a project of this sort will inevitably bring his or her own perspectives and views to the project. I try to be careful not to say that any particular interpretation is the "right" one, but rather to present the material in a way that is as unbiased as possible and then examine various interpretations.

Part 1 of this book examines in detail samādhi as presented in the Pāli suttas, without regard to the commentaries. Next samādhi is presented separately from the perspective of the Visuddhimagga, without consideration of what is in the suttas, so that the material can be viewed on its own. The two texts are then compared in a section discussing controversies surrounding these topics, such as what is jhāna; are there two paths of practice—tranquillity and insight—or one path that synthesizes the two; and is jhāna necessary for liberating insight.

In a few places bold text is used to highlight certain words or phrases that are of particular relevance within a quoted passage to the topic being discussed.

Part 2 of the book consists of interviews with well-known meditation teachers. Once readers understand the texts and range of understandings, they can see how and where each teacher falls within the overall landscape of teachings on the topic.

This book is targeted toward the general reader—meditators, of course, but anyone wishing to understand the range of teachings and mix of ideas on this topic so central to meditation practice. One of the challenges with a project of this nature is to delve thoroughly into the material without creating an overly academic or scholarly work, making it accessible to the general reader who might have only a basic exposure to Dharma teachings while still providing a comprehensive presentation of the material. I hope both purposes have been served.

It is of utmost importance that any study of texts or teachings be practical. Study of the old texts can be an interesting exercise in its own right, but study is of little practical value unless it serves to support the application of the teachings. But study is of great practical help if it brings a perspective and framework within which to understand and come to know the fruits of the teachings directly.

The great Thai meditation master Ajahn Chah said that study without practice is like a ladle in a pot of soup. The ladle is in the pot of soup every day, but it does not know the taste of the soup. We can immerse ourselves in Dharma study and talks, but if we want to experience the taste of the Dharma, we must put those teachings into practice through reflection and meditation.

A Note on Abbreviations

Texts from the Pāli Canon:

AN	Aṅguttara Nikāya (Numerical Discourses)
DN	Dīgha Nikāya (Long Discourses)
Dhp	Dhammapada
MN	Majjhima Nikāya (Middle-Length Discourses)
SN	Saṃyutta Nikāya (Connected Discourses)
Patis	Paṭisambhidāmagga

Postcanonical Texts:

Vism	Visuddhimagga
Vim	Vimuttimagga
Pm	Paramatthamañjūsā (Commentary to the Visuddhimagga)

References to DN and MN are to sutta number.

References to AN are to nipāta and sutta number.

References to SN are to saṃyutta and sutta number.

References to Vism are to chapter and paragraph number.

References to Patis are to treatise and paragraph.

References to Vim are to page number in the Chinese text.

ACKNOWLEDGMENTS

I AM DEEPLY APPRECIATIVE OF AND GRATEFUL TO ALL THOSE WHO contributed to this project, including:

Ajaan Ṭhānissaro, Bhikkhu Bodhi, and Gil Fronsdal, who most kindly and generously reviewed the initial draft of this book, providing extensive comments and invaluable insight.

Ajaan Ṭhānissaro, Bhante Gunaratana, Ajahn Brahmavaṃso, Pa Auk Sayadaw, Jack Kornfield, Sharon Salzberg, Christina Feldman, and Leigh Brasington, for sharing their teachings.

Barbara Gates, who reviewed some initial writing and provided feedback on the organization and structure of the book.

Special thanks to Joseph Goldstein for his many years of teaching, and to my wife, Kathy Grayson, for her patience and support in living with someone writing a book.

I am sincerely grateful to Shambhala Publications, and in particular to Emily Bower, without whose support this project would not have been possible. To the extent this book is helpful to Dharma practitioners, the project has been worthwhile. For any shortcomings in this book I alone am responsible.

INTRODUCTION

I considered . . . could jhāna be the path to enlightenment? Then came the realization: "That is the path to enlightenment."

The Buddha, Mahāsaccaka Sutta

EVEN BY THE ARDENT STANDARDS OF HIS DAY, THE AUSTERITIES and asceticism the soon-to-be Buddha had undertaken in the course of his spiritual quest were extreme, leaving him emaciated and weak, but no closer to his goal. After six years of seeking higher truth, he had been unable to achieve "any superhuman states, any distinction in knowledge and vision worthy of the noble ones."[1] Now he remembered a time as a child, resting in the cool shade of a rose-apple tree, when he spontaneously entered the first jhāna—a deep, meditative state characterized by powerful concentration, profound calm, and bliss—while watching his father lead a plowing ceremony. Realizing this was where the path to enlightenment lay, not in self-mortification, he took some food to regain strength and turned his attention in a new direction.

And so, on the night of his great awakening, the Bodhisattva entered the first jhāna, the second jhāna, the third, and the fourth. And when his mind was thus "purified, bright, unblemished, rid of imperfection, malleable, wieldy, steady, and attained to imperturbability," he directed it to the recollection of past lives, to the knowledge of beings living, dying, and being reborn in all sorts of circumstances, and finally, to the knowledge of the destruction of the taints. "When I knew and saw thus, my mind was liberated from the taint of sensual desire, from the taint of being, and from the taint of ignorance. When it was liberated, there came the knowledge:

'It is liberated.' I directly knew: 'Birth is destroyed, the holy life has been lived, what had to be done has been done, there is no more coming to any state of being.'"[2]

What is the nature of this jhāna the Buddha effortlessly stumbled upon in his youth and that became the basis for his great awakening and final enlightenment? Intensive concentration practices were well known and practiced by a number of renowned teachers of his day. The Buddha had practiced and excelled in several such meditations, declaring in each case that it did not lead to liberation. What was it about this jhāna that, rather than being a dead end leading merely to pleasant states of consciousness, became the pathway to enlightenment?

From soon after the Buddha passed into final Nibbāna, and continuing to this day, disagreements and disputes have arisen about the nature of jhāna and its proper place in the path to liberation. The more we listen, read, study, and practice, the less we may feel we understand what the "real," "correct" teaching is on the role and place of samādhi in Buddhist meditation and on the nature of jhāna. Everyone wants to follow the true path and to practice the authentic teachings. But what are they? Unraveling the mix of views and opinions about what exactly samādhi is and its proper place in meditation practice can be difficult.

Upon embarking on meditation in any of its forms, one regularly encounters a wide range of practices and teachings on samādhi. Typically translated as "concentration," samādhi is the quality of a mind that is calm and settled without distraction. There are so many teachers, each of whom seems to embody a depth of realization, teaching a range of often contradictory practices. Conflicting views exist regarding how much samādhi is necessary in meditation practice, and whether the meditator should emphasize concentration or insight practices. Virtually all Buddhist meditation teachers stress the need for some degree of mindfulness and concentration that are developed together to cultivate insight. However, there is a diverse assortment of teachings and opinions regarding how to meditate so as to develop these qualities in the ideal way.

Initially, we may begin by practicing a technique or in a style we were taught without understanding the essential place of concentration in meditation practice or the various methods for its cultivation. Some teachers maintain that jhāna might be of interest in some cases, but is not of particular importance or interest for insight meditation, teaching that concentration develops simply through moment-by-moment attention to whatever experiences arise. Through mindfulness you develop all the concentration you need. Others stress that deep samādhi is indispensable and, regardless of the technique or style of meditation you are engaged in, it is important to give attention to purposefully developing concentration. Among those advocating jhāna, there is no consensus on what the jhānas are or how to go about attaining them. Because there is no general agreement among teachers, students may become confused about the degree or type of samādhi they should cultivate, and how to incorporate concentration into their meditation practice. As our meditation practice matures, an understanding of the range of teachings and approaches to samādhi becomes increasingly important.

Rather than become disheartened or discouraged, we can appreciate the diversity of approaches and wide assortment of skillful means available to us. The Buddha himself recognized that individuals have widely varying natural abilities and tendencies, and that practice unfolds in different ways among individuals. Recognizing that there is no single right or best technique among these various approaches, our task, then, is to find a style of meditation practice best suited to our individual temperament and needs. To do so, it is necessary to familiarize ourselves with the range of practices and teachings regarding samādhi.

We should investigate any teacher, path, or practice critically in order to make our best judgment as to what is wise and skillful, and then put those teachings into practice. Their value and truth are verified through our own direct experience and our ability and willingness to look clearly and honestly at the results of our practice. Dharma practice is not a matter of finding the one "true and correct" interpretation of the doctrine and practice that is out there waiting for us to discover, if only we could find it, but instead, it's the ability to examine ourselves honestly, recognizing our strengths and limitations so that we may apply our efforts in the most fruitful directions.

The Buddha taught contextually. In any given situation, for any particular person, how the Buddha dealt with that situation, how he would teach and what he would say depended on the circumstances. Sometimes the Buddha would answer a question directly. Sometimes he answered a question with a question, or he might refuse to answer at all. At times he would tell people specifically what to do; other times he would simply tell them to do as they saw fit. The Buddha taught in an assortment of ways and offered many different practices. How he taught depended on the circumstances and what would be most effective to move people from ignorance and suffering to freedom and liberation.

Samādhi is an important aspect of meditation practice in any of its variations. The concepts of letting go and nonclinging are simple. Our conditioning and habit of mind are strong, though, and it is so easy for us to get caught over and over again in our daily lives. We need to acknowledge this and know it is the nature of being human. Understanding conditioning is the necessary first step, but it is not enough. We must find a way to recondition our minds, and ultimately free ourselves from conditioning altogether. It is through the power of a sustained, concentrated attention that the fruits of meditation practice are realized, so samādhi plays an indispensable role in mental training. Samādhi gives us strength of stability and continuity so that the mind is really resting in the current of nonclinging. Samādhi is associated with an assortment of insight and concentration practices, as well as combinations of both, so it is important to understand the range of teachings, the potential and limitations of the various practices, and our own aims and intentions for meditation.

Attaining samādhi, or any other meditative state, is not the ultimate goal of Buddhist meditation, and we should not make samādhi more important than it is. But we should not diminish its importance either. The habitual tendencies of grasping to pleasant experiences, getting rid of unpleasant ones, and the underlying root cause of ignorance are deeply conditioned in us. Samādhi is an important tool in gaining freedom from these tendencies because a certain degree of mental calm and steadiness is required in order to directly perceive these fundamental dharma truths and break free of the subtler tendencies toward clinging. The untrained mind is scattered and easily pulled moment by moment from one thought, sensation, or experience to another. A powerful, steady awareness is needed for strengthening the supportive conditions necessary for the mind to see more clearly into the subtler layers of ignorance. For most people, perseverance and patience are required to gradually strengthen the mind's power of concentration.

The many styles of meditation in the Pāli tradition can roughly be divided into three categories: practices that emphasize tranquillity or calm, those that emphasize insight, and those that develop both in concert. Some of us may be drawn toward intensive concentration practice, later making a conscious shift to insight as a distinct form of meditation. Others will emphasize the cultivation of insight from the beginning of our practice without devoting much effort specifically to concentration, allowing samādhi to naturally strengthen through the sustained, moment-by-moment application of attention toward all the changing experiences that arise and pass away during meditation practice. A third style of practice strengthens tranquillity and insight together.

Historical Background

Tradition tells us that within the first few hundred years after the Buddha's death, eighteen distinct schools had evolved. Of the early Buddhist schools, only the Theravāda (meaning "School of the Elders") has survived as a living tradition. Theravāda is the form of Buddhism practiced today primarily in Thailand, Myanmar (Burma), Sri Lanka, Cambodia, and Laos. The Theravāda scriptural writings, preserved in the Pāli language, are known as the Tipiṭaka, meaning "Three Baskets," or the Pāli Canon.

According to tradition, a council of five hundred elder monks was held shortly after the Buddha's death to recite and agree upon the content of his teachings. At this First Council, Ānanda, who had been the Buddha's attendant and companion during the last twenty-five years of his life, was questioned on and recited the Buddha's teachings. Upāli, renowned for his mastery of the rules of behavior, recited the monastic rules for the monks and nuns. The Buddha's discourses and teachings as recollected by Ānanda evolved into the Sutta (Pāli; Sanskrit, *sutra*) or discourse portion of the Canon, and the monastic rules into the Vinaya, the monastic code of conduct. Much more is unknown about the history and development of early Buddhism than is known, so the origins and evolution of the Pāli Canon are murky and little understood. These early verses were transmitted orally and continued to evolve. Only several hundred years later, when written down, were they fixed in the final form transmitted to us today as the Theravāda Pāli Canon.

After the Buddha died, his disciples engaged in analysis of his teachings by various methods, some of which were incorporated into the suttas. The third "basket" of teachings, the Abhidhamma, was also added to the Canon at this time. The Abhidhamma is an extensive technical, systematized analysis of the doctrine. When the Canon was finally written down, its contents were then fixed and thus could no longer be added to. However, further study and analysis continued, giving rise to a large body of commentarial literature.

Approximately nine hundred years after the Buddha's death, in the fifth century C.E., Buddhaghosa, a prolific commentator in the Theravāda tradition, produced his most important work, the Visuddhimagga (Path of Purification), a monumental treatise that attempts to describe the entirety of the Buddhist path of practice as understood in the Pāli commentarial tradition. Today the Visuddhimagga is a central text, extremely influential for Theravāda Buddhists, inspiring and shaping meditation practice throughout the Buddhist world.

As the canonical source for all the teachings, the suttas are authoritative. The Visuddhimagga carries tremendous weight in Theravāda Buddhism—particularly in Burma and Sri Lanka, less so in Thailand—though the commentarial work is not universally considered authoritative or accepted as a correct interpretation of the Buddha's doctrine.

There are disagreements over interpretations and meanings in the texts, over which texts are authoritative, and over whether the various sources can or should be reconciled. One of the confusions is caused by the fact that the Visuddhimagga and the suttas have been mixed together in many people's understanding. How one approaches these texts depends on one's perspective.

Methodology Used in This Book

There is no one place where the Buddha sets out a complete outline of his teaching and fills in all the details. Some of the suttas give a general sketch of the path as a whole (see, for instance, DN2); others fill in a few details here and there. In this sense, individual sutta passages are like pieces of a mosaic or puzzle that have to be fit together to form a coherent whole. If we want to gain a coherent and detailed picture of what the Buddha taught, we have to adopt an interpretative strategy to get at their full and proper meaning. Buddhaghosa applied one interpretative strategy, drawn from the Abhidhamma, in his Visuddhimagga and other commentaries. Some people feel that he did an excellent job, but there are those who feel that some of the information contained in the suttas does not fit into Buddhaghosa's system and interpretation. Thus there are two ways of approaching the information contained in a particular sutta: one is to interpret it in light of the system of the commentaries; the other is to try to use other suttas from the Canon itself to provide context for the information in question. This assumes that the suttas are generally consistent in their approach, and that a reading that can explain the suttas in a mutually consistent way is preferable to one that insists that they are inconsistent. This assumption may or may not be historically valid, but it does produce a more useful guide to practice than one that insists on taking surface inconsistencies as genuine inconsistencies. For this pragmatic purpose, I am going to apply this approach in the parts of the book devoted to analyzing what the suttas have to say about samādhi and jhāna.

The material in this book is presented in two main parts:

Part 1 focuses on samādhi in the Pāli suttas and the Visuddhimagga. Each of these will be investigated and discussed systematically, looking at the various ways and contexts in which samādhi is presented, both in its own right and in relation to other aspects of Dharma teachings. A chapter is devoted to summarizing and discussing disagreements and controversies surrounding samādhi.

Part 2 consists of interviews with eight well-known contemporary vipassanā and Theravāda meditation teachers. Some of the teachers included are known for their emphasis on samādhi and jhāna, while others do not expressly identify themselves as concentration teachers but rather as "general" meditation or Dharma teachers. This section of the book is intended to be practical, bringing the theoretical information in the first section to life, offering a range of views and practices from respected teachers, and highlighting various approaches to and applications of samādhi in meditation practice.

In reading the comments of these teachers, it is clear that there is quite a range of approaches to teaching and practice among them. Some adhere strictly to the Visuddhimagga's interpretation of doctrine and practice, while others do not agree with this explanation of the suttas, instead practicing and teaching in a style that does not rely on the commentaries for understanding. Still others find some, but not all, aspects of the Visuddhimagga quite useful, and so have blended and integrated portions of the original texts and the latter commentaries in how they teach. Not all would agree with the interpretations and conclusions I have drawn in the first section of this book.

The diverse views and approaches presented here are a real testament to the value and effectiveness of a wide assortment of skillful means. All of these teachers are well trained and practiced. All are grounded in a genuine depth of experience and wisdom.

Discussions will continue regarding the correct interpretation of the foundational texts and which style of practice yields the best results. There is one Buddhist path, comprising a great mosaic of systems and methods, and we are fortunate to live in a time when we can be exposed to the many teachings and approaches to Dharma practice.

PART ONE

SAMĀDHI IN THE PĀLI TEXTS

I

■

Samādhi in the Pāli Suttas

There are five detrimental things that lead to the decay and disappearance of the true Dhamma. What are the five? Here the bhikkhus [monks], the bhikkhunīs [nuns], the male lay followers, and the female lay followers dwell without reverence and deference towards the Teacher . . . towards the Dhamma . . . towards the Sangha . . . towards the training . . . without reverence and deference towards concentration. These are the five detrimental things that lead to the decay and disappearance of the true Dhamma.

The Buddha, Kassapasaṃyutta (SN16.13)

THE TERM *SAMĀDHI* BASICALLY MEANS "UNDISTRACTEDNESS." WHILE there is a range of views about the degree to which samādhi should be strengthened, what the best practices are that lead to right samādhi, and how best to incorporate it into one's meditation practice, there is no disagreement about the importance of cultivating the ability of the mind to settle. *Samādhi,* generally translated as "concentration," is derived from the Pāli prefix *sam,* meaning "together," and the root *dhā,* meaning "to put" or "place." It is related to the Pāli verb *samādahati,* meaning "to put together, to bring together, to concentrate." Thus, samādhi entails the unifying of the mind in a steady, undistracted awareness.

This key feature of samādhi, an undistracted singleness of mind, is understood in at least a couple of different ways. Some view it as an exclusive focus on a single object, while others as a broader state of awareness in which the mind remains steady and unmoving, yet aware of a wide range of phenomena around the meditation object. The Pāli term usually rendered as "one-pointedness of mind," *cittass' ekaggatā,* can be alternatively translated as "unification of mind." These two terms, "one-pointedness" and "unification of mind," are often used synonymously, but can also have different connotations. A one-pointed mind rests firmly and steadily fixed on the object of its attention. Practices such as focusing on the breath, gazing at colored disks, saying mantras, and visualizing build mental stability and calm and undistracted awareness. Concentration can ultimately be strengthened so that it will not waver from the object of its attention at all, to the point that no awareness of any other experience can arise. A mind concentrated in this way is called "one-pointed" because it is totally focused and fixed at one point on a single object.

A unified mind is also settled and undistracted, although not necessarily firmly focused on a single point. Rather than fixing the attention solely on one object or experience, the mind itself becomes still. All its faculties are brought together and integrated, remaining settled, unwavering, and clearly aware as a wide range of changing experiences unfold. In this case the mind itself is unmoving, but not the flow of experience. The distinction between these two forms of an undistracted mind is of particular importance in understanding the nature of the deepest levels of samādhi, known as *jhāna,* and will be discussed in detail in chapter 2.

Samādhi is cultivated through a variety of practices and attainments, leading to very pleasant states of tranquillity and happiness, as well as deepening mindfulness and liberating insights. The suttas give four distinct approaches to developing samādhi, along with the results one may expect from each, illustrating that there is not just one type of concentration or one correct or best practice for developing samādhi.[1] First, happiness is attained in this present life through developing the intrinsically pleasant meditative absorption states known as the four jhānas. Focusing one's attention on the perception of light, a second type of samādhi practice that cultivates a mind full of brightness, leads to knowledge and vision. Contemplating the arising, endurance, and passing away of feelings, perceptions, and thoughts, a third type of practice, gives rise to mindfulness and clear comprehension. And fourthly, through understanding the arising and passing away of the five aggregates (Pāli: khandhas), samādhi culminates in the destruction of the āsavas, forces of ignorance and clinging that keep us bound in suffering.

Perhaps the first mode, the attainment of jhāna, is about how to practice concentration, while the other three are talking about ways of applying that practice to other ends. Illustrations in support of this interpretation are found in the story of the Buddha's awakening, showing how jhāna practice can be used to foster knowledge and vision.[2] The Buddha recounts that after attaining jhāna "ignorance was banished and true knowledge arose, darkness was banished and light arose, as happens in one who abides diligent, ardent, and resolute."[3]

As an example of how developing jhāna gives rise to insight into the arising and passing away of the five aggregates:

> The destruction of the taints (āsavas) occurs in dependence on the first jhāna . . . a monk enters and dwells in the first jhāna . . . whatever states are included there comprised by form, feeling, perception, volitional formations or consciousness (the five aggregates): he views those states as impermanent, as suffering . . . as empty, as non-self.[4]

Of these four approaches, this leaves only the third: the topic of concentration used to develop mindfulness and clear comprehension. Given the fact that these qualities are emphasized in the formula for the third and fourth jhānas (to be discussed in detail in the following chapter), and that the contemplation described for developing this third mode of concentration (contemplating the arising, endurance, and passing away of feelings, perceptions, and thoughts) is similar to the contemplation described for the fourth (understanding the arising and passing away of the five aggregates), it is easy to relate jhāna practice to all three of the above applications.

The Importance and Place of Samādhi in Buddhist Meditation

We have only to look at how often samādhi is mentioned and the extent to which it is emphasized throughout the Pāli Canon to understand its essential place in meditation practice. The suttas are unambiguous regarding the importance of samādhi in the path of spiritual practice. The suttas state explicitly that it is not possible to attain the deepest stages of realization without a high degree of concentration, calm, and unification of mind:

> Without the peace of concentration in high degree, without attaining to calm, without winning one-pointedness . . . [that one] shall enter and abide in mind-emancipation, insight emancipation . . . that cannot be.[5]

Jhāna is especially advantageous to realization, being "entirely conducive to disenchantment, to dispassion, to cessation, to tranquility, to realization, to enlightenment, to Nibbāna."[6] With attainment of jhāna the mind is "concentrated, purified and cleansed, unblemished, free from impurities, malleable, workable, established, and having gained imperturbability,"[7] and can thus penetrate profoundly into the nature of the mind and body, allowing the deeper insights to arise.

The Buddha said that through the attainment of the jhānas many of his disciples reached the consummation and perfection of direct knowledge.[8] Yet, without jhāna:

> If there is no right concentration (jhāna, as discussed below), then the basis for knowledge and vision of things as they really are is destroyed for one who lacks right concentration. If there is no knowledge and vision of things as they really are, then the basis for revulsion and dispassion is destroyed for one who lacks such knowledge and vision. If there is no revulsion and dispassion, then the basis for the knowledge and vision of liberation is destroyed for one who lacks revulsion and dispassion.[9]

The powerful rapture, pleasure, and happiness inherent in jhāna act as strong antidotes to sensual pleasures. Even though one might clearly realize that sense pleasures ultimately provide little satisfaction, until one experiences rapture and pleasure associated with jhāna one might still be attracted to them.

> Even though a noble disciple has seen clearly as it actually is with proper wisdom how sensual pleasures provide little gratification, much suffering, and much despair, and how great is the danger in them, as long as he still does not attain to the rapture and pleasure that are apart from sensual pleasures, apart from unwholesome states, or to something more peaceful than that, he may still be attracted to sensual pleasures.[10]

Once the meditator experiences jhāna's superior joy and delight, one is not inclined to seek after the inferior sources of worldly pleasures. Their former appeal is greatly lessened.

Finally, the stability and calm of samādhi help buttress the mind against any unsettling experiences that might arise as the deeper levels of insight unfold. Until equanimity and nonclinging have matured, it can be quite disconcerting when our ordinary, everyday perceptions, to which we have been so accustomed, give way to direct experiences of impermanence, unsatisfactoriness, and selflessness. Through the power of samādhi the meditator can remain steady and equanimous as the progression of insight unfolds.

Warnings on the Dangers and Misuse of Samādhi

A number of suttas emphasize the importance of establishing a clear intention of purpose and balanced effort, accompanied by an awareness of the potential pitfalls surrounding the cultivation of samādhi. Wholesome intention comes from an understanding of Dharma teachings and of one's own goals and motivations for meditation practice. The Buddha stated that the essence of his teaching is insight and wisdom leading to liberation, not the attainment of concentration for its own sake.[11] If samādhi and jhāna become objects of clinging, they are no longer powerful aids on the path to awakening, but impediments. Samādhi should be cultivated but not identified with or clung to.

A tranquil, peaceful mind is extremely pleasant, and even the initial stages of samādhi can be seductive, increasing craving rather than freeing the mind. The meditator may begin practicing in order to have more of these concentration experiences and attain certain meditative states for their own sake.

> This holy life does not have gain, honor, and renown for its benefit, or the attainment of virtue . . . or the attainment of concentration for its benefit . . . . But it is this unshakeable deliverance of mind that is the goal of this holy life, its heartwood, and its end.[12]

"Right effort" refers to the right amount of effort, and also to effort aimed in the proper direction. Applying oneself skillfully in meditation practice entails making the effort to develop the wholesome qualities of the mind and heart that lead to wisdom, without a sense of overstriving. Right effort does explicitly include the skillful use of desire to produce wholesome and suppress unwholesome states in the mind:

> What . . . is right effort? . . . [a monk] generates desire for the non-arising of unarisen evil unwholesome states; he makes an effort, arouses energy, applies his mind, and strives. He generates desire for the abandoning of arisen evil, unwholesome states . . . for the arising of unarisen wholesome states . . . for the maintenance of arisen wholesome states, for their non-decay, increase, expansion, and fulfillment by development.[13]

Desire serves a useful and important purpose in motivating us in Dharma practice, as long as it is applied skillfully and in the proper direction. Desire becomes a hindrance when it leads to craving.

Right effort balances application and effort with relaxation and ease. Balanced effort means we can dedicate ourselves and persevere in the often hard and demanding work of meditation, all the while remaining peaceful and content with our present-moment experience and however progress unfolds. The meditator who does his or her best without clinging to or identifying with expectations or results is generally composed, tranquil, and avoids creating suffering along the path leading to the end of suffering.

The suttas liken a person who becomes enamored with the attainment of concentration to a person seeking heartwood from a great tree. Such a person, mistaking something that will not serve his purpose for the thing he seeks, passes over the heartwood and takes away only the inner bark.[14] Attachment to subtler meditative experiences can lead us to meditate in order to have those experiences, rather than as wholesome mental cultivation in service of liberation.

Rarified meditative states are compelling, and we can become enthralled with them, leading to subtle and not-so-subtle arrogance and identification.

> Being diligent, he achieves the attainment of concentration. He is pleased with that attainment of concentration and his intention is fulfilled. On account of it he lauds himself and disparages others thus: "I am concentrated, my mind is unified, but these other bhikkhus are unconcentrated, with their minds astray." He becomes intoxicated with that attainment of concentration, grows negligent, falls into negligence and being negligent, he lives in suffering.[15]

One who "lauds himself and disparages others because of his attainment [of concentration and meditative states] . . . [t]his too is the character of an untrue man. . . . But a true man considers thus: 'Non-identification even with the attainment of [the deepest states of concentration] has been declared by the Blessed One . . .' So, putting non-identification first, he neither lauds himself nor disparages others because of his attainment . . . This is the character of a true man."[16]

These warnings are not meant to dissuade us from cultivating samādhi, but as guides to inform our practice. Upon undertaking any journey we are wise to familiarize ourselves with the territory, paying particular attention to areas of special interest or those that are best avoided altogether. Understanding the mental terrain of meditation, concentration, and consciousness can enhance the effectiveness of our practice and aid us greatly in avoiding unnecessary suffering.

The Buddha was clear that the bliss of jhāna should not be feared, but should be pursued.[17] The dangers surrounding attachment to jhāna are much less perilous than those surrounding attachment to sense pleasures. It has been pointed out that no one has ever killed anyone, stolen things, had illicit sex, told lies, or taken intoxicants due to attachment to jhāna, whereas every day people all over the world are breaking the precepts because of their attachment to sensual pleasures.

Developing Concentration

To attain any degree of samādhi, the meditator must begin by diminishing, and then proceeding to remove, the hindrances to samādhi. The hindrances are unwholesome forces that hinder or obstruct our clarity and equanimity. These confused or agitated states of mind are sensual desire, ill will, sloth and torpor, restlessness and worry, and doubt. It is challenging, if not impossible, for the mind to settle down if it is entangled in these hindrances. The first step in eliminating them is to establish a firm basis of moral discipline and practice.

> If there is no sense control, O monks, then the basis for virtue is destroyed for one who lacks sense control. If there is no virtue, then the basis for right concentration is destroyed for one who lacks virtue.[18]

Virtue

Sīla, meaning "morality" or "virtue," is foundational for the entire path of Buddhist teachings and practice. Creating the supportive conditions essential to cultivating a concentrated mind begins with virtue. A solid foundation in moral behavior is vital in order to make progress in meditation practice and the development of samādhi. Right concentration is based and dependent upon virtue. It is not possible to attain right samādhi without virtue.[19]

Living in a way that creates less suffering and more harmony for ourselves and others is a worthy endeavor for its own sake and the first step in fostering advantageous circumstances for meditation practice. Virtuous living secures the meditator against actions that lead to remorse and worry, which prevent the cultivation of inner calm. The meditator will be unable to settle down and achieve even the early stages of concentration if the mind is agitated and remorseful. Virtuous living produces joy and happiness, two proximate causes for the arising of concentration.

> For one who is virtuous . . . non-remorse will arise. . . . For one free of remorse . . . It is a natural law that gladness will arise . . . [leading naturally to] . . . joy . . . [naturally the] body will be serene . . . [one will feel] happiness . . . the mind will be concentrated. . . . It is a natural law for one with a concentrated mind to know and see things as they really are . . . [and thus] experience revulsion and dispassion . . . [leading naturally to] knowledge and vision of liberation . . . the preceding qualities flow into the succeeding qualities; the succeeding qualities bring the preceding qualities to perfection, for going from the near shore to the far shore (Nibbāna).[20]

The section of the Noble Eightfold Path consisting of right speech, right action, and right livelihood is called "the morality group." For monastics, sīla refers to the behavioral guidelines codified in the Pāṭimokkha, the 227 training rules of conduct for monks and 311 for nuns that guide many aspects of life, as well as the thousands of rules contained in the full Vinaya Piṭaka.

For lay Buddhists, sīla refers to adherence to at least five training precepts, which are abstaining from five unwholesome actions: killing, stealing, sexual misconduct, lying, and intoxication; and in the cultivation of their opposites: nonharming, respect for what does not belong to us, abstaining from sexual misconduct, wise and true speech, and abstinence from intoxicants. Sīla should not be viewed as a list of commandments but, rather, as practical training principles for developing a wise and peaceful heart and mind.

Guarding the Sense Doors

Guarding the sense doors covers not only what you do while meditating, but also how you relate to sensory input throughout the day.

> How . . . [is one] a guardian of the sense-doors? . . . [O]n seeing a visible object with the eye, [one] does not grasp at its major signs or secondary characteristics. Because greed and sorrow, evil unskilled states, would overwhelm him if he dwelt leaving this eye-faculty unguarded, so he practices guarding it, he protects the eye faculty, develops restraint of the eye-faculty. On hearing a sound . . . on smelling an odor . . . on tasting a flavor . . . on feeling an object with the body . . . on thinking a thought . . .[21]

In addition to speaking and acting with wisdom and care, we need to find the proper environment conducive to cultivating samādhi. Especially in the early stages of development, the mind is easily disturbed, so protecting the senses from overstimulation, known as "guarding the sense doors," adds a level of external support. The Buddha often recommended practicing in secluded places and solitary dwellings, such as at the root of a tree, in caves or charnel grounds, in the dense jungle, or in the open air.[22]

If we are being constantly bombarded by the flood of sensory input we normally deal with in our daily lives, it is that much more difficult for the mind to settle into the deeper levels of samādhi. Once concentration is strong, the mind is much less susceptible to external disturbances.

As one continues to train using some meditation object, such as the breath, concentration strengthens to the point where the mind becomes focused solely on the meditation object and is not easily distracted. At this stage the meditator is said to have attained internal seclusion from sense pleasure, since the mind is no longer disturbed by external experiences.

An ideal environment for the nonmonastic meditator is the silent, intensive meditation retreat, where one can devote oneself exclusively to meditation practice, although it is certainly possible for the dedicated practitioner to make substantial progress in daily life. Guarding the sense doors in daily practice means finding a time and place in which we can put aside all concerns and focus exclusively on the meditation subject, at least for the duration of the meditation session.

Setting Aside the Hindrances

Having established the practice of morality and created a supportive environment for guarding the sense doors, we must abandon the five hindrances before we can make substantial progress in meditation.

> There are these five corruptions of the mind corrupted by which the mind is . . . not rightly concentrated . . . What five? Sensual desire . . . ill will . . . sloth and torpor . . . restlessness and remorse . . . doubt.[23]

The standard jhāna definition says that seclusion from sensuality and unwholesome mental states is a prerequisite for entering the first jhāna. As samādhi matures, the mind becomes stable, composed, and serene. As a result, the meditator becomes temporarily free from unwholesome mind-states, called "defilements," and is not swayed or agitated by the arising of various experiences.

As we begin meditation practice, the mind is often unstable, liable to distraction, and vulnerable to the hindrances. Hindrances are overcome through both abandoning and suppressing them. A degree of concentration suppresses the hindrances, but setting aside or abandoning the hindrances to a certain degree is a necessary precondition for developing concentration.

By their very nature, the hindrances tend to undermine the clarity we need to deal with them effectively. We tend to become caught up in sense desire, ill will, agitation, dullness, or doubt, so our ability to recognize these states when they occur and to discern a skillful course of action is impaired. Effort is needed in the beginning. Overcoming the hindrances strengthens concentration through persistent and patient practice, noticing the hindrances when they arise, letting go of them the best we can, and, when distracted, bringing the attention back over and over again to the meditation object.

The hindrance of sensual desires is overcome by abandoning them; ill will, by compassionate love and concern for the welfare of all living beings; sloth and torpor, by perceiving light while remaining mindful and clearly aware; restlessness and worry, through a calmed mind; and doubt, by knowing what is wholesome and what is unwholesome.[24]

"Abandoning covetousness for the world, he abides with a mind free from covetousness; he purifies his mind from covetousness. Abandoning ill will and hatred, he abides with a mind free from ill will, compassionate for the welfare of all living beings; he purifies his mind from ill will and hatred. Abandoning sloth and torpor, he abides free from sloth and torpor, percipient of light, mindful, and fully aware; he purifies his mind from sloth and torpor. Abandoning restlessness and remorse, he abides unagitated with a mind inwardly peaceful; he purifies his mind from restlessness and remorse. Abandoning doubt, he abides having gone beyond doubt, unperplexed about wholesome states; he purifies his mind from doubt."[25]

Right Samādhi

The suttas state that concentration is a condition for seeing directly and clearly into the true nature of things; in some places the ability of samādhi to facilitate insight is particularly stressed:

> Bhikkhus, develop concentration. A bhikkhu who is concentrated understands things as they really are. And what does he understand as they really are? He understands as it really is . . . "[all formations] . . . are impermanent." . . . Bhikkhus, develop concentration. A bhikkhu who is concentrated understands things as they really are.[26]

How are we to understand this apparent contradiction with the many other teachings stating that insight, not meditative states of concentration alone, leads to the deepest level of understanding?

Samādhi is the mind concentrated and unified. Ordinary concentration alone does not lead to liberating understanding, merely suppressing the hindrances and leading to temporary experiences of deep peace and well-being lasting as long as the concentration is maintained. Of the many forms of concentration, it is "right concentration" (Pāli: sammā samādhi) of the Noble Eightfold Path that is of importance in Buddhist meditation. Right concentration is a special kind of concentration, incorporating and supported by other factors, including mindfulness. Unless clearly stated otherwise, we should assume that when the suttas refer to concentration, they are referring to right concentration. It is right concentration that is essential for the deeper attainments in meditation and that, in and of itself, is a cause and condition for liberating insight:

> The knowledge and vision of things as they really are, too, has a proximate cause; it does not lack a proximate cause. And what is the proximate cause for knowledge and vision of things as they really are? It should be said: concentration.[27]

It is not only the strength of concentration that makes it "right," but the context within which it is applied. Before his enlightenment, the Buddha studied with two renowned teachers, Āḷāra Kālāma and Uddaka Rāmaputta, each of whom had attained profound states of meditative concentration and tranquillity, apparently equal in depth to levels of jhāna.[28] But their "jhāna," the pure concentration and stillness of their attainments, could not equal right concentration, because they lacked right view.

The suttas state explicitly that right concentration is the attainment of the four jhānas:

> And what, monks, is Right Concentration? Quite secluded from sensual pleasures, secluded from unwholesome states, a monk enters and abides in the first jhāna [which is characterized by] rapture and pleasure born of seclusion, and accompanied by thought and examination. With the stilling of thought and examination, he enters and abides in the second jhāna [which is characterized by] rapture and pleasure born of concentration, and accompanied by inner composure and singleness of mind, without thought and examination. With the fading away of rapture, he abides in equanimity, mindful and clearly aware, feeling pleasure with the body, he enters and abides in the third jhāna, of which the noble ones declare:

> "Equanimous and mindful he abides in pleasure." With the abandoning of pleasure and pain, and with the previous disappearance of joy and grief, he enters and abides in the fourth jhāna, [which has] neither-pain-nor-pleasure and purity of mindfulness and equanimity. This is called Right Concentration.[29]

This is the standard definition of the four jhānas given throughout the suttas.

Although unification of mind is a principal facet of right concentration, it is not the sole defining feature. Right concentration integrates and synthesizes a range of numerous qualities, which support and strengthen one another.

> What is noble right concentration with its supports and its requisites, that is, right view, right intention, right speech, right action, right livelihood, right effort, and right mindfulness? Unification of mind equipped with these seven factors is called noble right concentration with its supports and its requisites.[30]

It has been suggested that the suttas define right concentration in two different ways, and that this passage is an alternative definition of right concentration that does not necessarily include the four jhānas.[31] When viewed within the context of the standard definition repeated throughout the discourses, that right concentration is the four jhānas, this passage means that jhāna is a state accompanied by these seven other factors of the eightfold path.

It should be noted that even in this definition, concentration has reached a stage in which the mind is one-pointed. And in the sutta in which this definition appears, noble right intention is defined as follows:

> And what, Bhikkhus, is right intention that is noble, taintless, supramundane, a factor of the path? The thinking, thought, intention, mental absorption, mental fixity, directing of mind, verbal formation in one whose mind is noble, whose mind is taintless, who possesses the noble path and is developing the noble path.[32]

This definition includes some factors associated with jhāna, strengthening the interpretation that there is one, consistent definition in the suttas of right concentration as jhāna.

It is not merely concentration, but right concentration, that is indispensable. Right concentration is jhāna, with its unification of mind and other associated factors, within the context of the eightfold path. Therefore it is important to understand what jhāna is and how to attain it, which is the subject of the following chapter.

Samādhi in Important Buddhist Lists and Discourses

In addition to its place as the last factor in the Noble Eightfold Path, samādhi appears prominently throughout the suttas dealing with mental cultivation. Concentration is a significant element in important lists, such as the four bases of power (Pāli: iddhipāda), the five faculties (Pāli: indriya), also known as the five strengths (Pāli: bala), and the seven factors of enlightenment (Pāli: bojjhanga).

In several places the suttas state that the entire Buddhist path fundamentally entails abandoning the five hindrances, developing the four foundations of mindfulness, and realizing the seven factors of enlightenment so as to gain true knowledge and release.

> All those who escaped from the world [in the past], or escape [now], or will escape [in the future], did so, do so and will [continue] to do so by abandoning the five hindrances, which are defilements of the mind that weaken wisdom, and, with minds well established in the four establishings of mindfulness, by developing the seven awakening-factors thus present.[33]

Each of these three facets of the meditative path—abandoning the five hindrances, establishing the four foundations of mindfulness, and realizing the seven factors of enlightenment—entails some degree of samādhi. Precisely what and how much concentration is a subject of much debate.

Seven Factors of Enlightenment

The seven factors of enlightenment is one of the most important lists in Buddhist teaching.

> Just as all the rafters of a peaked house slant, slope, and incline towards the roof peak, so too, when [one] develops and cultivates the seven factors of enlightenment, he slants, slopes, and inclines toward Nibbāna.[34]

> What is the path and the way that leads to the cessation of craving? It is: the seven factors of enlightenment.[35]

The seven factors of enlightenment are as follows: (1) mindfulness (Pāli: sati-sambojjhanga), (2) investigation or discrimination of dhammas, or discernment of dhamma (Pāli: dhamma-vicaya-sambojjhanga), (3) energy (Pāli: viriya-sambojjhanga), (4) rapture (Pāli: pīti-sambojjhanga), (5) tranquillity (Pāli: passaddhi sambojjhanga), (6) concentration (Pāli: samādhi-sambo-jjhanga), and (7) equanimity (Pāli: upekkhā-sambojjhanga). Mindfulness is the balancing factor, followed by three energizing factors—investigation of the dharma, energy, and rapture—and three calming factors—tranquillity, concentration, and equanimity.

The seven factors of enlightenment are presented in the suttas as both a basic list of mental qualities and a list of progressive steps to be developed sequentially. As a simple list, the seven factors of enlightenment represent the factors that, when developed and cultivated, lead to the ultimate goal of true knowledge and deliverance.[36] These are the factors to develop in order to reach full awakening. Though an awakened mind transcends all these qualities, it may have them on hand to use as needed. In that sense they should be thought of, even in their fruition, as factors of the path leading to enlightenment, rather than descriptions of an enlightened mind.

As a series of successive steps, the seven factors of enlightenment is an encapsulation of the path of meditation practice, the cultivation and maturing of one factor being the supportive conditions for the unfolding and development of the next, leading up to right concentration. Beginning with sustained mindfulness, meditators closely examine the nature of their mind, body, and all experiences, strengthening the investigation or discernment factor. As the mind turns toward and investigates more and more deeply the nature of the body and mind, energy is aroused, and through repeated and persistent energy and effort, rapture arises. For one whose mind is uplifted by rapture, the body becomes tranquil and the mind becomes tranquil. When tranquil, the mind becomes concentrated, and with a concentrated mind one becomes equanimous.

Each of the enlightenment factors can appear at any point in the development of meditation, most likely in a nascent form in the early stages of mental cultivation. Though there is no explicit reference to jhāna in the list, the seven factors of enlightenment can be viewed as a condensed summary of the step-by-step path leading up through the cultivation of right concentration and the four jhānas. This is not the only possible way of understanding the seven factors, but there is ample reason to interpret the list in this way.

Beginning with mindfulness—a key element in the cultivation and an aspect of jhāna—the list culminates, as does the standard jhāna definition, in equanimity.

The seven factors of enlightenment and jhāna are both developed based on virtue[37] and arise dependent upon abandoning the five hindrances, so the same supportive conditions necessary for developing samādhi are necessary for developing all seven factors. Like jhāna, cultivation of the seven factors of enlightenment both obstructs the hindrances and strengthens the wholesome factors of awakening.

> I do not see even one thing that, when developed and cultivated, leads to the abandoning of the things that fetter so effectively as this: the seven factors of enlightenment.[38]

Cultivating the seven factors of enlightenment is an antidote to the hindrances, which, in turn, leads to deepening samādhi.

The seven enlightenment factors, in their stepwise successive form, correlate directly to the progressive development of jhāna and right concentration, as seen in this passage from the Sāmaññaphala (Fruits of the Homeless Life) Sutta:

> When he **knows** (Pāli: passati) the five hindrances are absent within him, gladness arises, and being glad, **rapture** (Pāli: pīti) arises. Because of rapture his **body becomes tranquil, with his body tranquillized** he feels happiness,[39] and with happiness **his mind becomes concentrated.** Quite secluded from sensual pleasures, secluded from unwholesome states, he enters and abides in the first jhāna [which is characterized by] rapture and pleasure born of seclusion, and accompanied by thought and examination.[40]

Continuing from the formula in the jhāna definition, the second jhāna is characterized by **rapture** and pleasure, born of **concentration.** With attainment of the third jhāna one abides in **equanimity, mindful** and clearly aware. And the fourth jhāna is characterized by **purity of mindfulness** and **equanimity.**

In the following passage, the Buddha recounts his period of meditation practice before his enlightenment:

> Tireless **energy** was aroused in me and unrelenting **mindfulness** was established, my body was **tranquil** and untroubled, my mind **concentrated** and unified. Quite secluded from sensual pleasures, secluded from unwholesome states, I entered upon and abided in the first jhāna . . . the second jhāna . . . the third jhāna . . . the fourth jhāna.[41]

Thus, six of the seven enlightenment factors appear directly in these introductory passages to the jhāna formulation or in the jhāna formula itself. Though discernment or discrimination of the dharma is not explicitly mentioned in these examples, a correspondence with the above passages can be seen. The Pāli term *passati,* from "When he **knows** the five hindrances are absent within him," means "to see." Seeing, in and of itself, does not necessarily equate to discernment, but there is a secondary meaning to *passati,* which is "to recognize, realize, or know." The term *vipassanā,* meaning "insight," is derived from this term. In this sense *passati,* "knowing," is near in meaning to *vicaya,* "discernment" or "discrimination." The seven factors of enlightenment give us a concise summation of the process of mental cultivation through jhāna.

Satipaṭṭhāna (Foundations of Mindfulness) Sutta

The Satipaṭṭhāna Sutta is one of the most detailed of the discourses focusing on meditation practice. Its importance is highlighted in the beginning and closing sections, where the Buddha declares the four foundations of mindfulness to be "the direct path for the purification of beings, for the surmounting of sorrow and lamentation, for the disappearance of pain and grief, for the attainment of the true way, for the realization of Nibbāna." The four foundations of mindfulness fulfills the seven factors of enlightenment, so the seven factors of enlightenment can be considered to be the culmination of practice and the foundations of mindfulness the method of practice leading to that culmination.

This sutta appears in two places in the Pāli Canon: as the Satipaṭṭhāna Sutta in the Middle Length Discourses[42] and as the longer Mahā (Great) Satipaṭṭhāna Sutta in the Long Discourses.[43] These two are identical except that the Mahāsatipaṭṭhāna Sutta expands the section on the Four Noble Truths to explain all four truths in detail. Further details can be gathered from the Connected Discourses, which devotes an entire collection of suttas to further explain and discuss the four foundations of mindfulness.[44]

There is some debate as to whether the term *satipaṭṭhāna* refers mainly to the activity of being mindful, to the process of contemplating the objects of meditation in and of themselves in a particular way, or to the objects of that mindfulness practice.[45] Although satipaṭṭhāna obviously requires both the action itself and the objects of mindfulness, this is an important distinction, because it informs where the emphasis of our practice should be placed. *Satipaṭṭhāna* is often translated as the "establishing of mindfulness," to emphasize it as the activity of being mindful in a prescribed way.

Beginning with mindfulness of breathing, the sutta presents comprehensive instruction on the practice of mindfulness meditation, refining awareness systematically through each of the four foundations of mindfulness: contemplation of the body, feelings, the mind, and mind-objects (also called dhammas, or phenomena).

Contemplation of the body, the first of the four satipaṭṭhānas, consists of six distinct practices: mindfulness of (1) breathing, in four steps; (2) the four postures; (3) general activities, such as eating and drinking, defecating and urinating, and talking; (4) deconstruction and analysis of the body into constituent parts; (5) deconstruction and analysis of the body into its four constituent elements of earth, air, fire, and water; and (6) nine contemplations of a corpse in varying degrees of decay.

Contemplation of feelings, the second foundation, refers to mindful investigation of the pleasant, unpleasant, or neutral feeling tone accompanying any experience. In the third foundation of mindfulness—contemplation of the mind (Pāli: citta)—the meditator is instructed to understand the presence or absence of lust, hatred, and delusion, as well as whether the mind is contracted, distracted, great or narrow, unsurpassed, concentrated or unconcentrated, and liberated or unliberated. The last of the four satipaṭṭhānas is contemplation of dhammas, generally translated as "mind-objects" or "mental qualities." This foundation of mindfulness consists of contemplating and understanding the five hindrances, the five aggregates, the six sense spheres, the seven factors of enlightenment, and the Four Noble Truths.

Throughout all of these practices, the meditator should be actively involved in the process, and not merely a passive observer. The third and fourth steps in mindfulness of breathing, the first of the contemplations of the body, are to *train* experiencing the whole body and tranquillizing the body formation, pointing toward an engaged role in the practice. In the contemplation of the hindrances and seven factors of enlightenment, the meditator is told to be aware of how to prevent the hindrances from arising, and of how to bring the seven factors of enlightenment to the culmination of their development. Though the sutta itself only instructs us to understand these, that understanding points toward taking an active role in working with them. In the expanded version, the Mahāsatipaṭṭhāna Sutta, knowing as it really is the fourth noble truth, the way leading to the cessation of suffering, includes the understanding that right effort entails arousing energy and exertion for the arising and sustaining of wholesome mental states, and for preventing and overcoming the arising of unwholesome mental states. The meditator should clearly be actively engaged in the process.

Samādhi in the Satipaṭṭhāna Sutta

Though the meditator should be active and involved throughout the four satipaṭṭhāna practices, he or she is not directly instructed anywhere to strengthen or diminish any of the experiences that arise and pass away, including samādhi, but to just mindfully be aware and clearly understand whatever experience is present. Based on the sutta itself, we cannot determine what level of samādhi the sutta wants us to develop. For that we have to look elsewhere.

When engaged in the satipaṭṭhāna contemplations, if the mind does not become concentrated, the defilements are not abandoned, the mind does not pick up the sign of concentration, and the meditator "does not gain pleasant dwellings in this present life, nor does he gain mindfulness and clear comprehension."[46] The suttas expect the meditator to develop a strong degree of concentration and tranquillity.

The first practice of the sutta, breath meditation, is presented in four steps, beginning with bare awareness to understand when breathing in and out long and short in the first two steps. As concentration is strengthened through these preliminary practices, the practitioner experiences the whole body in the third, and tranquillizes the bodily formation in the fourth. The bodily formation is defined in other suttas as in-breathing and out-breathing,[47] so this practice culminates in calming the breath, and subsequently the whole body, entailing a degree of samādhi.

Establishing the foundations of mindfulness is the path leading to the realization of the seven factors of enlightenment. If we interpret the seven factors of enlightenment as a condensed outline of the path for jhāna development, then the Satipaṭṭhāna Sutta describes the method for developing jhāna. "What is concentration? What is the basis of concentration? . . . Unification of mind is concentration; the four foundations of mindfulness are the basis of concentration."[48]

> Having thus abandoned these five hindrances, imperfections of the mind that weaken wisdom, he abides contemplating the body as a body, ardent, fully aware, and mindful, having put away covetousness and grief for the world. He abides contemplating feelings as feelings . . . mind as mind . . . mind-objects as mind-objects. . . . Just as the elephant tamer plants a large post in the earth and binds the forest elephant to it by the neck in order to subdue his forest habits . . . so these four foundations of mindfulness are the bindings for the mind . . . in order that he may attain the true way and realize Nibbāna. . . .[49]

The image of binding the mind strengthens the association between the foundations of mindfulness and jhāna. Mindfulness is a practice leading to concentration, and the four foundations of mindfulness are the framework for developing jhāna.

> In one of right view, right intention comes into being; in one of right intention, right speech comes into being; . . . in one of right mindfulness, right concentration comes into being.[50]

After having abandoned the five hindrances and contemplated the four foundations of mindfulness, the meditator is then instructed to contemplate the body, feelings, mind, and mind-objects without thinking thoughts about them and, finally, to enter the second through fourth jhānas, with no explicit mention of the first jhāna:

> Abide contemplating the body as a body, but do not think thoughts connected with the body; abide contemplating feelings as feelings . . . mind as mind . . . mind-objects as mind-objects but do not think thoughts connected with mind-objects . . . With the stilling of applied and sustained thought, he enters and abides in the second jhāna . . . the third jhāna . . . the fourth jhāna.[51]

The last statement in this passage begins with the second jhāna, with no mention of the first. The second jhāna, which is without thought and examination, is not attained without going through the first, so the first jhāna must be attained at some point. The implication is that the first jhāna was already attained through cultivating the foundations of mindfulness. The second jhāna is then reached by continuing with the four foundations of mindfulness as objects, but with relinquishment of thought and examination.

When contemplating the four foundations of mindfulness, if discomfort in the body, sluggishness, or distraction arises, one "should then direct his mind towards some inspiring sign. When he directs his mind towards some inspiring sign, gladness is born. When he is gladdened, rapture is born. When the mind is uplifted by rapture, the body becomes tranquil. One tranquil in body experiences happiness. The mind of one who is happy becomes concentrated. He reflects thus: 'The purpose for the sake of which I directed my mind has been achieved. Let me now withdraw it.' So he withdraws the mind and does not think or examine. He understands: 'Without thought and examination, internally mindful, I am happy.'"[52] Meditating without thinking suggests a level of samādhi associated with jhāna. Rapture, happiness, and tranquillity are all factors connected with jhāna. The first jhāna is accompanied by thought and examination; "without thought and examination" is associated with the second and higher jhānas.

Samādhi is directly mentioned in the Satipaṭṭhāna Sutta in only three places. In the third foundation, of mind, one understands "concentrated mind as concentrated mind, and unconcentrated mind as unconcentrated mind."[53] The Pāli term used here for concentration is *samāhitaṃ,* meaning "having attained samādhi." From this alone it is not clear whether the passage means "knowing whether or not one has attained a particular stage of samādhi" or just "knowing whether or not concentration has been attained to any degree at all." We might suppose that *samāhitaṃ* refers to having attained jhāna, since the satipaṭṭhāna practices are the path leading to fulfillment of the seven factors of enlightenment, and in any case the suttas probably are not interested in having the meditator develop anything other than right samādhi. Regardless, the only explicit instruction here is to notice whatever degree of samādhi there is, rather than to cultivate any specific degree of samādhi.

The second place where samādhi is mentioned is in the fourth foundation, in the section on the seven factors of enlightenment.

> If the concentration awakening factor is present in him, he knows "there is the concentration awakening factor in me"; if the concentration awakening factor is not present in him, he knows "there is no concentration awakening factor in me"; he knows how the unarisen concentration awakening factor can arise, and how the arisen concentration awakening factor can be perfected by development.[54]

Again, the instruction is to know and understand the presence, absence, and skillful means to cultivate concentration. The implication is that we should act on that understanding to develop the concentration factor of enlightenment to its ultimate fruition.

The third place where samādhi is discussed is in the expanded section of the Mahāsatipaṭṭhāna Sutta detailing the eightfold path, which restates that right samādhi is jhāna. This could be interpreted to mean that satipaṭṭhāna is the practice leading to jhāna, and that jhāna is a fruit of satipaṭṭhāna practice. Here, too, the practitioner is not directed to develop jhāna, or any particular meditative state. The instruction is to

> know as it really is: "This [the Noble Eightfold Path] is the way of practice leading to the cessation of suffering" . . . [which is] Right View . . . Right Concentration. And what is Right Concentration? . . . the first jhāna . . . the second jhāna . . . the third jhāna . . . the fourth jhāna . . . This is called Right Concentration.[55]

One should know and understand that right concentration is jhāna, regardless of the degree of samādhi actually attained.

From these instances of samādhi in the Satipaṭṭhāna Sutta, we would not expect the sutta to point us toward passive realization that samādhi properly culminates in jhāna, without actually attaining jhāna.

The Role of Concentration in Overcoming the Hindrances

Samādhi and freedom from the hindrances are closely associated. In the introductory section of the sutta, one is instructed to meditate "ardent, clearly aware, and mindful, having put aside covetousness and grief for the world" when practicing each of the four categories for mindfulness meditation. *Abhijjhā,* the Pāli term used here for "covetousness," has the general meaning of wanting or liking. And *domanassa,* the term for "grief," means discontent. Together they convey a general meaning of "wanting and disliking." Different terms are typically used in referring to the first two of the five hindrances, *kāmacchanda* for "sensual desire" and *byāpāda* for "ill will" (although there are some places where the suttas use *abhijjhā* instead of *kāmacchanda*[56]). Even if we equate "likes and dislikes" from the sutta introduction with "sense desire and ill will" from the list of hindrances, the sutta formulation still does not mention the last three hindrances, sloth and torpor, restlessness and worry, and doubt, so it is not clear from the sutta itself that "having put aside covetousness and grief for the world" equates with suppressing all of the hindrances.

We have seen in a previous quote from the Buddha that anyone who has ever attained enlightenment has done so by abandoning the five hindrances and then establishing the four foundations of mindfulness in order to realize the seven factors of enlightenment. Additionally, "Having abandoned these five hindrances, imperfections of the mind that weaken wisdom, he abides contemplating the body as a body [the first foundation of mindfulness], ardent, fully aware, and mindful, having put away covetousness and grief for the world. He abides contemplating feelings as feelings [the second foundation of mindfulness] . . . mind as mind [the third foundation] . . . mind-objects as mind-objects [the fourth foundation], ardent, clearly aware, and mindful, having put away covetousness and grief for the world."[57]

The Satipaṭṭhāna Sutta cannot expect us to completely eradicate the five hindrances before beginning mindfulness meditation, since the sutta includes contemplation of various hindrances and unwholesome mind-states as integral practices. In the third foundation, on the mind, the meditator knows the presence or absence of the hindrances of lust and hatred, and the fourth foundation of mindfulness of mind-objects contains various contemplations of the five hindrances. The fact that one practices the four satipaṭṭhānas after abandoning the five hindrances does not preclude practicing them while the hindrances are still prone to arise.

If it is clear that the hindrances must be greatly diminished or removed for successful mindfulness practice, the sutta does not tell us how that should be accomplished. Should they be subdued by the force of concentration, or allowed to appear as long as the practitioner is not bothered or distracted by them? In one discourse the definition of *satipaṭṭhāna* is modified, substituting "ardent, clearly aware, and mindful, having put away covetousness and grief for the world" with "ardent, clearly comprehending, unified, with limpid mind, concentrated, with one-pointed mind, in order to know the body as it really is . . . feelings . . . mind . . . in order to know phenomena as they really are."[58] Modifying the introductory section in this way, substituting "having put away covetousness and grief for the world" with language denoting concentration, reinforces the idea that abandoning the hindrances, "having put away covetousness and grief for the world," is accomplished through attaining a level of samādhi that would suppress the ability of the hindrances to arise.

However, since the four foundations of mindfulness are the basis for concentration, a high degree of concentration cannot be expected prior to beginning satipaṭṭhāna practice, for that would then render unreachable the very practices one needs to attain that degree of concentration. The Satipaṭṭhāna Sutta cannot expect the meditator to attain a substantial degree of concentration prior to beginning its practices, which are the practices that lead to a substantial degree of concentration.

Until all potential for the hindrances to arise is ultimately eliminated, in order to practice they are temporarily cut off by right effort and skillfully suppressing or abandoning. The hindrances do not have to be eradicated in order to take up the foundations of mindfulness practices, but the mind needs to be free enough from them to become settled. The first step is to tentatively overcome them by minimizing their intensity through suppressing or abandoning. Once their effects have faded or ceased altogether, they can no longer act as hindrances, but when they do arise, they can be known mindfully and integrated into the insight meditation practice. At that point, one continues to practice and attains samādhi. In this way the four foundations of mindfulness are the basis of concentration, which is unification of mind.

Ānāpānasati (Mindfulness of Breathing) Sutta

Mindfulness of breathing is often taught merely as a preparatory practice, since it is the initial practice in the first of the four foundations of mindfulness practices.[59] As a means to develop some concentration and the beginning stages of mindfulness, it can be seen as preliminary to the greater body of satipaṭṭhāna practices. But the Ānāpānasati Sutta declares that, when developed and cultivated, mindfulness of breathing alone fulfills the entire four foundations of mindfulness, which, in turn, fulfill the seven factors of enlightenment:

> When mindfulness of breathing is developed and cultivated, it is of great fruit and benefit. When mindfulness of breathing is developed and cultivated, it fulfills the four foundations of mindfulness. When the four foundations of mindfulness are developed and cul-

> tivated, they fulfill the seven factors of enlightenment. When the seven factors of enlightenment are developed and cultivated, they fulfill true knowledge and deliverance.[60]

Concentration by mindfulness of breathing leads to jhāna and the formless attainments;[61] ānāpānasati should be viewed not as a preliminary practice but as a complete method to develop right concentration and insight necessary for enlightenment. Mindfulness of breathing encompasses more than just the experience of the breath, and is more than an introductory practice for the foundations of mindfulness meditations; it is essentially a manifestation of the entire satipaṭṭhāna. Mindfulness of breathing is the means by which the hindrances are abandoned and the entirety of the four foundations of mindfulness is accessed and developed, bringing the seven factors of enlightenment to fruition.

Of all the meditation practices in the first foundation of mindfulness—contemplation of the body—mindfulness of breathing is perhaps the most common. Developing concentration through mindfulness of breathing is given particular emphasis in the suttas. The Buddha states that before his own enlightenment he dwelled in samādhi through mindfulness of breathing:

> Concentration by mindfulness of breathing, when developed and cultivated, is of great fruit and benefit [when practiced and developed as presented in the Ānāpānasati Sutta]. . . . I, too, before my enlightenment, while I was still a bodhisatta, not yet fully enlightened, generally dwelt in this dwelling.[62]

In the Ānāpānasati Sutta, the meditator proceeds through sixteen steps of mindful breathing, the initial four steps of breath meditation in the Satipaṭṭhāna Sutta followed by an additional twelve steps introduced in this sutta. The sutta is structured as four groups of four steps each. The sutta declares that the foundation of mindfulness of the body from the Satipaṭṭhāna Sutta is fulfilled through the practices in the first tetrad, mindfulness of feelings through the practices in the second, mindfulness of mind in the third, and mindfulness of mind-objects in the fourth.

Breathing in and out, the meditator:

FIRST TETRAD

1. Knows long breath
2. Knows short breath
3. Trains experiencing the whole body[63]
4. Trains tranquillizing the bodily formation

SECOND TETRAD

5. Trains experiencing rapture
6. Trains experiencing pleasure
7. Trains experiencing mental formations
8. Trains tranquillizing mental formations

THIRD TETRAD

9. Trains experiencing the mind
10. Trains gladdening the mind
11. Trains concentrating the mind
12. Trains liberating the mind

FOURTH TETRAD

13. Trains contemplating impermanence
14. Trains contemplating dispassion
15. Trains contemplating cessation
16. Trains contemplating letting go

Breath meditation generally combines mindfulness and concentration, either of which may be emphasized depending upon which aspects of breath are emphasized. In the Ānāpānasati Sutta, mindfulness of breathing contains elements of both concentration and insight. This sutta is open to a variety of interpretations and opinions regarding how the system should be practiced and what degree of samādhi the meditator should develop at each step. The steps can be viewed as a description of how breath meditation naturally unfolds through the simple act of mindful breathing, reflecting the natural deepening of concentration, awareness, and insight that occurs on its own merely by focusing on the in-breath and out-breath as a meditation object. Or it can be viewed as steps to be practiced systematically (hence the word *trains*), whereupon practicing one stage, the meditator consciously takes up the instructions for the next. In either case, some degree of concentration is clearly an important aspect of every step in the sequence.

As is evident in the structure of the Ānāpānasati Sutta, tranquillity and clarity of concentration are supportive conditions for insight to arise. The first twelve of the sixteen steps are easily recognized as concentration practices, while the last four—contemplation of impermanence, fading away, cessation, and letting go—are clearly insight practices, having been built upon the previous steps of concentration.

As concentration deepens, rapture and pleasure, two of the jhāna factors, arise in steps 5 and 6. So, though not explicitly stated in the sutta, this stage is commonly understood as the beginning of jhāna. The first steps of the sutta are often classified purely as concentration practices leading to jhāna. The initial four steps are identical to the beginning breath meditation sequence in the Satipaṭṭhāna Sutta, leading to a certain degree of samādhi since, through mindfulness of long in- and out-breaths (step 1), short in and out breaths (step 2), and experiencing the whole body (step 3), the bodily formation (breathing) is tranquillized (step 4). Because rapture and pleasure, as well as the tranquillity, gladdening, and concentration of the mind in later steps, occur to some degree throughout a wide range of samādhi, including well before entering jhāna, these steps do not necessarily correlate to jhāna. However, it is a reasonable interpretation since ānāpānasati fulfills satipaṭṭhāna, which fulfills the seven factors of enlightenment.

2

Jhāna in the Pāli Suttas

Jhāna is called the pleasure of renunciation, the pleasure of seclusion, the pleasure of peace, the pleasure of enlightenment. I say of this kind of pleasure that it should be pursued, that it should be developed, that it should be cultivated, that it should not be feared.

The Buddha, Laṭukikopama Sutta (MN66)

Just as the river Ganges slants, slopes, and inclines towards the east, so too one who develops and cultivates the four jhānas slants, slopes, and inclines towards Nibbāna.

The Buddha, Jhānasaṃyutta (SN53.1)

THE FOUR JHĀNAS ARE DISTINCTIVE MEDITATIVE STATES OF HIGH concentration in which the mind becomes unified. These are remarkable states of extraordinary rapture, happiness, and peace, characterized by a steady mental clarity and a profound sense of well-being. The experience of jhāna is inspiring, as the concentrative potential of the mind comes to fruition. Upon attaining any of the four jhānas, progress seems effortless as meditation takes on a power and momentum of its own. Jhāna is often referred to as an absorption state, since the mind in jhāna is so deeply concentrated that it "absorbs" into the meditation object. Much disagreement has arisen over precisely what the nature of this meditative state is and its proper place in Buddhist meditation practice.

The word *jhāna* (Pāli; Sanskrit, *dhyana*) is derived from the verb *jhāyati,* meaning "to meditate or contemplate." In a few places the term *jhāna* retains its general meaning as a type of meditation or mental absorption, including some that would be described as wrong or unskillful.

For instance, before his enlightenment, when he was practicing extreme asceticism, the Buddha practiced a jhāna called the "breathingless jhāna," in which he would hold his breath, a form of wrong meditation that caused severe pain and did not lead to enlightenment.[1] The Buddha disapproved of a type of jhāna in which the mind is obsessed by the five hindrances, which could be considered mental absorption in anger, lust, and so forth, but is not really a meditation.[2] These types of jhāna are of interest as examples of meditations to avoid.

> Not every kind of jhāna was praised by the Blessed One, nor was every kind of jhāna criticized by the Blessed One .... What kind of jhāna did he praise? A monk enters and remains in the first jhāna ... in the second jhāna ... in the third jhāna ... in the fourth jhāna. ... The Blessed One praised that kind of jhāna.[3]

Of most importance, and the sense in which jhāna is most commonly used, is right concentration, the four jhānas in the context of the Noble Eightfold Path. Throughout the suttas the four jhānas are always defined in terms of the presence or absence of various associated attributes, using the following standard formula:

> Quite secluded from sensual pleasures, secluded from unwholesome states, a monk enters and abides in the first jhāna [which is characterized by] rapture and pleasure born of seclusion, and accompanied by thought and examination. With the stilling of thought and examination, he enters and abides in the second jhāna [which is characterized by] rapture and pleasure born of concentration, and accompanied by inner composure and singleness of mind, without thought and examination. With the fading away of rapture, he abides in equanimity, mindful and clearly aware, feeling pleasure

> with the body, he enters and abides in the third jhāna, of which the noble ones declare: "Equanimous and mindful he abides in pleasure." With the abandoning of pleasure and pain, and with the previous disappearance of joy and grief, he enters and abides in the fourth jhāna, [which has] neither-pain-nor-pleasure and purity of mindfulness and equanimity.

Four jhānas are enumerated in this definition, along with a number of qualities and factors associated with each.

The Mahāvedalla Sutta specifies certain elements from the definition as jhāna factors.

> How many factors does the first jhāna have? The first jhāna has five factors ... there occur thought, examination, rapture, pleasure, and unification of mind. That is how the first jhāna has five factors.[4]

This is regarded as the standard list for the five jhāna factors. The first four—thought, examination, rapture, and pleasure (Pāli: vitakka, vicāra, pīti, and sukha)—are found in the jhāna formula. The fifth factor—unification of mind (Pāli: cittass' ekaggatā)—does not occur in the standard formula, but another similar term—singleness of mind (Pāli: ekodi-bhāva)—appears in the definition of the second jhāna (see the section entitled "The Jhāna Definition in Detail" on page 38 for a discussion of these two terms). As meditation progresses, the mind continues to become more strongly concentrated with each jhāna. The first four jhāna factors are abandoned or fade away with progression through the four jhānas; unification of mind persists as a factor in all jhānas. Unification of mind is never said to be abandoned or to fade away, so it is never lost and must be an attribute of all the subsequent jhānas.

The suttas differentiate carnal rapture, pleasure, and equanimity, which are dependent upon sense pleasure, from the rapture, pleasure, and equanimity associated with jhāna, which are free from carnal desire:

> There is carnal rapture ... pleasure ... equanimity ... there is spiritual rapture ... pleasure ... equanimity. What is carnal rapture ... pleasure ... equanimity? [It is] rapture ... pleasure ... equanimity that arises in dependence on these five cords of sensual pleasure

> [the five senses]. What is spiritual rapture? . . . [one] enters and dwells in the first jhāna . . . [and] the second jhāna. What is spiritual pleasure? . . . [one] enters and dwells in the first . . . the second . . . and the third jhāna. What is spiritual equanimity? [one] enters and dwells in the fourth jhāna.[5]

In addition to the five jhāna factors and the other descriptive qualities in the definition, the Anupada Sutta describes eleven additional features present in each of the jhānas, which serve to more fully expand the description and illustrate the nature of these states. These are sense contact, feeling, perception, volition, mind, intention, determination, energy, mindfulness, equanimity, and attention.[6] From this list we can see that the jhānas are dynamic states, with many associated mental factors. These additional aspects will be important in helping us to understand the nature of jhāna, especially in comparison to descriptions of jhāna in the later commentarial works.

The four jhānas are developed in successive order, with attainment of and stabilization in the lower jhānas forming the foundation for the next higher jhāna. The suttas compare the meditator who tries to develop a higher jhāna before consolidating and strengthening the previous one to an unwise, foolish cow searching for new pasture but unskilled at wandering in the rugged mountains.[7] Such a cow would neither successfully find the new pasture nor be able to find its way back to the old one. Similarly, the meditator will not successfully attain any stage of jhāna if the previous level has not been developed properly.

Progress through the four jhānas is through the systematic diminishment of the coarser factors, allowing the subsequent subtler and deeper jhāna states to emerge. Each jhāna is reached through the eradication of its impediments, which are factors to be abandoned, and the development and strengthening of its associated states, factors to be "entered into."

> Five factors are abandoned and five are present in the first jhāna. Sensual desire, ill-will, sloth and torpor, restlessness and remorse, and doubt (these are the five hindrances) are abandoned; thought, examination, rapture, pleasure, and unification of mind are present. That is how five factors are abandoned and five are present in the first jhāna.[8]

The jhāna factors function to obstruct the hindrances and absorb the mind into the meditation subject. Unwholesome mental states do not have an opportunity to arise since the mind in jhāna is so deeply concentrated, steady, and clear.

As we proceed through the formula, in addition to the jhāna factors themselves, which fade away in succession as we progress through the levels, the definition introduces additional elements, adding further to the description and the overall distinct quality of each successive stage. In the second jhāna, two factors are eliminated, thought and examination, leaving the three remaining factors of rapture, pleasure, and unification of mind, and adding the new element of inner composure. The third jhāna abandons the factor of rapture, leaving pleasure and unification of mind, while naming for the first time the qualities equanimity, mindfulness, and clear awareness (also called "clear comprehension"). In the fourth jhāna, pleasure is abandoned, leaving neither-pain-nor-pleasure and unification of mind, and adding purity of mindfulness and equanimity. Each jhāna is defined in terms of its associated factors, all of which must be present for the meditative state to be considered jhāna.

The First Jhāna

In several suttas, descriptions of the jhānas are elaborated and embellished with beautiful similes.[9] These images and metaphors serve two functions. The first is to elucidate the nature of the jhāna experience, shedding further light on the standard definitions. The similes highlight that jhāna is not a state in which awareness of the body has been lost. Rather than losing connection with the body as one enters jhāna, the meditator gains heightened awareness of it as the jhāna factors gradually develop and suffuse throughout the body. The second purpose of the similes is to clarify the way to attain and progress through the jhānas. In some of the suttas, the similes begin with "I have proclaimed to my disciples the way to develop the four jhānas." The similes not only supplement the jhāna definition, shedding light on their nature, they also clarify the way to attain and to progress through the successive stages.

The simile continues, expanding on the standard definition of the first jhāna to illustrate how the associated factors of pleasure and rapture are strengthened by permeating them throughout the body:

> Quite secluded from sensual pleasures, secluded from unwholesome states, a monk enters and abides in the first jhāna [which is characterized by] rapture and pleasure born of seclusion, and accompanied by thought and examination. He makes the rapture and pleasure born of seclusion drench, steep, fill, and pervade this body, so that there is no part of his whole body unpervaded by the rapture and pleasure born of seclusion. Just as a skilled bath man or a bath man's apprentice heaps bath powder in a metal basin and, sprinkling it gradually with water, kneads it till the moisture wets his ball of bath powder, soaks it and pervades it inside and out, yet the ball itself does not ooze; so too, a bhikkhu makes the rapture and pleasure born of seclusion drench, steep, fill, and pervade this body, so that there is no part of his whole body unpervaded by the rapture and pleasure born of seclusion.

Suffusing jhāna factors throughout the body is both a characteristic of and the way to progress through the higher stages of jhāna. Once the first jhāna is attained, in order to deepen it and proceed to the second, the meditator suffuses the body with rapture and pleasure, solidifying the first jhāna and strengthening the factors leading into the second. Rapture and pleasure are the jhāna factors that remain once thought and examination have subsided when the meditator enters the second jhāna. The image of a man gradually kneading bath powder into a moist ball emphasizes the extent to which these factors should be suffused throughout the body, as well as the transformative nature of these meditative states. Just as the bath powder is transformed into a moist ball, so, too, the concentration, calm, and associated factors transform the mind of the meditator. A focused and unified mind is tremendously powerful, enabling clear seeing.

A good deal of effort is needed leading up to jhāna, at which point the practice achieves a momentum of its own. But the first jhāna can still be unsteady, and the meditator is liable to fall out of it into lower levels of samādhi. A degree of diligence and effort is required at this stage to solidify the jhāna attainment. The image of a man working gives us a very active sense of the meditator arousing energetic effort. The simile highlights the energetic quality of the first jhāna.

The Jhāna Definition in Detail

> Quite secluded from sensual pleasures, secluded from unwholesome states, a monk enters and abides in the first jhāna [which is characterized by] rapture and pleasure born of seclusion, and accompanied by thought and examination.

"Quite secluded from sensual pleasures" refers to both external and internal seclusion, as we have discussed in chapter 1. The appropriate conditions for meditation practice must be established. This means finding a place, such as a meditation center or monastery, where the normal distractions of daily life can be avoided. The mind cannot settle down and still itself to the degree necessary for jhāna if it is receiving an incessant stream of inputs. And then we must guard the sense doors, protecting our focus from other sights, sounds, thoughts, or sensations that arise in our experience.

Internal seclusion begins as our attention focuses inward. As concentration deepens, the mind becomes quiet and is said to be "secluded from unwholesome states." This is called "internal seclusion" because, with this degree of samādhi, the mind has reached a strong enough degree of stillness that it is not susceptible to the hindrances.

Vitakka-vicāra

The Pāli terms for the expression "thought and examination," the first two jhāna factors, are *vitakka-vicāra*. These are problematic terms, difficult to arrive at the original intended meaning as used in the definition of jhāna. *Vitakka* (from the Pāli root *takka,* meaning "to think") means "reflection, thought, thinking, or initial application of mind." *Vicāra* (from the Pāli root *car,* "to move about") means investigation, examination, consideration, deliberation, or sustained application.

Although the term *vitakka* is sometimes used alone in the suttas, the term *vicāra* rarely is. These terms, when used together, as in the jhāna definition, should be taken as one expression. Together, they are variously translated as "reflection and investigation," "thinking and pondering," "thought and examination," "applied and sustained thought," "thought-conception and discursive thinking," "connecting and sustaining," "initial and sustained mental application," and "directed thought and evaluation."

Two distinct meanings are suggested from these various renderings, one indicating mental activities such as thinking, reflecting, and so on, and the other referring to the mental activity of connecting and sustaining the attention on a meditation subject. Since there is controversy over how these terms should be interpreted and understood, "thought and examination" were chosen for the translation of the jhāna definition used here, being close to the literal meanings.

Etymologically, it is hard to get away from at least some sense of discursive thinking in the meaning of vitakka-vicāra, so the probable meaning is that thinking, or some other forms of mental activity, is present in the first jhāna. Support for this idea can be found in the suttas, which state:

> With the stilling of thought and examination, he enters and abides in the second jhāna, [which is characterized by] rapture and pleasure born of concentration, and accompanied by inner composure and singleness of mind, without thought and examination. This is called noble silence.[10]

Thought and examination, in the everyday sense, are called the "verbal formation," leading from ordinary thinking to speech:

> Why are thought and examination the verbal formation? . . . First, one thinks and examines, and then begins speaking; that is why thought and examination are the verbal formation.[11]

Elsewhere the suttas state that speech ceases for one who has entered the first jhāna.[12] These two statements can be brought into harmony by observing that verbal mental formations precede external speech. In the first jhāna, one may still verbalize internally, but one does not break into speech.

Jhāna is attained by directing the mind to some meditation object in order to strengthen concentration, so clearly the connecting and sustaining aspects of vitakka-vicāra are essential in practices leading up to jhāna.

"Vitakka-vicāra as jhāna factors" refers to qualities present upon having entered the first jhāna, rather than the qualities of mind and practices required for its realization. We should make a distinction between connecting and sustaining the attention in order to attain jhāna, and the qualities vitakka-vicāra once jhāna has been attained.

Upon attainment of the first jhāna, either the qualities of connecting and sustaining the mind on its meditation object, or the mental activities of directed thought and evaluation, or both are present. In jhāna any mental activity is integrated and synthesized with all the other associated jhāna and supporting factors.

Vitakka-vicāra should never be understood as thinking or musing in the ordinary sense. The salient unifying feature unique to vitakka-vicāra as jhāna factors is the function of applying and sustaining the mind to its object, rather than just recognition that thinking is present in the first jhāna. Vitakka-vicāra is not mere thought; it is applied thought and sustained thought. Applied thought is inclusive of all mental activity, and entails directing and focusing the whole mind, including its thinking capability, wholeheartedly and exclusively on the meditation object. Sustained thought denotes maintaining the full continuous, stable, and undistracted mental faculty on that object. Though the Pāli suttas do not state this explicitly, regardless of how one renders vitakka-vicāra, even as the presence of thinking and pondering, it seems that it always includes the aspect of connecting and sustaining.

Pīti-sukha

Rapture and pleasure, the third and fourth jhāna factors, are said to be born of seclusion because they are a natural outcome of a mind that is secluded from the hindrances. A mind free from desire, aversion, agitation, sluggishness, and doubt is invariably happy and peaceful, and readily engaged in the process and progression in meditation. The Pāli term for rapture is *pīti,* also translated as "bliss, joy, delight, zest, and exuberance." The term for pleasure is *sukha,* rendered variously as "happiness, joy, agreeable, pleasure, and bliss." From these various meanings, we can see that pīti and sukha are understood as being similar, though not identical.

Pīti is quite strong energetically, often experienced as intense bliss, energy, light, or manifesting in various other ways. Its rapturous quality keeps the mind keenly involved in the meditative experience in the first two jhānas. Sukha, which is by no means weak, is milder, more even and more settled than pīti. Pīti is often seductive during the initial stages of development, but may later feel too coarse as the mind settles into subtler levels of happiness in the later stages of concentration. Pīti could be a mental or physical quality; the suttas nowhere make this distinction, and some later practice traditions insist that pīti is a physical phenomenon. The happiness or pleasant experience of sukha can also be either mental or physical. Sukha is defined in the third jhāna as purely a physical experience.

Sukha has been translated as "pleasure" in the jhāna definition in order to emphasize its connection with the body, especially in the jhāna similes, where rapture and pleasure are suffused throughout the body. Pīti and sukha are jhāna factors present in the first two jhānas, but are also important qualities leading up to jhāna. *Sukha* is translated as "happiness" in those contexts, highlighting its function as a supportive condition leading to concentration:

> Concentration has a proximate cause . . . happiness. Happiness has a proximate cause . . . tranquility. Tranquility has proximate cause . . . rapture. Rapture has a proximate cause . . . gladness.[13]

Gladness naturally arises when the five hindrances are absent.

> When the five hindrances are absent within him, gladness arises, and being glad, rapture (pīti) arises. Because of rapture his body becomes tranquil, with his body tranquillized he feels happiness (sukha), and with happiness his mind becomes concentrated. Quite secluded from sensual pleasures, secluded from unwholesome states, he enters and abides in the first jhāna [which is characterized by] rapture and pleasure born of seclusion, and accompanied by thought and examination.[14]

Rapture arises prior to entering the first jhāna, is a supportive conditioning factor leading to its attainment, and is sustained until reaching the third jhāna.

Ekaggatā

Cittass' ekaggatā, the fifth jhāna factor, is translated as "one-pointedness, singleness, and unification of mind." Sustained undistractedness is what most determines whether or not a particular meditative state is jhāna. All of the jhāna factors are present to varying degrees of intensity throughout a wide range of levels of samādhi. Even in the early stages of meditative development, the power of applied and sustained attention increases as the mind begins to settle, resulting in a greater calm that can be pleasant or blissful. Well before attaining jhāna the meditator experiences longer periods of undistracted awareness as the ability to remain steady on the meditation object increases. An undistracted mind, in concert with the other factors, is a characteristic distinquishing jhāna from the lower levels of samādhi. While in jhāna the mind is not subject to wandering.

Some traditions maintain that ekaggatā means being aware of only one point; others, that it indicates maintaining a single center in a larger range of awareness. The term *one-pointedness* suggests a stable focus on a single object, in which no other awareness arises besides the meditation subject. One-pointedness is single-minded concentration, the ability of the mind to remain, without distraction, unwavering and steady on the fixed object of its attention.

Ekaggatā translated as "unification of mind" includes this meaning, but can also suggest another connotation. Rather than a mind fixed on one object, in which the experience of changing phenomena is lost, in this state the mind itself is unmoving, not the objects of experience, as all mental faculties come together, are unified and synthesized into an integrated whole. Even while the experience of objects is ever-changing, the mind itself remains still, present, and clear.

Ekaggatā is used in several places in the suttas to describe all levels of jhāna.[15] The term does not appear in the jhāna definition itself, though. *Cetaso ekodibhāvaṃ* is a similar term, also used to describe the focused application and undistracted nature of the mind in jhāna, which is explicitly mentioned at only one place, in the definition of the second jhāna. An injunction related to ekodibhāvaṃ, cittaṃ ekodiṃ karohi, occurs in reference to the first jhāna in the Moggallānasaṃyutta. Here the Buddha exhorts the struggling Moggallāna, who became one of the Buddha's two chief disciples, "Do not be negligent regarding the first jhāna. Steady your mind in the first jhāna, *unify your mind in the first jhāna,* concentrate your mind in the first jhāna"[16] (italics are mine). Translated as "singleness of mind," "unification of mind," and "one-pointedness of awareness," *ekodibhāvaṃ* is similar in meaning to *ekaggatā,* and is also open to interpretation as meaning either a narrow, fixed attention or a still mind with a broader awareness.

In this discussion, the term "unification of mind" is being used whenever referring to *ekaggatā,* and "singleness of mind" is being used for the term *ekodibhāvaṃ* in the jhāna definition, to emphasize in both cases the aspect of mind that is unmoving, but clearly aware of a broad range of changing phenomena. One-pointedness will be used specifically to refer to states of single-pointed awareness fixed on a single object.

The Second Jhāna

> With the stilling of thought and examination, he enters and abides in the second jhāna [which is characterized by] rapture and pleasure born of concentration, and accompanied by inner composure and singleness of mind, without thought and examination.

Progress through the stages of jhāna is not accomplished by adding new factors, but by abandoning some of the factors already there. The second jhāna is attained upon the elimination or fading away of two factors, thought and examination, leaving three remaining factors of rapture, pleasure, and unification of mind. Inner composure, a new element introduced for the second jhāna, is not a jhāna factor, but is highlighted in the formula as a prominent feature in this state.

The meditator attains the second jhāna and, again, pervades the body, this time with rapture and pleasure born of concentration: "He makes the rapture and pleasure born of concentration drench, steep, fill, and pervade this body, so that there is no part of his whole body unpervaded by the rapture and pleasure born of concentration. Just as though there were a lake whose waters welled up from below and it had no inflow from east, west, north or south and would not be replenished from time to time by showers of rain, then the cool fount of water welling up in the lake would make the cool water drench, steep, fill, and pervade the lake, so that there would be no part of the whole lake unpervaded by cool water; so too, a bhikkhu makes the rapture and pleasure born of concentration drench, steep, fill, and pervade this body, so that there is no part of his whole body unpervaded by the rapture and pleasure born of concentration."

The tone has shifted from the simile of the first jhāna, reflecting the deepening calm associated with the second jhāna. The seclusion of the second jhāna is much more stable than that of the first, and the image of cool water gives the impression of a well-established tranquillity and settledness. One does not have to put in the same effort as in the first jhāna; meditation has achieved a momentum and progresses more on its own. As the meditator deepens into the second jhāna, the mind becomes more "cool" with the subsiding of thought and examination.

The rapture and pleasure of the first jhāna are said to be born of seclusion. The second jhāna is characterized by rapture and pleasure born of concentration. With the stilling of thought and examination, the mind is more concentrated and unified than in the first jhāna. The kneading mentioned in the first simile stands for the function of vitakka and vicāra. In the second jhāna, where these two activities are dropped, the suffusing is more effortless, as when cool waters naturally fill the lake simply by flowing from the unified focus of the spring. In this image water is welling up from a deep internal place, conveying much more a sense of being self-contained and suffusing the body from within.

Having connected and sustained the mind on its meditation object, vitakka-vicāra drops away upon attaining the second jhāna, leaving only the jhāna factors rapture, pleasure, and unification of mind. Because thought and examination, the verbal formation, are no longer present, the second jhāna is called "noble silence." The importance of removing vitakka-vicāra in attaining the second jhāna is emphasized with the repetition that the second jhāna is attained with the stilling of vitakka-vicāra, and results in a state without vitakka-vicāra.

As concentration deepens, the mind becomes more still. The mind in the second jhāna is free from discursive thought. If vitakka-vicāra is viewed as connecting and sustaining the mind on its meditation object, we can see that this, too, drops away in the deeper levels of samādhi. Concentration has been sufficiently strengthened so that it need not be tethered to an object by the factors of vitakka and vicāra, since it naturally remains steady through singleness of mind. At this stage the awareness remains stable and unbroken. The Samaṇamaṇḍikā Sutta states that wholesome intentions, a form of mental activity, cease without remainder with the subsiding of vitakka-vicāra upon entering the second jhāna.[17]

Upon attaining the second jhāna, one gains inner composure and singleness of mind. The Pāli term used here for inner composure, *sampasādana,* also means "tranquillity," and is translated variously as "self-confidence," "internal assurance," and "serene purity" (from *pasādana,* which means "a happy state or purity"). Composure and concentration are not identical, but are associated. Confidence and composure are both fruits of a concentrated mind, as well as factors strengthening concentration, as the meditator's practice bears fruit, the much more stable mind is further secluded from the hindrances, and direct, clear seeing and knowing deepens.

In the standard formula for the first jhāna, concentration is not mentioned at all, although it has been strengthened to a high degree manifesting as mental unification. Concentration appears twice in the formula for the second jhāna, emphasizing its prominence, once directly and a second time indirectly as singleness of mind. Although, by normal standards the mind is extraordinarily concentrated in the first jhāna, because vitakka-vicāra is active, concentration is subject to agitation. Concentration is mentioned in the formula for the second jhāna because, with the stilling of vitakka-vicāra, the mind becomes much better established, unwavering, and secure, reaching a much deeper level.

In the second jhāna, rapture and pleasure are born of concentration, arising in dependence on the concentration, rapture, and pleasure of the first jhāna, and also in dependence on and supported by the concentration of the second jhāna itself. In the first jhāna, rapture and pleasure were said to be born of seclusion, a consequence of being sheltered from the hindrances. Because the meditator has already obtained rapture and pleasure born of seclusion in the first jhāna, the rapture and pleasure of the second jhāna is born of a deeper level of concentration. Since vitakka-vicāra has subsided and concentration has strengthened, the rapture and pleasure of the second jhāna are of a distinctive nature, and may be, but are not necessarily, of a finer, quieter texture.

An Alternate Scheme for the First Two Jhānas

A threefold classification of samādhi introducing an intermediate stage between the first and second jhānas, which appears to be an alternative arrangement for the first two jhānas, is briefly mentioned in a few places.[18] This threefold system does not appear in the jhāna formula, or anywhere else other than in these suttas, and is only briefly mentioned without providing any explanatory detail.

There is concentration with thought and examination (as in the first jhāna), concentration without thought but with examination only, and concentration without thought and examination (as in the second jhāna). Concentration with thought but without examination does not fit into the standard jhāna scheme.

The term *samādhi,* not *jhāna,* is used here, so this formula might not necessarily be referring to an alternative jhāna system. However, though these three types of samādhi mostly appear only as a simple list, in one sutta it states that the Buddha, just before his enlightenment, "developed concentration with thought and examination; concentration without thought but with examination only . . . without thought and examination . . . with rapture . . . without rapture . . . accompanied by enjoyment . . . developed concentration accompanied by equanimity."[19] With the exception of enjoyment (Pāli: sāta), which does not appear in the jhāna formula, this sequence roughly follows the progression through the four jhānas in the standard definition.

The Third Jhāna

With the fading away of rapture, he abides in equanimity, mindful and clearly aware, feeling pleasure with the body, he enters and abides in the third jhāna, of which the noble ones declare: "Equanimous and mindful he abides in pleasure."

Upon entering the third jhāna, the simile continues: "He makes the pleasure divested of rapture drench, steep, fill, and pervade this body, so that there is no part of his whole body unpervaded by the pleasure divested of rapture. Just as in a pond of blue or red or white lotuses, some lotuses that are born and grow in the water thrive immersed in the water without rising out of it, and cool water drenches, steeps, fills, and pervades them to their tips and their roots, so that there is no part of all those lotuses unpervaded by cool water; so too, a bhikkhu makes the pleasure divested of rapture drench, steep, fill, and pervade this body, so that there is no part of his whole body unpervaded by the pleasure divested of rapture."

The sense of the image has shifted again. The intense bliss of rapture associated with the second jhāna can feel agitating, and at some point the mind settles down further, giving way to a less forceful, subtler, and more satisfying experience. At this stage rapture has calmed down as the mind becomes more deeply immersed in stillness. The pleasure of the third jhāna pervading the body is subtler than the bliss of rapture. Just as a lotus that is completely submerged in cool water requires no source outside of itself, nothing has to come in from the outside. The coolness and calmness has become so deeply established that there is no sense of "suffusing" or "upwelling," but the body is completely suffused.

With attainment of the third jhāna, rapture has faded away, leaving two remaining jhāna factors, pleasure and unification of mind. With the subsiding of rapture, pleasure comes to prominence, being mentioned twice here in the formula. The suttas describe pleasure as a proximate cause for concentration, emphasizing that concentration continues to be strengthened and unification of mind remains a factor throughout all four jhānas. Three new elements, not considered jhāna factors, are introduced in the formula: equanimity, mindfulness, and clear awareness, also known as clear comprehension or alertness.

Equanimity strengthens and becomes noticeable in the third jhāna, as the mind becomes contented and serene. The term *equanimity* has a range of meanings. It can refer to neutral feelings, which are neither pleasant nor unpleasant. More important here, it denotes nonreactivity, where the mind rests mindful and clearly aware throughout a wide range of experiences without preference for any of them, including ones that can be very pleasant or painful. It should not be mistaken for lack of sensation, or a disassociated state, especially given that the formula mentions physical pleasure as a component of the third jhāna.

Mindfulness, keeping in mind the meditation subject, is present in all four jhānas, but this is the first time it is mentioned in the standard definition, emphasizing that it comes to prominence in the third jhāna with the subsiding of rapture. The Anupada Sutta states that mindfulness is one of eleven qualities, in addition to the jhāna factors and other attributes listed in the definition, associated with all the jhānas.[20] Mindfulness tends to be less apparent until the subsiding of the agitation of thought and examination, and the intensity of rapture in the comparatively coarse first two jhānas. Mindfulness and clear awareness are closely related and are often mentioned in conjunction.

The Fourth Jhāna

> With the abandoning of pleasure and pain, and with the previous disappearance of joy and grief, he enters and abides in the fourth jhāna, [which has] neither-pain-nor-pleasure and purity of mindfulness and equanimity.

Finally, upon attaining the fourth jhāna, "He sits pervading this body with a pure bright mind, so that there is no part of his whole body unpervaded by the pure bright mind. Just as though a man were sitting covered from head to foot with a white cloth, so that there would be no part of his whole body not covered by the white cloth; so, too, a bhikkhu sits pervading this body with a pure bright mind, so that there is no part of his whole body unpervaded by the pure bright mind."

In the similes for the first three jhānas, the body is pervaded by various jhāna factors. Now the style of the simile has shifted and there is no sense of making effort or doing anything. The pure bright mind covers everything, indicating the powerful lucidity, clear nature of mindfulness, and clear awareness accompanying this jhāna.

In one sutta, the simile ends with an inspiring promise of fruition from the practice and cultivation of jhāna meditation, through which many of the Buddha's disciples reached the culmination of direct knowledge.[21]

In the discussion of the third jhāna we saw that *equanimity* can refer either to neutral feelings, which are neither pleasant nor unpleasant, or to a nonreactive mind. The formula for the fourth jhāna introduces two new elements—neither-pain-nor-pleasure and purity of mindfulness and equanimity—which together serve to underscore the presence of both aspects of equanimity. Neither-painful-nor-pleasant, also called "equanimous feeling," is the neutral bodily feeling remaining after pleasure, pain, joy, and grief are all eliminated. At this stage, with strong equanimity firmly established, mindfulness is said to be purified. The mind is detached, in the sense of not being pulled into or away from experiences, but is not disconnected or disassociated. Because the mind is not reactive, it is naturally clear and awake, able to be more present and mindful, unmoving and unperturbed by any experience.

The first four jhāna factors have been eliminated in the fourth jhāna, leaving only unification of mind. Even though it is not mentioned at this point in the formula, the fourth jhāna is characterized by a high level of concentration and calm, so mental unification remains as a jhāna factor. Neither-painful-nor-pleasant feeling is sometimes considered a second factor in the fourth jhāna, replacing pleasure, which has been eliminated.

Beyond the Four Jhānas
Three Divergent Paths of Development

Upon mastery of the four jhānas, three further paths of training and development are possible. These three divergent paths each have distinct goals and associated practices.

First, beyond the four jhānas already discussed, four additional higher immaterial or formless attainments are described. In the suttas, these formless states are called "āruppas" (*āruppa* means "without form"). In the later commentaries, the four jhānas are called "rūpa jhānas," and the āruppas retain their designation, although in a few instances they are referred to as "arūpa jhānas."

The first of the āruppas is called "the base of the boundlessness of space," in which awareness of the body falls away, leaving only the experience of limitless space. According to the suttas, the base of the boundlessness of space is attained by not attending to any sensory stimulation, transcending all perceptions of form, and perceiving boundless space directly."[22] The next āruppas are called respectively "the base of the boundlessness of consciousness," "the base of nothingness," and, finally, a state so subtle that it can only be called "the base of neither-perception-nor-nonperception."

The āruppas are purely mental states, achieved by transcending any perceptions of form and sensory awareness. These are extremely subtle meditative states, not defined in terms of the factors associated with the four jhānas. The four jhānas were attained in order, by systematically eliminating the grosser jhāna factors. Moving from the fourth jhāna to the āruppas does not involve the abandoning of further jhāna factors, but rather a shift in the object of concentration. One means of doing this is by directing the equanimity of the fourth jhāna to the desired formless state.[23] In the āruppas body awareness is lost as the meditator focuses on the quality of the formless state. Based on the concentration of the fourth jhāna, the object of concentration becomes the āruppa itself.

The second training accessible upon attainment of the four jhānas is development of the supernormal powers or higher knowledge (*abhiññās* in Pāli).

These amazing powers, widely described in the Pāli suttas, are rarely discussed by Western meditation teachers, though they are not unknown. Three higher knowledges are listed in some suttas: recollection of past lives, knowledge of death and rebirth of beings, and the knowledge of the destruction of the corruptions.[24] Other suttas expand this list into six abhiññās: (1) the various psychic powers, known as iddhis; (2) the divine ear; (3) the ability to read minds; (4) the ability to remember past lives; (5) the divine eye (which is the same as knowledge of death and rebirth of beings); and (6) the knowledge of the destruction of the corruptions.[25]

The first higher power is the iddhis, attainments of supernormal or psychic power far surpassing the capabilities of normal human beings. These powers are not considered miraculous, but are derived from realization of natural laws hidden from the minds of ordinary people. The list of iddhis includes the power to create multiple copies of oneself; pass through fences, walls, and mountains; dive into and out of the earth; walk on water; fly cross-legged through the air; and touch the sun and the moon. The divine ear, the second of the six higher powers, is the ability to hear heavenly and human sounds, both far away and near. The third power is the ability to know the minds of others, whether they are filled with passion, hate, delusion, are narrow or broad, expanded or unexpanded, surpassed or unsurpassed, concentrated or unconcentrated, and liberated or unliberated. The fourth power is the ability to recollect past lives, extending as many lifetimes back as one wishes. The divine eye, the fifth power, is the ability to see the death and rebirth of beings.

The sixth higher power is the destruction of the corruptions, which leads directly to enlightenment. The Pāli term for the corruptions, *āsava,* means "to flow out or onto," and is variously translated as "taints," "influxes," "cankers," "corruptions," "floods," "intoxicants," "fermentations," "effluents," and "biases." Three corruptions are most often listed in the suttas:[26] sense desire, craving for existence, and ignorance. A fourth corruption, corruption of views, is sometimes added.

Along with the abhiññās, the suttas mention two additional insights and attainments accessible upon mastery of the four jhānas.[27] The first is the insight knowledge that "this body of mine, made of material form, consisting of the four great elements (earth, air, fire, and water), procreated by a mother and father, and built up out of boiled rice and porridge, is subject to impermanence, to being worn and rubbed away, to dissolution and disintegration, and this consciousness of mine is supported by it and bound up with it." The second attainment is the knowledge of the mind-made body, which is the ability to create from the physical body another mind-made body, complete in every respect.

The āruppas and the first five supernormal powers, developed through refined concentration, are not prerequisites for achieving the end of suffering. While they are profound meditative achievements, they remain subject to the same laws governing all other conditioned phenomena. Even these extraordinary attainments are limited in that they are impermanent and thus inherently unsatisfactory. The sixth supernormal power, the knowledge of the destruction of the corruptions, is attainable not through concentration alone but through insight, and thus is linked with the third path beyond jhāna.

The third path of training and development is insight, the path leading to Nibbāna, which is the ultimate goal of the Buddha's teachings. Through the application of mindfulness, and supported by the steadiness and concentration of jhāna, the meditator's awareness is able to penetrate beneath the ordinary, everyday way in which we view all experience in order to clearly perceive the three characteristics of existence, impermanence, unsatisfactoriness, and selflessness. It is through this direct seeing into the true nature of reality that the subtler levels of hatred, greed, and delusion are overcome, leading directly to liberation through nonclinging.

3

Samādhi in the Visuddhimagga

So wise men fail not in devotion
To the pursuit of concentration:
It cleans defiling stains' pollution,
And brings rewards past calculation.

Visuddhimagga XI, 125

AS THE UNDERSTANDING AND INTERPRETATION OF THE BUDDHA'S teachings evolved over the centuries, later commentaries appeared, each with their particular interpretations of the doctrine. The Visuddhimagga (Path of Purification), a voluminous work written around the fifth century C.E., has remained the most influential of the postcanonical Pāli works. While not a commentary, but rather an independent treatise, it is a cornerstone of the commentarial method. For some Theravāda Buddhists, the entire teaching is funneled through this one commentarial lens, coloring the perspective and greatly influencing the understanding and style of meditation practice.

The Visuddhimagga's basic framework is based on the Relay Chariots Discourse (Pāli: Rathavinīta Sutta[1]) in the Middle Length Discourses of the Pāli Canon.[2] In it, the path of spiritual development is likened to someone using a series of seven chariots to reach a destination. With the first chariot one reaches the second, with the second chariot one reaches the third, and so on until with the seventh chariot one reaches the final destination. Similarly, spiritual progress unfolds in seven stages, with each step being cultivated in order to bring one to the next.

The seven stages of purification are as follows: (1) purification of virtue, (2) purification of mind, (3) purification of view, (4) purification by overcoming doubt, (5) purification by knowledge and vision of what is the path and what is not the path, (6) purification by knowledge and vision of the way, and (7) purification by knowledge and vision. Each of these represents a deeper level of insight and wisdom leading to final Nibbāna.

The Pāli suttas do not provide details to explain this scheme or its seven elements. For that we have to turn to the commentaries. Briefly, according to the Visuddhimagga, "purification of virtue" entails observance of whatever precepts or moral rules of behavior one has undertaken, five or more precepts for laypeople, or the monastic code of discipline for monks and nuns. "Purification of mind" is the attainment of "access concentration" (to be explained under "Three Levels of Concentration" on page 56) and of the jhānas. "Purification of view" is the understanding that a living being is merely a convention or an appearance based on the five aggregates. "Purification by overcoming doubt" is purity through elimination of doubt regarding the conditioned cycle of births and deaths. "Purification by knowledge and vision of what is the path and what is not the path" is the understanding that distinguishes between the wrong path based upon attaining certain seductive meditative states and the right path of insight into impermanence, unsatisfactoriness, and selflessness (Pāli: anicca, dukkha, and anattā, respectively). "Purification by knowledge and vision of the way" consists of a series of insights leading up to Nibbāna, and "purification by knowledge and vision" is attainment of one of the four stages of enlightenment.

The Visuddhimagga is a comprehensive and detailed manual based on this structure, with roughly half of it devoted to developing concentration and jhāna. The Pāli suttas, while often clear and precise, can be vague at times, without a lot of explanatory detail and open to various interpretations. The Visuddhimagga, in contrast, is meticulous and specific. The Visuddhimagga is a practical manual, filled with detailed descriptions of the various stages of samādhi and clear-cut instructions for meditation practice.

Tranquillity and Insight
Two Paths of Meditation Practice

The Visuddhimagga divides meditation practice into two distinct, separate paths, tranquillity (Pāli: samatha), in which concentration is cultivated to a high degree without regard to insight; and insight (Pāli: vipassanā), in which samādhi can sometimes be de-emphasized. In samatha meditation, attention is focused on an unmoving object, called a "kasiṇa," or on other meditation subjects, depending on the meditator's temperament, in order to develop and highly refine concentration until the attainment of jhāna. *Fixed* concentration is cultivated, concentration on a fixed object so intense that awareness of no other experience can arise, resulting in one-pointed focus and states of profound tranquillity and peace where all experience of changing physical and mental activity ceases. Subtle states of steady, undistracted awareness can ultimately be achieved, but awareness of changing phenomena is lost as the mind is fixed or absorbed into its meditation object and mental activity becomes still. The initial objects for focusing attention in order to achieve these states can be physical or mental. A list of forty meditation subjects is given.

Insight meditation may be practiced either after developing at least the first jhāna, or directly, without ever having practiced toward or attained any of the jhānas. In either case, insight meditation employs *momentary* concentration (Pāli: khaṇika samādhi), where samādhi is strengthened to a degree corresponding to that achieved in access concentration (see page 56), so that the mind is relatively stable, concentrated, and present for the moment-by-moment changing expression of unfolding experience, but not so much that it becomes fixed on an unchanging object. One is able to practice insight with momentary concentration, since the experience of changing phenomena is retained. Meditation progresses by observing with clear, steady mindfulness the full range of physical and mental experiences that arise, in order to reveal their changing and selfless nature. It is through insight, the direct experiential realization into the selfless and constantly changing nature of all things, both internal and external, that wisdom arises and clinging is abandoned. According to the system of the Visuddhimagga, insight cannot occur in jhāna because the mind is absorbed in fixed concentration. For one who has attained jhāna, insight is developed upon emerging from the fixed concentration of jhāna back to momentary concentration, and then considering the defects of jhāna and of all conditioned experience.

One who practices insight based upon the attainment of at least one of the jhānas is called "one who takes calm as his vehicle" (Pāli: samatha-yānika). One who practices insight without developing jhāna is called a "bare-insight worker" or "one whose vehicle is insight" (Pāli: sukkha-vipassaka or suddha-vipassanā-yānika, respectively). Attainment of insight without jhāna is called "dry" insight, because it is said to be "unmoistened" by the moisture of jhāna. None of these terms appear in the Pāli suttas.

One finds very few details about the dry-insight worker and khaṇika-samādhi in the commentarial literature, whether in the commentaries themselves or in the subcommentaries. Between them, however, more is said in the subcommentaries. In general, the Visuddhimagga, the commentaries, and the subcommentaries all seem to treat these topics as if there was already an understanding of them shared by the commentator and his readers. To come to a more analytical understanding, one has to piece together scattered references throughout all of these works.

Three Levels of Concentration

In the path of samatha—tranquillity—samādhi develops in three stages as meditation progresses. The first level of samādhi is *preparatory* concentration (Pāli: parikamma samādhi). This is the initial, undeveloped degree of concentration found in the normal, untrained mind. It is the ordinary level of concentration we have in daily life when focusing our attention on any object and is the level of concentration we bring to meditation practice when we first begin. Preparatory concentration varies greatly from one person to another since each individual has a different degree of natural concentration ability.

The second level of samādhi is *access* or *neighborhood* concentration (Pāli: upacāra samādhi). At this point the meditator is neighboring or close to accessing jhāna. One retains awareness of the full range of internal and external experiences, but is no longer distracted or agitated by them. The mind is still liable to wander, but much more infrequently, and if the mind does drift from its object, it tends not to be for long. It is at the level of access concentration that the hindrances are temporarily suppressed and a clear, undistracted awareness can be brought to any meditation object.

The third level of samādhi is *fixed* or *attainment* concentration (Pāli: appanā samādhi), which is the concentration existing during jhāna.

The bare-insight worker does not use samatha meditation at all, or uses it just for settling into the meditation. This meditator, at the very outset, takes up the practice of attending to the rise and fall of the five aggregates (or other phenomena), and this contemplation eventually brings khaṇika samādhi and the insight knowledges. In dry-insight practice, samādhi is developed along with insight contemplation, but does not reach the level of the jhānas. Technically, though, one who develops access concentration and then goes on to insight is a samatha-yānika, for the commentaries include access concentration among the attainments of samatha.

The commentary to the Visuddhimagga (Paramatthamañjūsā) sees the force of khaṇika samādhi to be equivalent to that of full absorption, presumably of the first jhāna, and that is on the commentarial understanding of jhāna.

> "Momentary unification of the mind": concentration lasting only for a moment. For that too, when it occurs uninterruptedly on its object in a single mode, and is not overcome by opposition (the five hindrances), fixes the mind immovably, as if in absorption.[3]

Khaṇika samādhi seems to be more vulnerable to opposition, to the influx of the five hindrances, than jhāna, because the mind has not removed itself from the hindrances to the same degree that jhāna has. But its force of stabilization is otherwise seen as equivalent to that of absorption.

Three Signs of Concentration

The term *nimitta* is used in the suttas in various ways, referring to the characteristic or outward appearance of an object; to a portent, foreshadowing, or sign preceding an event; and to the basis or theme of something. In the Visuddhimagga, *nimitta* is used in a special sense, referring to three specific signs obtained through meditative concentration practice.

The sign accompanying preparatory concentration is called "the preliminary sign" (Pāli: parikamma nimitta). The preliminary sign is the meditation object experienced at the initial stages of meditation practice. For example, in mindfulness-of-breathing meditation, the preliminary sign is the breath, wherever in the body one is focusing on it.

As concentration strengthens, a mental image of the meditation object begins to arise that can be perceived even with eyes closed. In the case of a nonvisual meditation object, such as the breath, a mental image of color or light arises in the mind. This mental image is called "the learning sign" or "acquired image" (Pāli: uggaha nimitta). At this stage, although concentration has begun to strengthen, it is still comparatively unsteady, as is the learning sign itself.

Access concentration is characterized by a steady mental image, called "the counterpart sign" (Pāli: paṭibhāga nimitta). The counterpart sign is unmoving, flawless, extremely clear, and steady. For the development of jhāna in the path of tranquillity, once the counterpart sign appears, the meditator continues to focus on it exclusively.

Concentration has strengthened to a great degree in order for the learning or counterpart sign to emerge. Both are strictly mental images. The Visuddhimagga distinguishes between them as follows:

"The difference between the earlier learning sign and the counterpart sign is this. In the learning sign any fault in the kasiṇa is apparent. But the counterpart sign appears as if breaking out from the learning sign, and a hundred times, a thousand times, more purified, like a looking-glass disk drawn from its case, like a mother-of-pearl dish well washed, like the moon's disk coming out from behind a cloud, like cranes against a thunder cloud. But it has neither color nor shape; for if it had, it would be cognizable by the eye, gross, susceptible of comprehension and stamped with the three characteristics. But it is not like that. For it is born only of perception in one who has obtained concentration, being a mere mode of appearance. But as soon as it arises the hindrances are quite suppressed, the defilements subside, and the mind becomes concentrated in access concentration."[4]

The counterpart sign appears differently depending upon the meditation object and the meditator; different meditators can have different kinds of signs even when using the same object.

Developing Samādhi

"Concentration should be developed by one who has taken his stand on virtue that is quite purified. He should sever any of the ten impediments that he may have. He should then approach the Good Friend, the giver of a meditation subject, and he should apprehend from among the forty meditation subjects one that suits his own temperament. After that he should avoid a [dwelling place] unfavorable to the development of concentration and go to live in one that is favorable. Then he should sever the lesser impediments and not overlook any of the directions for development."[5]

Preparation for meditation practice begins by purification of virtue, which is the first of the seven stages of purification. Purification of virtue entails self-restraint and strict adherence to the five minimum training precepts for laypeople, which are nonharming, nonstealing, sexual restraint, verbal restraint, and abstinence from intoxicants. These may be increased to ten or more precepts as desired. Monastics adhere to a detailed code of conduct involving several hundred training rules covering all aspects of behavior. As the purification of virtue matures and is internalized, it manifests additionally as "virtue as volition," the mental attitudes of nonharming, nonstealing, and so on, accompanying the bodily expression of self-restraint.

The next step in creating the supportive conditions for developing concentration is to sever the ten impediments of dwelling, family, gain, class, building (doing construction work), travel, kin, affliction, books, and supernormal powers. The first nine of these are impediments for developing samādhi, while the last is a hindrance only for the development of insight. None of these are inherently impediments, but only so if the meditator has become attached to them or they preoccupy the mind. For example, a dwelling "is an impediment only for anyone whose mind is exercised about the building, etc., that goes on there, or who has many belongings stored there, or whose mind is caught up by some business connected with it. For any other it is not an impediment."[6]

Once virtue has been purified and the ten impediments have been severed, a suitable meditation subject must be obtained from a qualified person, someone who is as far advanced in his or her own meditation and spiritual practice as can possibly be found. This person is known as "the Good Friend," and should be trusted to select an appropriate meditation subject from among the forty subjects specified, according to what is best suited for the aspirant's temperament. The six temperaments are as follows: greedy, hating, deluded, faithful, intelligent, and speculative.

Now that a meditation subject has been selected, a dwelling should be chosen suitable to the meditator's individual temperament. A person with a greedy temperament should select an ugly, unsightly place that arouses loathing when seeing it. One with a hating or a faithful temperament should select a place that is beautiful and makes one happy when seeing it. The deluded type will do best in a place that is not shut in, with a view of all four directions. For the intelligent type, any dwelling is suitable, whereas the speculative temperament should seek a deep cavern screened by woods, a place not open with a lot of views, since this person's mind tends to wander.

Finally, any lesser impediments should be severed, meaning that any details such as mending worn clothes, cleaning the living quarters, or grooming should be attended to. Now the meditator is ready to begin the formal meditation practice.

Meditation Subjects to Develop Samādhi

The Visuddhimagga spells out forty meditation subjects for samatha meditation. Each subject is best suited to people of particular temperaments and not others, and each leads to different levels of samādhi.

The forty meditation subjects are as follows:

Ten kasiṇas: earth, water, fire, air; the four colors blue, yellow, red, white; light; and limited space

Gratitude (?)

Ten kinds of bodily decay, also called "ten kinds of foulness": bloated corpse, livid corpse, festering corpse, and so forth
Ten recollections: Buddha, Dharma, Sangha, virtue, generosity, deities, mindfulness of death, mindfulness of the body, mindfulness of breathing, and peace
Four divine abidings: loving-kindness, compassion, sympathetic joy, and equanimity
Four immaterial states: the base of boundless space, the base of boundless consciousness, the base of nothingness, and the base of neither-perception-nor-nonperception
One perception: repulsiveness in nutriment
One defining: of the four elements

Under the guidance of an experienced teacher, one of these meditation subjects will be selected according to the student's temperament, aptitude, and needs.

Table 1: Meditation Subjects Suitable for Various Temperaments

TEMPERAMENT	RECOMMENDED MEDITATION SUBJECT
Greedy	Any color kasiṇa, beginning with blue, whose color is not pure; 10 kinds of foulness; mindfulness of the body
Aversive, hateful	Any color kasiṇa, beginning with blue, whose color is quite pure; divine abidings
Deluded	Any large-size kasiṇa; mindfulness of breathing; measureless kasiṇas
Faithful	Any color kasiṇa, beginning with blue, whose color is quite pure; divine abidings; any of the 10 recollections, especially the first 6
Intelligent	Any meditation subject; mindfulness of death, recollection of peace, 4 elements, repulsiveness of nutriment

Speculative	A small kasiṇa; any color, beginning with blue, whose color is not pure; mindfulness of breathing; limited kasiṇas
All Temperaments	Any kasiṇa; any of the 4 immaterial states

Jhāna in the Visuddhimagga

The four jhānas of the Pāli suttas have been renamed "rūpa jhānas" (fine-material or formal jhānas) in the Visuddhimagga. The sutta's four "āruppas" (immaterial or formless attainments of boundless space, boundless consciousness, nothingness, and neither-perception-nor-nonperception) are also usually called "āruppas" here, and are grouped with the four rūpa jhānas to form "the eight attainments" (Pāli: aṭṭha samāpatti). In a few instances the āruppas are called "arūpa (formless) jhānas" (the term *arūpa jhāna* is more typical of the Pāli subcommentaries than it is of the commentaries). Some meditation teachers designate the four āruppas as "jhānas 5–8," a nomenclature that does not seem to appear in the commentarial texts, so the term may have originated among modern meditation teachers.

All of the forty meditation subjects previously discussed can lead to access concentration, but only thirty lead to the first jhāna or beyond (see table 2). The ten that lead no farther than access concentration can be used for cultivating each practice's wholesome mental qualities for their own sake.

Table 2: Attainments Possible Through the Various Practices

MEDITATION SUBJECT	DEGREE OF SAMĀDHI THAT MAY BE ATTAINED
8 of the 10 recollections (not including mindfulness of breath and body), perception of repulsiveness in nutriment, and defining of the 4 elements	Access concentration only
10 kinds of foulness and mindfulness of the body	First jhāna only

First 3 divine abidings (loving-kindness, compassion, and sympathetic joy)	Up to third jhāna
Mindfulness of breathing, 10 kasiṇas	First 4 jhānas
Fourth divine abiding (equanimity)	Fourth jhāna only (first 3 jhānas must have been previously attained through one of the first 3 divine abiding meditations).
The 4 immaterial states	The 4 āruppas (access concentration and lower jhānas must have been previously attained through any of the kasiṇas, except limited space)

Access concentration, which is characterized by the arising of the particular counterpart sign associated with the meditation subject being employed, is the beginning point for further development into full jhāna absorption. Once access concentration has been reached, the meditator enters jhāna by focusing the attention solely on the counterpart sign until the mind is immersed or absorbed into that counterpart sign.

With the arising of the counterpart sign, the meditator has attained the level of access concentration. It should be noted that only twenty-two of the forty meditation subjects have associated counterpart signs: the ten kasiṇas, ten kinds of foulness, mindfulness of the body, and mindfulness of breathing. The remaining subjects also lead to access concentration, but have various signs other than counterpart signs.

Twelve contemplations have signs accompanying access concentration consisting of the individual essences or special qualities of the meditation subject. These are eight of the ten recollections (excepting mindfulness of the body and of breathing), the perception of repulsiveness in nutriment, the defining of the four elements, the base of boundless consciousness, and the base of neither-perception-nor-nonperception. The remaining six meditation subjects have signs that are classified in other ways. In the four divine abidings, access concentration is breaking down the barriers to those states. The bases of boundless space and nothingness take space and nothingness as their objects and signs, respectively.

Jhāna in the Visuddhimagga is a purely mental meditative state of fixed samādhi, in which the mind has become so intensely concentrated and focused on the mental image of the counterpart sign that all other experiences, including body awareness, are cut off. Fixed concentration is developed such that the mind is fixed or absorbed into the counterpart sign. The jhāna factors each have a function in absorbing the mind, but the object of experience is the counterpart sign itself.

For reference, the jhāna definition from the suttas is repeated here:

"Quite secluded from sensual pleasures, secluded from unwholesome states, a monk enters and abides in the first jhāna [which is characterized by] rapture and pleasure born of seclusion, and accompanied by applied and sustained thought.[7] With the stilling of applied and sustained thought, he enters and abides in the second jhāna [which is characterized by] rapture and pleasure born of concentration, and accompanied by inner composure and singleness of mind, without applied and sustained thought. With the fading away of rapture, he abides in equanimity, mindful and clearly aware, feeling pleasure with the body, he enters and abides in the third jhāna, of which the noble ones declare: 'Equanimous and mindful he abides in pleasure.' With the abandoning of pleasure and pain, and with the previous disappearance of joy and grief, he enters and abides in the fourth jhāna, [which has] neither-pain-nor-pleasure and purity of mindfulness and equanimity."

The Jhāna Factors in Detail

Vitakka-vicāra

Jhāna is attained through sustained concentration on and mental absorption into the counterpart sign, so the sustaining and connecting aspects of the jhāna factors vitakka-vicāra are emphasized in the Visuddhimagga, rather than discursive and other mental qualities suggested by the terms *applied* and *sustained thought*. Continuously connecting and sustaining the mind on the chosen meditation object are especially important aspects of practices leading up to the attainment of jhāna and fixed concentration.

"[In] applied thought (vitakka), hitting upon is what is meant. It has the characteristic of directing the mind onto an object. It is manifested as the leading of the mind onto an object. [In] sustained thought (vicāra), continued sustainment is what is meant. It has the characteristic of continued pressure on the object. It is manifested as keeping consciousness anchored on that object."[8]

Six similes are used to further clarify the nature of vitakka and vicāra, and how they are related. The initial contact of the mind onto the meditation object is likened to the initial striking of a bell, and the continued sustainment of directed attention is like the subsequent ringing of the bell. Similarly, vitakka is comparable to a bird spreading its wings when about to fly or a bee diving toward a lotus when it first catches its scent, while vicāra is like the bird soaring with outstretched wings or the bee buzzing around the flower after diving toward it. Vitakka is like the hand that takes hold and grips a tarnished metal dish; vicāra is like the other hand that rubs it with powder, oil, and a woolen pad. Vitakka is like the potter's supporting hand, and vicāra like the hand that moves back and forth when making a dish. Vitakka is like the pin that remains fixed at the center of a compass, and vicāra is like the pin that revolves around when drawing a circle.

Vitakka functions to initiate mental contact, and vicāra follows. Vitakka carries the mind toward and draws awareness onto the meditation object, creating the initial impression of the mind upon the object. Vicāra secures it there, continuing and sustaining that impression. Vitakka brings the awareness close to the object, and vicāra maintains a continuous, focused degree of concentration. Together they serve to immerse the mind into the counterpart sign, leaving behind the physical object as the mind absorbs into jhāna. Once the level of jhāna has been attained, vitakka-vicāra reflect the qualities of mind continuously connected and sustained in one-pointed concentration, "directing the mind on to the object in an extremely lucid manner, and sustained thought does so pressing the object very hard."[9]

Pīti (Rapture)

Rapture is purely a mental state that "refreshes, thus it is rapture. It has the characteristic of endearing. Its function is to refresh the body and the mind; or its function is to pervade. It is manifested as elation."[10]

Rapture develops in stages as the cultivation of concentration progresses. Five distinct types of rapture are specified, in order of increasing intensity: minor, momentary, showering, uplifting, and pervading. Minor rapture is able to raise the hairs on the body. Momentary rapture is like flashes of lightning occurring at various moments. Showering rapture breaks over the body repeatedly in surges, like waves breaking on the seashore. Uplifting rapture has the power to levitate the body and move it from place to place. Rapture reaches its peak at the level of pervading rapture, at which stage it fills and suffuses the entire body. Of these five types, it is pervading rapture that is referred to as a jhāna factor "which is the root of absorption and comes by growth into association with absorption."[11]

"This fivefold rapture, when conceived and nurtured, perfects the twofold tranquility, that is, bodily and mental tranquility. When tranquility is conceived and matured, it perfects the twofold pleasure, that is, bodily and mental pleasure. When pleasure is conceived and matured, it perfects the threefold concentration, that is, momentary concentration, access concentration, and absorption concentration."[12]

Sukha (Pleasure)

Pleasure, as a jhāna factor, is a pleasant feeling that has the characteristic of gratifying, its function is to intensify associated states, and it is manifested as aid for those states. *Sukha* is also translated and understood as "happiness."

"Whenever the two are associated, rapture is the contentedness at getting a desirable object, and pleasure is the actual experience of it when got . . . If a man exhausted in a desert saw or heard about a pond on the edge of a wood, he would have rapture; if he went into the wood's shade and used the water, he would have pleasure."[13]

Ekaggatā (One-pointedness)

The Visuddhimagga emphasizes the presence of the fifth jhāna factor, one-pointedness, in the first jhāna. "Although one-pointedness is not actually listed among these factors (in the formal definition) . . . it is a factor, too."[14]

The Eight Attainments

The First Attainment

THE FIRST JHĀNA

"The words 'quite secluded from sensual pleasures' . . . express bodily seclusion, while the words 'secluded from unwholesome states'. . . express mental seclusion."[15] Having arrived at access concentration, the meditator has already created strongly supportive conditions for meditation and seclusion by reducing or eliminating external distractions, and focusing solely on the initial meditation subject. From the point of access concentration, all the attention is focused on the counterpart sign, further secluding the meditator from sensual stimulation. As the mind absorbs into the counterpart sign upon entering the first jhāna, the process of seclusion from sensual impressions is strengthened even further, so the first jhāna is said to be born of seclusion since it is well protected from the hindrances.

Upon entering the first jhāna all five factors come to fruition, working in concert, each contributing to the overall quality of the state.

"Applied thought directs the mind onto the object; sustained thought keeps it anchored there. Rapture produced by the success of the effort refreshes the mind whose effort has succeeded through not being distracted by those hindrances; and pleasure intensifies it for the same reason. Then one-pointedness aided by this directing onto, this anchoring, this refreshing and this intensifying, evenly and rightly centers the mind with its remaining associated states on the object consisting in unity. Consequently possession of five factors should be understood as the arising of these five, namely, applied thought, sustained thought, rapture, pleasure and one-pointedness."[16]

Jhāna can be reached through effort, but it will not last unless the mind has been purified from the mental states that obstruct concentration. If jhāna has been entered before completely purifying and suppressing the hindrances, then the meditator "soon comes out of that jhāna again, like a bee that has gone into an unpurified hive, like a king who has gone into an unclean park. But when he enters upon a jhāna after completely purifying his mind of states that obstruct concentration, then he remains in the attainment even for a whole day, like a bee that has gone into a completely purified hive, like a king who has gone into a perfectly clean park."[17]

When jhāna is accessed for the first time, it usually can only be sustained for a few moments before the meditator reverts to access concentration. With continued practice, jhāna can be entered more and more readily, and can be sustained for longer periods. Eventually, the meditator has complete facility and control, which is known as "mastering the jhāna." It is crucial that each jhāna be mastered before attempting to move on to the next.

"There are five kinds of mastery. There is mastery in adverting, in attaining, resolving, in emerging, in reviewing. He adverts to the first jhāna where, when, and for as long as he wishes he has no difficulty in adverting, thus it is mastery in adverting. He attains the first jhāna where, when, and for as long as he wishes . . . He resolves upon [the duration of] the first jhāna when, where . . . He emerges from the first jhāna . . . He reviews the first jhāna . . . thus it is mastery in reviewing."[18]

At the point of mastery the meditator is ready to move to the second jhāna, beginning by reviewing the flaws in the first jhāna in order to break any attachment to it. Reviewing can only take place after the practitioner has emerged from jhāna, and so is no longer absorbed in the jhāna factors and is thus able to reflect on what has just been experienced. The first jhāna should be regarded as "threatened by the nearness of the hindrances, and its factors are weakened by the grossness of the applied and sustained thought."[19] As the first jhāna is reviewed in this way with mindfulness and full awareness, applied and sustained thought will appear gross and undesirable, and the second jhāna, with its rapture, pleasure, and singleness of mind, will appear peaceful.

Reflecting in this way, the attention is focused on whatever meditation subject is being used, developing its counterpart sign again. The practice method is the same as when cultivating the first jhāna, that is, bringing the sign to mind again and again, and keeping it there, except now the intent of abandoning applied and sustained thought and of attaining the second jhāna is maintained.

The Second Attainment

THE SECOND JHĀNA

"With the stilling of applied and sustained thought, he enters and abides in the second jhāna [which is characterized by] rapture and pleasure born of concentration, and accompanied by inner composure and singleness of mind, without applied and sustained thought."

The two jhāna factors applied and sustained thought subside upon entering the second jhāna, leaving the three factors rapture, pleasure, and one-pointedness. Inner composure, which is not a jhāna factor, comes to prominence at this stage.

The first jhāna inspires faith through the extraordinary experience of what has been achieved, which matures into inner composure and confidence with the arising of the second jhāna, since the agitation of applied and sustained thought is stilled. A profound degree of stillness and focus characterize any degree of absorption, but in the first jhāna an element of agitation remains. "Although the first jhāna was born of associated concentration too, still it is only this concentration that is quite worthy to be called 'concentration' because of its complete confidence and extreme immobility due to absence of disturbance by applied and sustained thought. So only this [jhāna] is called 'born of concentration'."[20]

Upon attaining the second jhāna the procedure for moving to the third is the same as previously discussed for moving from the first to the second jhāna. The second jhāna should be mastered in the same five ways as described for the first jhāna, and then its flaws are reviewed in order to break any subtle attachment to it.

"Once this [the second jhāna] has been obtained in this way, and he has mastery in the five ways already described [for the first jhāna], then on emerging from the now familiar second jhāna he can regard the flaws in it thus: This attainment is threatened by the nearness of applied and sustained thought; 'Whatever there is in it of rapture, of mental excitement, proclaims its grossness', and its factors are weakened by the grossness of the rapture so expressed. He can bring the third jhāna to mind as quieter and so end his attachment to the second jhāna and set about doing what is needed for attaining the third."[21] As the second jhāna is reviewed in this way with mindfulness and full awareness, rapture will appear gross and undesirable, and the third jhāna, with its pleasure and singleness of mind, will appear peaceful.

By focusing attention again on the meditation subject and its sign of concentration, with the intention of abandoning rapture, the meditator attains the third jhāna.

The Third Attainment

THE THIRD JHĀNA

"With the fading away of rapture, he abides in equanimity, mindful and clearly aware, feeling pleasure with the body, he enters and abides in the third jhāna, of which the noble ones declare: 'Equanimous and mindful he abides in pleasure.'"

One jhāna factor, rapture, has been abandoned upon entering the third jhāna, leaving the two factors of pleasure and one-pointedness. Just as inner composure and concentration came to prominence in the second jhāna, the salient feature of the third jhāna is equanimity, which is mentioned here for the first time in the jhāna definition.

Ten types of equanimity are specified, roughly grouped into three categories. The first category consists of various types of equanimity manifesting as nonpreference or neutrality toward any experience. The second category is equanimity of energy, meaning being neither too strenuous nor too lax in effort; and the third is equanimity as a feeling, which refers to experiencing neither-pain-nor-pleasure. "Of these kinds of equanimity, it is equanimity of jhāna that is intended here. That has the characteristic of neutrality. Its function is to be unconcerned. It is manifested as uninterestedness. Its proximate cause is the fading away of rapture."[22]

This is also the first mention of "mindful and fully aware" in the formula. The Visuddhimagga tells us that "this mindfulness, and this full-awareness exist in the earlier jhānas as well—for one who is forgetful and not fully aware does not attain even access, let alone absorption, yet, because of the [comparative] grossness of those jhānas the mind's going is easy [there], like that of a man on [level] ground, and so the functions of mindfulness and full awareness are not evident in them. But it is only stated here because the subtlety of this jhāna, which is due to the abandoning of the gross factors, requires that the mind's going always includes the functions of mindfulness and full-awareness, like that of a man on a razor's edge."[23]

Since upon entering any of the jhānas the mind becomes absorbed into the jhāna factors, awareness of the physical body is lost. Yet the jhāna definition states that the meditator enters the third jhāna while "still feeling pleasure with the body." The Visuddhimagga says this refers to the mental body while in jhāna, and to the material body only once one has emerged from jhāna.[24]

"Once this [the third jhāna] has been obtained in this way, and once he has mastery in the five ways already described, then on emerging from the now familiar third jhāna, he can regard the flaws in it thus: This attainment is threatened by the nearness of rapture; 'Whatever there is in it of mental concern about pleasure proclaims its grossness', and its factors are weakened by the grossness of the pleasure so expressed. He can bring the fourth jhāna to mind as quieter and so end his attachment to the third jhāna and set about doing what is needed for attaining the fourth."[25] As the third jhāna is reviewed in this way with mindfulness and full awareness, pleasure will appear gross and undesirable, and the fourth jhāna, with its equanimity as feeling and one-pointedness, will appear peaceful.

By focusing attention again on the meditation subject and its sign of concentration, with the intention of abandoning pleasure, or by using the divine abiding of equanimity as a meditation subject (providing the third jhāna has been attained through one of the other three divine-abiding practices) the meditator attains the fourth jhāna.

The Fourth Attainment

THE FOURTH JHĀNA

"With the abandoning of pleasure and pain, and with the previous disappearance of joy and grief, he enters and abides in the fourth jhāna, [which has] neither-pain-nor-pleasure and purity of mindfulness and equanimity."

A very high level of concentration and serenity characterizes this final formal jhāna, in which one factor, pleasure, has been abandoned, leaving only equanimity, meaning mental balance and neutrality, and one-pointedness. The equanimity that came to prominence in the third jhāna reaches full fruition in the fourth, being nonreactive to both pleasant and unpleasant feelings and culminating in a pure mindfulness.

Pleasure and pain, and joy and grief have all disappeared with the establishment of the fourth jhāna. "Pleasure and pain" refers to bodily pleasure and pain; joy and grief are mental pleasure and mental pain. Pain is abandoned with attainment of the first jhāna, grief with attainment of the second jhāna, pleasure with attainment of the third jhāna, and joy finally with the attainment of the fourth.[26]

"This equanimity exists in the three lower jhānas, too; but just as, although a crescent moon exists by day but is not purified or clear since it is outshone by the sun's radiance in the daytime . . . so too, this crescent moon of equanimity consisting in specific neutrality exists in the first jhāna, etc., but it is not purified since it is outshone by the glare of the opposing states consisting in applied thought and sustained thought, etc. That is why no one among these [first three jhānas] is said to have purity of mindfulness due to equanimity. But here this crescent moon consisting in specific neutrality is utterly pure because it is not outshone by the glare of the opposing states consisting in applied thought, etc. . . . that is why this jhāna is said to have purity of mindfulness due to equanimity."[27]

The Fifth Attainment

THE BASE OF BOUNDLESS SPACE

Beyond the four formal jhānas there are four further stages of absorption, known as "the āruppas" (formless or immaterial states) or "arūpa jhānas," which can be pursued once the fourth jhāna has been attained and fully mastered. These attainments, which transcend even the subtlest traces of physical form, are only possible if the fourth jhāna has been reached using any of the kasiṇas, with the exception of the limited-space kasiṇa. None of the other forty meditation subjects may be used to reach the fourth jhāna if the meditator wishes to continue on toward the immaterial jhānas.

The first of these formless absorptions is the base consisting of boundless space. The meditator wishing to develop this jhāna begins by reflecting on the insecurity and danger of physical substance, in order to become dispassionate toward materiality. Continuing in this way, dispassion arises even toward the materiality of the kasiṇa.

"When he has thus become disgusted with (dispassionate towards) the kasiṇa materiality, the object of the fourth jhāna, and wants to get away from it, he achieves mastery in the five ways. Then on emerging from the now familiar fourth jhāna of the fine-material sphere he sees the danger in that jhāna in this way 'This makes its object the materiality with which I have become disgusted', and 'It has joy as its near enemy', and 'It is grosser than the Peaceful Liberations'. There is, however, no [comparative] grossness of factors here [as in the case of the four fine-material jhānas]; for the immaterial states have the same two factors as this fine-material [fourth jhāna]."[28]

Once the danger in the fourth jhāna has been clearly seen and attachment to it has ended, the attention is again turned to the kasiṇa that is being worked with, and it is extended in a manner similar to that used for attaining the lower four jhānas. Only now the kasiṇa itself is extended, rather than the counterpart sign that was extended when developing the formal jhānas.

"When he has spread out the kasiṇa to the limit of the world-sphere, or as far as he likes, he removes the kasiṇa [materiality] by giving his attention to the space touched by it, [regarding that] as 'space' or 'boundless-space' . . . he does not advert to it [the kasiṇa] or give attention to it or review it, but gives his attention exclusively to the space touched by it . . . and when the kasiṇa is being removed, it does not roll up or roll away. It is simply that it is called 'removed' on account of his non-attention to it, his attention being given to 'space, space'."[29]

The attention is now turned again and again to the space left by the removal of the kasiṇa, using that space as the sign of concentration and striking it repeatedly with applied and sustained thought. Continuing in this way, the meditator attains access concentration using space itself as its object, and then, with "complete surmounting of perceptions of matter, with the disappearance of perceptions of resistance [to anything], with nonattention to perceptions of variety, [aware of] 'unbounded space', he enters upon and dwells in the base consisting of boundless space."[30]

The Sixth Attainment

THE BASE OF BOUNDLESS CONSCIOUSNESS

Cultivation of the sixth attainment proceeds in the same manner as did cultivation of the fifth, as the attention is turned from boundless space to boundless consciousness.

Once the fifth attainment has been fully mastered in the standard five ways, the meditator proceeds to contemplate the defects in the base of boundless space, reflecting that it is dangerously close to the fine-material absorptions (the fourth jhāna being the last and highest of them) and is not as peaceful as the base of boundless consciousness.

Then the attention is focused on the consciousness that pervades the space of the previous absorption. "He should give his attention to the base consisting of boundless consciousness as peaceful, adverting again and again as 'Consciousness, consciousness' to the consciousness that occurred pervading that space [as its object]; He should give it attention, review it, and strike at it with applied and sustained thought."[31]

Continuing to practice in this way, the hindrances become suppressed and the meditator gains first access concentration and then absorption. "By completely surmounting the base consisting of boundless space, [aware of] 'unbounded consciousness,' he enters upon and dwells in the base consisting of boundless consciousness."[32]

The Seventh Attainment

THE BASE OF NOTHINGNESS

Each of the absorptions has been attained by abandoning certain of their features, leaving a subtler remainder. Now the attention is turned to the only thing remaining once consciousness itself has been abandoned: nothingness.

"Suppose a man sees a community of bhikkhus [monks] gathered together in a meeting hall . . . then after the bhikkhus . . . have departed, the man comes back, and as he stands in the doorway looking at that place again, he sees it only as void, he sees it only as secluded . . . he sees only the nonexistence thus, 'This is void, secluded'—so too, having formerly dwelt seeing with the jhāna eye belonging to the base consisting of boundless consciousness the [earlier] consciousness that had occurred making the space its object, [now] when that consciousness has disappeared owing to his giving attention to the preliminary work in the way beginning 'There is not, there is not' he dwells seeing only its non-existence, in other words its departedness when this consciousness has arisen in absorption."[33]

After mastering the sixth attainment, upon emerging from it the meditator now reflects on its inherent deficiency of being close to the base of boundless space, which is a grosser attainment and not as peaceful as the base of nothingness.

The meditator should then "give his attention to the base consisting of nothingness as peaceful. He should give attention to the [present] non-existence, voidness, secluded aspect, of that same [past] consciousness . . . How does he do this? . . . Without giving [further] attention to that consciousness, he should [now] advert again and again in this way 'There is not, there is not' or 'Void, void' or 'Secluded, secluded'."[34] Continuing again in this way, the meditator gains first access concentration and then absorption into the base consisting of nothingness.

The Eighth Attainment

THE BASE OF NEITHER-PERCEPTION-NOR-NONPERCEPTION

All of the absorptions are profound states of extraordinary awareness that transcend our ordinary perceptions of reality. Beginning with the first jhāna, each successive stage of absorption is progressively harder to conceptualize. The eighth attainment, a meditative state defined by the simultaneous absence of both perception and nonperception, represents an extremely subtle state. "That jhāna with its associated states neither has perception nor non-perception because of the absence of gross perception and presence of subtle perception . . . This perception is 'neither perception' since it is incapable of performing the decisive function of perception, and it is 'nor nonperception' because it is present in a subtle form as a residual formation."[35]

Following the usual procedure, the base of nothingness must be mastered in five ways and then its inherent flaws contemplated by reflecting

"This attainment has the base consisting of boundless consciousness as its near enemy, and it is not as peaceful as the base consisting of neither perception nor non-perception or in this way 'Perception is a disease, perception is a boil, perception is a dart, . . . this is peaceful . . . that is to say, neither perception nor non-perception."[36]

At this point, as has been done throughout the progression through the absorptions, "He should give attention to the base consisting of neither perception nor non-perception as peaceful . . . As he directs his mind again and again on to that sign in this way the hindrances are suppressed, mindfulness is established, and his mind becomes concentrated in access. He cultivates that sign again and again, develops and repeatedly practices it. As he does so, consciousness belonging to the base consisting of neither perception nor non-perception arises in absorption."[37]

4

Controversies Surrounding Samādhi

Having released knots, a sage here in the world does not follow any faction when disputes arise. Calmed among those who are not calm, equanimous, he does not take up opinions, saying "Let others take them up."

The Buddha, Sutta Nipāta, 912

IT IS EASY TO SEE WHY THERE IS A RANGE OF VIEWS ABOUT SAMĀDHI and the nature of jhāna, and easy to understand why later commentators were eager to clarify the meaning of the Pāli suttas according to their own understandings. Many of the meditative states and techniques for attaining them are described very concisely in the suttas, using compressed formulas with little or incomplete explanatory detail, and so are only partially adequate as practical meditation guides. Sutta passages often rely on standard prescribed phrases, which served to assist in memorization for their oral transmission in the early centuries before they were finally codified in written form. A few of them sketch out a full map for the practice, but none of them fill in all the details. Although perhaps the details would have been enough for a practitioner during the time when the suttas were composed, the original meanings of some words, as intended within a sutta's context, may not be clearly understood by modern Pāli scholars (it is also quite possible that greater detail was provided orally, outside the formulaic pattern of the suttas). There is reason to suspect that certain passages were inserted at later dates. Unless we want to pick and choose the portions of the suttas we are inclined to accept as original, leaving the rest, we must accept the suttas as they exist today. We can find either inconsistency or congruency among the wide range of practices in the canonical and commentarial texts, depending on our viewpoint.

There is disagreement about what jhāna is, and the term is used to describe a range of experiences by various teachers. Jhāna is always defined by the standard formula, in which the presence or absence of five jhāna factors and other supplemental elements characterize the various levels of jhāna. Because these factors are present, to varying degrees, throughout a wide range of levels and types of samādhi, various meditation teachers, each presenting a different idea of what jhāna is, can legitimately claim to be teaching the "real" jhāna. There is no consensus on whether or not jhāna is necessary to realize the deeper stages of insight, and scriptural evidence can be found to support either view.

The scriptural sources can be conflicting. The Buddha of the early Pāli suttas taught contextually, varying his advice depending on his audience and the immediate circumstances. The suttas, therefore, are not entirely consistent, presenting an array of styles and approaches to practice that vary to suit the range of human temperaments, and lending themselves to various interpretations regarding the path of meditation.

Now that we have examined the range of ways samādhi and jhāna are described in the suttas and the Visuddhimagga, some of the controversy and disagreement surrounding samādhi and how it is taught can be discussed. The approach taken here is to remain open and receptive to reconciling the suttas and the Visuddhimagga, without having to do so, recognizing that there may be points of tension and incompatibility between the two. If the beginning premise is that the Visuddhimagga is the authority for understanding the suttas correctly, then the two sources must agree, and one will be predisposed to interpret the suttas in light of the Visuddhimagga. One will be disposed to construe the words and phrases of the suttas in the light of the explanations given by the Visuddhimagga. In the preceding chapters each has been viewed on its own terms, and they can now be compared in order to highlight their similarities and differences, convergences and inconsistencies. Various teachers and methods can then be surveyed without passing judgment on their interpretations.

The debates surrounding samādhi can roughly be summarized by three broad questions: (1) What is jhāna? (2) Are concentration and insight two distinct paths of meditation practice or one? (3) Is jhāna necessary for insight? The answers to all of these questions depend upon whether the Visuddhimagga is taken to be the authoritative interpretation of the suttas, and upon which interpretation of the suttas one adopts.

What Is Jhāna?

Competing views about the nature of jhāna arise, in part, because the descriptions given in the standard sutta definition can reasonably be understood and interpreted in more than one way. The passages do not contain a lot of detail. If we define jhāna only in terms of the jhāna factors, we may be confused. Though jhāna is defined by the standard formula, elsewhere the suttas make it clear that other factors must be present and working together. In order to understand what the suttas are conveying, the definition must be viewed within the context of the suttas' entire range of teachings and descriptions of samādhi and jhāna, which depict a dynamic state of sharpened clarity and awareness. Even if the definition is viewed within the wider framework of all the suttas' various depictions of jhāna, we are liable to disagree since the experience of jhāna is hard to describe.

A basic dispute regarding jhāna is whether one is aware of the body while in jhāna. There is controversy as to whether the mind is unified and aware of changing experience or one-pointed, whether it is a state of mindfulness and clear connection with body awareness or a purely mental state of fixed concentration in which there is no awareness of the body at all.

No suttas state explicitly that there is sense experience, as we normally understand it, in the jhānas. However, the suttas put much emphasis on mindfulness of the body as a key feature of the jhānas, emphasizing the integration of breath and whole-body meditation. An intimate connection with body awareness that is maintained and refined throughout all four jhānas is an essential component comprising jhāna in the suttas. This important aspect of jhāna is highlighted in the expanded jhāna similes, which repeatedly refer to the body being filled with rapture, pleasure, or awareness.

Heightened awareness of and connection with the body is both a characteristic of jhāna and a practice leading to it, as emphasized in the Kāyagatāsati (Mindfulness of the Body) Sutta, which states unambiguously that through attaining jhāna one develops mindfulness of the body.[1] The sutta begins with the exact text of the six contemplations on mindfulness of the body from the Satipaṭṭhāna Sutta: mindfulness of breathing, the four postures, full awareness of all activities, the constituent parts of the body, the four elements, and the nine contemplations of a decaying corpse. A new passage is added in this sutta at the end of each contemplation: "As he abides thus diligent, ardent, and resolute, his memories and intentions based on the household life are abandoned; with their abandoning his mind becomes steadied internally, quieted, brought to singleness, and concentrated. That is how a monk develops mindfulness of the body."

A seventh section is then added on jhāna, using the standard jhāna definition and similes, and concluding with the same phrase: "As he abides thus diligent... that too is how a monk develops mindfulness of the body." The sutta adds that one of the benefits of cultivating mindfulness of the body is the ability to obtain the four jhānas at will. Thus, the sutta states explicitly that body awareness is present in jhāna, which is the seventh in an ever subtler progression of practices and insights into the body. As the mind becomes tranquil and is brought to singleness, rather than losing awareness of the body in jhāna, mindfulness of the body is enhanced, as underscored by the jhāna similes.

In contrast to the suttas, the Visuddhimagga clearly describes jhāna as a state in which body awareness is lost as the mind absorbs into a nimitta, a mental image. Jhāna in the Visuddhimagga is a purely mental state characterized by fixed concentration in which no changing phenomena, including awareness of the physical body, can be experienced. All awareness of the body, and any changing experience, disappears as the mind absorbs into the nimitta and the jhāna factors, which is why one cannot do insight practice in Visuddhimagga jhāna. The Visuddhimagga reconciles this with the sutta descriptions, in which jhāna is a state of heightened body awareness, by stating that when the suttas refer to the body in conjunction with jhāna, they are referring to a metaphorical "mental" body:

"Now, as to the clause *he feels pleasure with his body* [from the definition of the third jhāna, the only place the body is mentioned in the standard formula]: here although in one actually possessed of the third jhāna there is no concern about feeling pleasure, nevertheless he would feel the pleasure associated with his mental body, and after emerging from the jhāna he would also feel pleasure since his material body would have been affected by the exceedingly superior matter originated by that pleasure associated with the mental body."[2]

It is possible to interpret jhāna in the Kāyagatāsati Sutta in this way, as referring to the mental body, since the word *kāya* means "group," "aggregate," "collection," or "body," and so could be used to refer to any group or "body," either physical or mental. However, the Kāyagatāsati Sutta is clearly about mindfulness of the physical body, beginning with the entire first satipaṭṭhāna on mindfulness of the body—mindfulness of breathing, four postures, all activities, and so on. In the seventh section on jhāna, there is no mention that the term *body* is going to have a new meaning in the following discussion. It is hard to conceive that the entire sutta would focus on mindfulness of the physical body and then switch to mindfulness of the "mental body" just in this last section on jhāna. It is unlikely that the Buddha would switch meanings for the word *kāya* without signaling that he is doing so, especially if it is so essential to jhāna that *kāya* not mean "physical body." Adding jhāna in the Kāyagatāsati Sutta emphasizes the connection of jhāna with mindfulness of the physical body.

So, while some sort of connection with or awareness of the body seems to be indicated in the suttas, the nature of this body awareness is less clear. Perhaps the suttas are referring to a subtler type of body awareness, not accessible through the normal sense apparatus.

Revisiting the Satipaṭṭhāna Sutta

One could argue that samādhi in the Satipaṭṭhāna Sutta is meant to be a pre-jhāna level. We have seen that the Kāyagatāsati Sutta begins by presenting all six contemplations in the first foundation of mindfulness from the Satipaṭṭhāna Sutta, adding at the end of each that "this is how one practices mindfulness of the body." The meditator is instructed in each of the six contemplations to bring the mind to singleness and concentration, further strengthening the argument that this sutta is talking about jhāna. But jhāna is then added to the Kāyagatāsati Sutta as a seventh contemplation, implying that jhāna is an attainment separate from the satipaṭṭhāna practices and that the Satipaṭṭhāna Sutta is concerned with a level of concentration below jhāna. Otherwise, why add jhāna as an additional practice? One answer is that jhāna is added here to indicate that jhāna is an outcome of the first six practices, as well as to highlight body awareness as a crucial aspect of jhāna.

The Jhāna Factors Vitakka-Vicāra

As I mentioned in chapter 2, there are two ways of interpreting the jhāna factor cittass' ekaggatā in relation to the practice of jhāna. The mind can become *one-pointed*—still and unmoving, intensely sustaining fixed concentration on a single object such that the experiences of change are lost. In another way of understanding ekaggatā, which we have called *unification of mind,* a broader awareness around the object is maintained. The mind itself becomes collected and unmoving, but not the objects of awareness, as mindfulness becomes lucid, effortless, and unbroken. In one case awareness of the flow of experience stops, while in the other case the mind itself stops, even while the ever-changing flow of experience continues.

The differences between these two views of ekaggatā are relevant to understanding the different ways in which vitakka and vicāra are understood to function in the first jhāna. If translated as "one-pointedness," meaning concentration fixed on a single point, including it as a factor of the first jhāna presents some problems since, it seems, one-pointedness is incompatible with vitakka-vicāra.

If we assume that *ekaggatā* means total, unmoving, one-pointed focus on a single object, exclusive of all else, then *vitakka* and *vicāra* must have a very circumscribed meaning, as nothing more perhaps than an instability in one's single focus. During any moments of true one-pointedness the mind is completely focused and "locked" on a single object, so it seems that no other mental activity could arise, including vitakka-vicāra in any of its usual senses, whether thinking and pondering, or connecting and sustaining the mind on an object. If a defining factor of the first jhāna is discursive thought, some sort of volitional activity, or other mental activity such as applying and sustaining the attention on a meditation subject, then by definition, it cannot be singly fixed in one-pointed concentration.

The mind cannot be simultaneously fixed in one-pointed concentration and engaged in some sort of activity.

Perhaps the list of five jhāna factors was a later addition to the Sutta Piṭaka, shifting the definition of *jhāna* away from the original meaning and adding a degree of inconsistency. Since the five-factor list is in the suttas, though, we must either accept this as an inconsistency or find an interpretation of the meanings of *vitakka-vicāra* and *ekaggatā* in which they can coexist.

Proponents of the Visuddhimagga approach to jhāna say that, in fact, vitakka and vicāra have functions other than those evident to us in normal sensory consciousness and that they perform these functions in the jhāna. Thus, vitakka and vicāra can be present in one-pointed concentration while one is engaged in activity, such as connecting and sustaining. In this understanding, a contradiction appears only if we limit vitakka and vicāra to active discursive functions.

The sutta simile for the first jhāna indicates a certain amount of purposeful movement within the context of the jhāna, engaged in spreading the sense of rapture and pleasure throughout the body. This would seem to indicate that vitakka and vicāra are more than a mere unstability or directing and sustaining the attention on an object, and instead that a certain amount of mental activity is a useful and essential part of the first jhāna. In this case, the second interpretation of "one-pointedness" as unification of mind may correspond better to the canonical descriptions of jhāna. If interpreted in this way, we can have a unified mind present along with the mental activity of vitakka-vicāra.

Are Samādhi and Insight Two Distinct Paths of Practice or One?

Interpretations vary regarding whether the cultivation of samādhi is an endeavor separate from the development of insight or whether samādhi and insight are two aspects of the same practice. Some say tranquillity and insight are two distinct practices, and that you must first develop jhāna and later switch to separate insight practices. Others disregard jhāna entirely and begin directly with insight practice, allowing concentration to strengthen naturally to the degree necessary through the application of mindfulness. Still others teach meditation in which concentration and insight are both emphasized and strengthened together. People have found evidence in the suttas to support all of these approaches.

The Visuddhimagga unambiguously separates meditation practice into two distinct types or paths of development, tranquillity and insight. The path of tranquillity focuses exclusively on the attainment of jhāna, defined as one-pointed concentration. The path of insight can be pursued either after attaining jhāna or directly, as the path of "dry" insight, in which case samādhi develops in conjunction with the contemplations leading to insight but does not reach the level of jhāna. The path of insight must be a separate endeavor from that of concentration in Visuddhimagga jhāna because sense contact is lost as the mind absorbs into fixed concentration, and insight cannot develop until emerging from jhāna and reflecting back on what has happened, considering the defects in the state and the desirability of not clinging to it. As the Visuddhimagga understands it, the mind can take only one fixed object, and this precludes the investigation of multiple, changing objects characteristic of vipassanā.

Though many of the suttas teach that liberating understanding arises through insight practice, supported by some degree of concentration, the suttas also place much emphasis on samādhi's important role in the development of insight:

> Bhikkhus, develop concentration. A bhikkhu who is concentrated understands things as they really are. And what does he understand as it really is? He understands as it really is: "This is suffering." He understands as it really is: "This is the origin of suffering." He understands as it really is: "This is the cessation of suffering." He understands as it really is: "This is the way leading to the cessation of suffering."[3]

If read without imposing any interpretation on them, the suttas seem to be saying that insight can occur within a jhāna. In the Anupada Sutta, Sāriputta is able to discern and analyze all the various qualities associated with each jhāna:

> And the states in the first jhāna: the thought, the examination, the rapture, the pleasure, and the unification of mind; the sense contact, the feeling, the perception, the volition, the mind, the intention, the determination, the energy, the mindfulness, the equanimity, and the attention, each of these states were continuously determined by him; those states were known to him as they arose, as they were present, and as they disappeared. He understood: "Truly, these states, not having existed, come into existence; having existed, they disappear." Regarding those states, he remained unattached, unrepelled, free, detached . . . in the second jhāna . . . in the third jhāna . . . and the states in the fourth jhāna . . . each of these states were continuously determined by him; those states were known to him as they arose, as they were present, and as they disappeared.[4]

In this way, it seems, Sāriputta was able to recognize, investigate, and develop insight into each of the jhānas and the first three āruppas while still in the particular meditative state. Only upon reaching the final āruppa, the state of neither-perception-nor-nonperception, and the state of cessation, could the attendant qualities be known only upon emerging from the state and reflecting back on what had just occurred.

Similarly, in another sutta, "The destruction of the taints occurs in dependence on the first jhāna . . . a monk enters and dwells in the first jhāna . . . whatever states are included there comprised by form, feeling, perception, volitional formations or consciousness (the five aggregates): he views those states as impermanent, as suffering . . . as empty, as non-self."[5]

There are suttas that could be interpreted to suggest that meditation should be practiced sequentially, developing samādhi until jhāna has been achieved and then switching to insight as a separate practice, just as presented in the Visuddhimagga. On the night of his enlightenment the Buddha practiced jhāna meditation before attaining numerous supernormal powers and then directing his mind toward insight into the Four Noble Truths to gain his final great breakthrough into full realization and ultimate liberation:

> I entered upon and abided in the first jhāna . . . in the second jhāna . . . in the third jhāna . . . in the fourth jhāna . . . When my concentrated mind was thus purified, bright, unblemished, rid of imperfection,

> malleable, wieldy, steady, and attained to imperturbability . . . I directed it to knowledge of the destruction of the taints. I directly knew as it actually is: "This is suffering"; . . . "This is the origin of suffering"; . . . "This is the cessation of suffering"; . . . "This is the way leading to the cessation of suffering"; . . . "These are the taints"; . . . "This is the origin of the taints"; . . . "This is the cessation of the taints"; . . . "This is the way leading to the cessation of the taints" . . . thus my mind was liberated.[6]

This is sometimes cited as evidence in the suttas that, although jhāna is a necessary prerequisite for insight, insight meditation is something distinct from, and practiced after, jhāna meditation.

A further example that could be interpreted as a sequential style of development is found in a stock passage recurring numerous times throughout the suttas, where a standard gradual path of practice proceeds progressively through the threefold division of the eightfold path: morality, concentration, and wisdom.[7] Beginning with morality, the seeker enters the homeless life and proceeds to live by the monastic rules of restraint and guarding the sense doors. He then finds a suitable place to begin formal sitting meditation practice, keeping mindfulness established and abandoning the hindrances. The disappearance of the hindrances leads to gladness, which leads to delight, leading in turn to tranquillizing the body, to joy, and finally to concentration. At this point, with the strengthening of concentration, the meditator develops the four jhānas. Only after mastering jhāna does he turn his attention to insight practices as he "inclines his mind towards knowing and seeing."

This is considered the complete model for graduated spiritual development, and is used to support the notion of two distinct types of meditative development as presented in the Visuddhimagga, where you must first develop jhāna and then switch to a separate style of insight practice. But this is not a generic instruction that one should first attain jhāna and then begin insight practice. Upon realization of the jhānas the mind is directed toward knowing and seeing, first that "the body is material, made up from the four great elements, born of mother and father, fed on rice and gruel, impermanent, liable to be injured and abraded, broken and destroyed, and this is my consciousness which is bound to it and dependent on it." He then creates a fully formed mind-made body and develops the iddhis, supernormal powers, and the abhiññās (see chapter 2). Finally, the meditator applies his mind to the knowledge of the destruction of the corruptions, culminating with insight into the Four Noble Truths and final enlightenment.

Neither the above passage from the night of the Buddha's enlightenment nor the standard graduated path of spiritual cultivation say that the meditator comes out of jhāna into a lower level of samādhi to practice insight as a distinct form of meditation, but only that insight practice begins after the attainment of jhāna and the iddhis (it also does not say that one has to go through the iddhis before gaining insight into the Four Noble Truths). We could interpret these formulations either to indicate that insight meditation is begun as a separate practice after leaving jhāna or that it is begun based upon and while still in jhāna, all depending on how jhāna is interpreted and defined. In the Visuddhimagga you cannot do insight practice while in jhāna, so we could construe this passage as meaning that this progressive path unfolds first through jhāna, and then leaves jhāna and shifts to insight meditation as a distinct practice. In the suttas, since insight can be interpreted to occur at any level of samādhi, including, as we have seen above, jhāna, insight is a progression and natural outcome of jhāna.

In the Sammādiṭṭhi (Right View) Sutta, Sāriputta delivers a discourse on sixteen dharma subjects and ways of understanding them, through which a person is endowed with right view and, thus, arrives at the true Dharma.[8] When any one of these truths has been realized, the Dharma practitioner attains final knowledge and deliverance by eradicating sensual desire, aversion, and ignorance, the root causes of suffering.

The first way a person possesses right view is through the understanding of what is wholesome and unwholesome conduct, and the root causes of each. The remainder of the sutta deals with fifteen additional dharma themes: nutriment, the Four Noble Truths, aging and death, birth, being, clinging, craving, feeling, contact, the six sense bases, mentality and materiality, consciousness, formations, ignorance, and the taints. Starting with aging and death, this list follows the steps of dependent origination in reverse order. The understandings associated with right view are insights into the cause, cessation, and way leading to the cessation of each of these fifteen dharma subjects. In each case, a person with right view understands that the way leading to its cessation is through the eightfold path, which includes right concentration.

The way to achieving these deep stages of understanding is not discussed at all. No mention is made of samādhi or jhāna, or any other practices leading to these insights. This might seem to suggest that concentration and jhāna are not necessary for enlightenment, strengthening the case for an insight path that is not dependent upon samādhi. But just because there is no mention of samādhi and jhāna does not necessarily imply that they are of no importance, or that these insights can be attained by means of a "dry" path of pure insight practice. This sutta is simply not concerned with describing the path leading to right view, but only in describing the nature of right view itself.

As in the Visuddhimagga, the suttas acknowledge that a person can develop either tranquillity or insight separately. Certain people are naturally inclined toward one or the other, and either can be emphasized. The suttas recognize that individuals differ in innate ability and skill in meditation, and so tranquillity and insight may not develop in a balanced way. Some practitioners will attain levels of deep tranquillity before discernment and insight have matured. Others will strengthen the factor of discernment leading to insight before tranquillity deepens.

> . . . he who has gained mental calm in himself, but not the higher wisdom of insight into things, should make an effort to establish the one and attain the other . . . he who has gained the higher wisdom of insight into things, but not mental calm in himself, should make an effort to establish the one and attain the other . . . he who has gained neither mental calm in himself nor the higher wisdom of insight into things should put forth intense desire, effort, exertion, impulse, unobstruction, mindfulness and attention for the attainment of those profitable states . . . he who has gained both these things should make an effort to establish those profitable states and further to destroy the taints.[9]

One can develop insight and then tranquillity, tranquillity and then insight, or both in concert. There is no stipulation that tranquillity at the level of jhāna must precede vipassanā. They can be developed in either order, but both are necessary in order to attain arahantship:

> [All who attain arahantship] do so in one of four ways . . . [one] develops insight preceded by serenity . . . or [one] develops serenity preceded by insight . . . or [one] develops serenity and insight joined in pairs . . . or [one's] mind is seized by agitation about the teaching. But there comes a time when his mind becomes internally steadied, composed, unified, and concentrated.[10]

There is not only one way that meditation practice can unfold, but regardless of how it develops, upon reaching its ultimate fruition both tranquillity and insight are bound together in balance, which is right concentration:

> [When] the view of a person . . . is right view. His intention is right intention . . . his concentration is right concentration . . . this Noble Eightfold Path comes to fulfillment in him . . . These two things—serenity and insight—occur in him yoked evenly together. He fully understands by direct knowledge those things that should be fully understood by direct knowledge.[11]

Whenever the Buddha talked about concentration, we can assume he was referring to right concentration, unless clearly stated otherwise. The suttas define right concentration as the four jhānas, meditative states imbued with many factors, including heightened mindfulness. Developing right concentration builds tranquillity and insight, leading to a deepening understanding of the Four Noble Truths.

We see a theme running throughout the suttas that through right concentration tranquillity and insight develop in concert, are practiced together and thus synthesized into a unified and complete practice and path. Jhāna in the suttas is not easily separated from insight: each supports the development of the other, and both are essentially integrated into one unified practice. Right samādhi entails integrating a depth of both tranquillity and insight. Whichever is developed should be retained while strengthening the other:

> Two things are conducive to awakening. What two? Tranquillity and insight. If tranquillity is developed . . . the mind becomes developed . . . and all lust is abandoned. If insight is developed . . . wisdom becomes developed . . . and all ignorance is abandoned . . . With the ending of lust the mind is liberated; with the ending of ignorance there is liberation by insight.[12]

Neither tranquillity nor insight unaccompanied by the other constitute right concentration, so if we develop either alone, we must make effort to strengthen the other. Calm and insight support each other and work together, and both must be cultivated in order to overcome anger, delusion, and lust.[13] A distinction is drawn in both the suttas and the Visuddhimagga between the practices leading to tranquillity and those leading to insight; tranquillity comes from trying to settle the mind, steady it, unify it, and concentrate it, while insight comes from regarding and investigating formations (Pāli: sankhāras)[14]—but, of course, settling the mind requires some insight into the verbal formations that disturb it, just as investigating formations requires a certain steadiness of mind.

Both are necessary, and both should be cultivated and brought into balance. Tranquillity is the calm and serenity achieved through one-pointedness and unification of mind, but mental calm alone does not constitute right concentration. This is why the development of insight needs to be specifically emphasized if the meditator develops pure tranquillity alone. On the other hand, if right concentration is developed, then tranquillity and insight can arise together.

Is Jhāna Necessary for the Deepest Stages of Insight?

> There is no jhāna for one without discernment.[15]
> There is no discernment for one without jhāna.
> One with both jhāna and discernment is close to Nibbāna.
>
> Dhammapada 372

Even if we divide meditation practice into two distinct paths, in which the attainment of insight entails practices distinct from concentration meditation, the question remains as to whether jhāna is a necessary precondition for engaging in the insight path. Enlightenment is always achieved through insight. Whether jhāna is necessary to attain the deeper stages of insight in meditation or will some lesser degree of concentration suffice is a question that overlaps with the disagreements over what constitutes jhāna. Some teach that jhāna is indispensable, while others teach that jhāna is of no particular importance to insight meditation.

Perhaps the strongest argument in favor of jhāna's essential role in awakening is that the Noble Eightfold Path defines right concentration as jhāna. The cultivation and attainment of jhāna is a fundamental part of the training, and, as such, we can reasonably conclude that it is an indispensable part as well. If that is true, the question remains at what point jhāna becomes indispensable. When, if ever, must jhāna be developed before further progress can be made, and what degree of insight and awakening can be attained without jhāna?

The Visuddhimagga acknowledges a path of the "bare-insight worker" leading to full enlightenment, where the meditator does not strive for nor attain jhāna, developing momentary samādhi no farther than a level equal to access concentration. For example, in reference to a specialized meditative state known as "cessation," in which there is a temporary halt to the experience of consciousness itself, the Visuddhimagga declares, "Who attains [the state of cessation]? No ordinary men, no Stream-Enterers or Once-returners, and no Non-returners and Arahants who are bare-insight workers, attain it."[16]

In order to find a similar dry-insight path in the suttas in which the deeper stages of samādhi play no part we have to look for occasional hints scattered throughout the suttas. The suttas contain examples of people attaining states of insight and awakening merely upon hearing a Dharma talk from the Buddha or another monk. Accounts are preserved of people from various walks of life attaining stream-entry after hearing a discourse from the Buddha.[17] In each of these cases there is no indication the people involved had any previous meditation experience or had attained any degree of concentration ability. In each case the hindrances seemed to be overcome prior to stream-entry solely through hearing a Dharma teaching.

According to the traditional account, the five ascetics, to whom the Buddha preached his first sermon on the Middle Way and the Four Noble Truths, attained at least the first stage of enlightenment, stream-entry, in this way. It may be that their minds had already become exceptionally purified and highly concentrated through the years of intensive austerities and other practices, so that their minds were ripe and receptive. Or it is possible they developed the jhānas in the one- or two-week interval between hearing the Buddha's first discourse and attainment of final arahantship. The story recounts only that enlightenment occurred upon listening to Dharma talks given by the Buddha.

Freedom from obsession with the five hindrances is among the factors associated with the fruition of stream-entry.[18] The hindrances can be removed by either suppression or eradication. The hindrances are temporarily suppressed throughout a range of samādhi up to jhāna. They can also be abandoned in a number of ways not dependent upon jhāna, through cultivating their opposites and through reflecting on wholesome qualities. Just through listening to the Dharma the five hindrances are said not to be present if one is fully attentive and engaged, with a sincere and serious attitude.[19]

All of these possible cases must be weighed against the large number of texts emphasizing the central role jhāna plays in achieving the stages of enlightenment. While people have found some evidence in the suttas for realization without jhāna, the Buddha emphasized jhāna throughout the suttas, so at the very least jhāna is a very important aspect of meditation practice.

A key question is whether attainment of the first stage of enlightenment requires prior attainment of the jhānas. The suttas are explicit that samādhi, in some measure, is indispensable for attainment of arahantship:

"Knowledge of the destruction of the taints occurs for one who is concentrated, and not for one who is not concentrated. So concentration is the path; non-concentration is no path at all."[20]

It is reasonable to assume the Buddha is referring to right concentration here, though that is not stated directly. The following passage, too, though not asserting that jhāna attainment is an absolutely indispensable condition for the attainment of arahantship, stresses the role jhāna plays in its realization:[21]

"I declare, O monks, that the destruction of the taints occurs in dependence on the first jhāna, the second jhāna, the third jhāna, the fourth jhāna; in dependence on the base of the infinity of space, the base of the infinity of consciousness, the base of nothingness, the base of neither-perception-nor-non-perception (the four āruppas); in dependence on the cessation of perception and feeling."[22]

There are no suttas that explicitly speak of arahants without jhāna, and proficiency in the jhānas is routinely ascribed to the arahants. In chapter 1 we saw that anyone who has ever been enlightened, or who ever will be, has done so through realization of the seven factors of enlightenment, which appears to be tantamount to the four jhānas. Right concentration of the eightfold path is defined as the four jhānas, and the four jhānas are integral to the complete model of monastic progressive training, as mentioned in the preceding section, as well as the threefold higher training: "There are these three trainings: the training in the higher virtue, the training in the higher mind, and the training in the higher wisdom . . . . And what is the training in the higher mind? . . . . one enters and dwells in the first jhāna . . . the second jhāna . . . the third jhāna . . . one enters and dwells in the fourth jhāna . . . this is the training in the higher mind."[23]

All of these examples seem to indicate that attainment of all four jhānas is necessary for arahantship. Other suttas, though, allow the possibility of arahantship with the attainment of any jhāna. The Jhāna Sutta, for example, states that one could attain any one of the four jhānas or lower three immaterial states, and then investigate the essential aspects of that state—form, feeling, perception, volitional formations, and consciousness—in various ways, for example as impermanent, as suffering, as empty, and as nonself, to name a few.[24] The destruction of the āsavas, and arahantship, follows directly if the meditator remains firm in the investigation. Similarly, in the Aṭṭhakanāgara Sutta, one may gain any one of the four jhānas, the four divine abodes (loving-kindness, compassion, appreciative joy, and equanimity), or the lower three immaterial attainments, and attain arahantship by contemplating that state as conditioned and volitionally produced, and thus impermanent and subject to cessation.[25] The implication is that the suttas describing right concentration and the training in higher mind as entailing the four jhānas should not be taken literally, but that attainment of any *one* of the jhānas is sufficient to attain the highest goal of liberation.

We might hesitate to read the suttas as definitely excluding the possibility of arahantship without jhāna, but at the least there is a strong suggestion it is so. Although jhāna may be a necessary condition for enlightenment, it alone is not a sufficient condition. The suttas define four kinds of persons, each of whom attains one of the four jhānas, but rather than the mind being freed, the person craves and clings to the jhāna experiences, "relishes it, longs for it and finds satisfaction in it."[26] After passing away, each person is reborn in a celestial realm corresponding to his or her particular meditative attainment, and after living in those realms for the duration of a normal life span (quite a long time in the deva realms), he or she is subject to rebirth in lower realms in unfortunate circumstances. Disciples of the Buddha, on the other hand, are similarly reborn in a deva realm if they attained jhāna in this lifetime, but are not subject to unfortunate rebirths and go on to final Nibbāna (are non-returners). This sutta makes it clear that meditative attainments are not to be sought after for their own sake, and also suggests that attainment of jhāna needs to be within the context of the full path, including virtue and discernment, in order to lead to the stage of non-return.

The suttas are conflicting regarding whether or not jhāna is necessary to reach the stage of non-returner. The Mahāmālunkyaputta Sutta states clearly that jhāna is a necessary condition for and the way leading to the state of non-returner (strengthening the argument for the necessity of jhāna for arahantship, as well) and that attainment of any one of the jhānas or the lower three immaterial attainments alone is sufficient:

"There is a path to the abandoning of the five lower fetters; that anyone, without coming to that path, to that way, shall know or see or abandon the five lower fetters—that is not possible . . . And what is the path, the way to the abandoning of the five lower fetters? [one] enters upon and abides in the first jhāna . . . whatever exists of [the five aggregates] he sees those states as impermanent, as suffering . . . he turns his mind away from those states . . . he attains the destruction of the taints. But if he does not . . . he enters and abides in the second jhāna . . . in the third jhāna . . . in the fourth jhāna . . . the base of infinite space . . . the base of infinite consciousness . . . the base of nothingness . . . this is the path, the way to the abandoning of the five lower fetters."[27]

The closing section of the Satipaṭṭhāna Sutta states that "if anyone should develop these four foundations of mindfulness . . . one of two fruits could be expected: either final knowledge here and now (Nibbāna), or if there is a trace of clinging left, non-return."[28] If Nibbāna or non-return are achieved dependent on jhāna, this passage is further evidence that the four foundations of mindfulness practices are meant to culminate in jhāna. If satipaṭṭhāna is viewed as a set of practices independent of jhāna, this passage could mean that jhāna is not essential for non-return, though that interpretation would be in direct conflict with the previous sutta passage.

A distinction is made between two types of non-returners: those who, after death, attain final Nibbāna with exertion and those who do so without exertion.[29] One attains Nibbāna with exertion by contemplating the unattractiveness of the body, repulsiveness of food, discontent with the entire world, impermanence in all formations, and the perception of death. A non-returner attains Nibbāna without exertion by attaining and dwelling in the four jhānas. This does not categorically mean that there are some non-returners without access to jhāna, though it seems to suggest so since they are contrasted with those who attain Nibbāna without exertion through the four jhānas.

The difference between a once-returner and a non-returner is the degree of samādhi developed: "[one] fully accomplished in virtue but only moderately accomplished in concentration and wisdom . . . with utter destruction of the three fetters and the attenuation of greed, hatred and delusion he becomes a once-returner . . . [one] fully accomplished in virtue and concentration (concentration is defined in a following sutta as the four jhānas) but only moderately accomplished in wisdom . . . with the utter destruction of the five lower fetters he becomes one due to be reborn spontaneously (in a celestial realm) and there attain final Nibbāna, without ever returning from that world (he becomes a non-returner)."[30]

Nowhere do the suttas tell us clearly either that the jhānas are required for the attainment of stream-entry or that they are unnecessary. The suttas do state categorically that the "stream" is defined as the Noble Eightfold

Path, which includes right concentration (jhāna): "The Noble Eightfold Path is the stream, that is, right view . . . right concentration . . . One who possesses this Noble Eightfold Path is called a stream-enterer."[31] This does not necessarily mean that the jhānas are prerequisites for stream-entry. Anyone possessing the eightfold path is a stream-enterer, but others might be so as well. Stream-entry could be attained well before mastering all aspects of the eightfold path, though the eightfold path must be incorporated to some degree.

The four factors with which a stream-enterer is fully endowed do not include concentration. The Buddha declared that a person possessing four qualities is a stream-enterer: confirmed confidence in the Buddha, the Dharma, and the Sangha, along with "virtues dear to the noble ones."[32] Attainment of samādhi to any extent is not mentioned.

Furthermore, in the Sotāpattisaṃyutta the Buddha teaches that a person who is a stream-enterer should make further effort to become concentrated. A noble disciple who is a stream-enterer, possessing confirmed confidence in the Buddha, the Dharma, the Sangha, and virtues dear to the noble ones, should not become complacent and should "make further effort for solitude by day and for seclusion at night. When he thus dwells diligently, gladness is born. When he is gladdened, rapture is born . . . the body becomes tranquil . . . [one] experiences happiness. The mind of one who is happy becomes concentrated."[33]

Although none of the four factors of stream-entry include insight, nowhere is it suggested that a stream-enterer is devoid of insight, but simply that his or her insight requires further work. In fact, there are a number of suttas that substitute for the fourth factor of stream-entry "the wisdom of arising and perishing that leads to the complete extinction of suffering."[34] The householder Dighāvu, an ill lay follower, declares to the Buddha that he possesses the four qualities of a stream-enterer. The Buddha then instructs him as follows: "Therefore, established upon these four factors of stream-entry, you should develop further six things that partake of true knowledge. Dwell contemplating impermanence in all formations, perceiving suffering in what is impermanent, perceiving non-self in what is suffering, perceiving abandoning, perceiving fading away, perceiving cessation."[35] All six of these contemplations are insight practices. Stream-entry entails attainment, but not mastery, of insight.

The same can be said of concentration. The stream is defined as the Noble Eightfold Path, which includes jhāna. But one can be a stream-enterer and only moderately accomplished in concentration: "[one] fully accomplished in virtue but only moderately accomplished in concentration and wisdom . . . . With the utter destruction of the three fetters he becomes a stream-enterer."[36] In a following sutta, concentration is defined as the four jhānas, so "moderately accomplished in concentration" would mean that the stream-enterer has some experience of jhāna but that jhāna is not yet fully mastered. Alternatively, "moderately accomplished in the four jhānas" might mean that the practitioner has done some work toward attaining jhāna, but has not yet reached that goal.

From the Suttas to the Visuddhimagga

We cannot know how the notion of samādhi and jhāna in the suttas evolved to the form we find in the later commentaries, but we can trace a few steps in that evolution.

Any experienced practitioner knows that meditative progress is marked at every stage by various signs, which are simply the experiences of the meditative states. How do we know if the mind is concentrated? It is through the direct experience of these samādhi states. The stability, calm, steadiness, rapture, clarity, and other characteristics of samādhi are the signs of concentration. These are not just accompanying signs; they are integral to and form the essence of the state itself. They are the experiences through which we know the mind is concentrated.

These signs can manifest in many ways, and vary widely depending on the individual's mental and psychological makeup, how the body is structured, previous life history, and numerous other factors. Signs of samādhi and jhāna can be experienced as sensations in the body, or can manifest through any of the other senses.

We have seen that access concentration in the Visuddhimagga is distinguished by a particular sign, the counterpart sign, precisely specified for each of the meditation subjects. The counterpart sign is the doorway leading to jhāna.

The counterpart sign for the ten kasiṇas is a mental image in all ten cases. For example, the earth kasiṇa sign is "like a looking-glass disk drawn from its case, like a mother-of-pearl dish well washed, like the moon's disk coming out from behind a cloud, like cranes against a thundercloud." The water kasiṇa sign is "like a crystal fan set in space, like the disk of a looking-glass made of crystal"; the fire sign is "motionless like a piece of red cloth set in space, like a gold fan, like a gold column." For the mindfulness-of-the-body meditation the counterpart sign has "the appearance of repulsiveness."

Breath meditation can have either a tactile or a visual counterpart sign, although the visual sign is stressed. "It appears to some like a star or a cluster of gems or a cluster of pearls, to others with a rough touch like that of silk-cotton seeds or a peg made of heartwood, to others like a long braid string or a wreath of flowers or a puff of smoke, to others like a stretched-out cobweb or a film of cloud or a lotus flower or a chariot wheel or the moon's disk or the sun's disk."

When the counterpart sign appears, the meditator lets go of any other meditation subjects or experiences and focuses on it exclusively.

The Visuddhimagga is predated by another important text, the Vimuttimagga (The Path of Freedom), which is generally dated around the first century C.E. The Vimuttimagga treatment of jhāna based on kasiṇa is similar to that of the Visuddhimagga, though it is less detailed. Breath meditation is approached similarly, too, with the arising of nimitta as a sign of concentration, but the Vimuttimagga shifts the emphasis away from the mental image, stressing the importance of remaining focused on the tactile sign. Here, the "subtle image" presumably is the paṭibhāga nimitta, the counterpart sign of access concentration: "One subject of meditation seizes the sign [of concentration] through contact. Namely, mindfulness of respiration . . . one subject of meditation seizes the sign through sight or contact. Namely, air kasiṇa."[37]

> To the yogin who attends to the incoming breath with mind that is cleansed of the nine lesser defilements **the image (nimitta) arises with a pleasant feeling similar to that which is produced in the action of spinning cotton or silk cotton. Also, it is likened to**

> **the pleasant feeling produced by a breeze. Thus in breathing in and out, air touches the nose or the lip and causes the setting-up of air perception mindfulness. This does not depend on color or form. This is called the image.** If the yogin develops the image and increases it at the nose-tip, between the eye-brows, on the forehead or establishes it in several places, he feels as if his head were filled with air. Through increasing in this way his whole body is charged with bliss. This is called perfection.
>
> And again, there is a yogin: he sees several images from the beginning. **He sees various forms such as smoke, mist, dust, sand of gold,** or he experiences something similar to the pricking of a needle or to an ant's bite. **If his mind does not become clear regarding these different images, he will be confused.** Thus he fulfills overturning **and does not gain the perception of respiration. If his mind becomes clear,** the yogin does not experience confusion. **He attends to respiration and he does not cause the arising of other perceptions. Meditating thus he is able to end confusion and acquire the subtle image. And he attends to respiration with a mind that is free. That image is free.** Because that image is free, desire arises. Desire being free, that yogin attends to respiration and becomes joyful. Desire and joy being free, he attends to respiration with equipoise. Equipoise, desire and joy being free, he attends to respiration, and his mind is not disturbed. If his mind is not disturbed, he will destroy the hindrances, and arouse the meditation (jhāna) factors. Thus this yogin will reach the calm and sublime fourth meditation, jhāna. This is as was fully taught above.[38]

The counterpart sign images that the commentaries emphasize as primary meditation objects appear as figurative descriptions, not meant to be taken literally, in the even earlier Paṭisambhidāmagga (a canonical book, probably of a relatively late date, in the Khuddaka Nikāya):

> Suppose there were a tree trunk placed on a level piece of ground, and a man cut it with a saw. The man's mindfulness is established by

> the saw's teeth where they touch the tree trunk, without his giving attention to the saw's teeth as they approach and recede, though they are not unrecognized by him as they do so; and he manifests endeavor, carries out a task and achieves a distinctive effect.[39]
>
> Whose mindfulness of breathing in and out is perfect, well developed, and gradually brought to growth according as the Buddha taught, it is he illuminates the world just like the full moon free from cloud.[40]

The Paṭisambhidāmagga goes on to explain that "just like the full moon free from cloud" means "Defilements are like clouds, the noble ones' knowledge is like the moon. The bhikkhu is like the deity's son who possesses the full moon. As the moon when freed from cloud, freed from mist, freed from smoke and dust, delivered from the clutches of the Eclipse-Demon Rāhu, gleams and glows and shines, so too the bhikkhu who is delivered from all defilements gleams and glows and shines. Hence 'just like the full moon free from cloud' was said."[41]

A similar passage occurs in the Aṅguttara Nikāya:

> There are four defilements of the sun and moon, defiled by which the sun and moon do not shine, blaze and radiate. What four? Clouds are a defilement of the sun and moon . . . Snow is a defilement . . . Smoke and dust is a defilement . . . Rāhu lord of the asuras[42] is a defilement of the sun and moon . . . Similarly, there are four defilements of ascetics and brahmins, defiled by which some ascetics and brahmins do not shine, blaze and radiate. What four? There are some who drink wine and liquor . . . there are some who indulge in sexual intercourse . . . who accept gold and silver . . . there are some who earn their living by wrong livelihood. These are four defilements of ascetics and brahmins, defiled by which some ascetics and brahmins do not shine, blaze and radiate.[43]

The aim of concentration meditation in the commentaries is to cultivate counterpart signs, either visual or tactile, as meditation objects, which the earlier Paṭisambhidāmagga and Aṅguttara Nikāya offer as purely symbolic images.

Conclusion

The Visuddhimagga presents a path of meditation and the states within it that is new and distinct from the Pāli suttas. During the centuries between the composition of the suttas and Buddhaghosa's great work, the understanding of jhāna evolved from being a state of undistracted awareness and profound insight into the nature of changing phenomena to states of extreme tranquillity in which the mind is utterly engrossed in the mental qualities of the jhāna itself. Whether the path of meditation developed to adapt to that change or the new understanding arose from a change in the way meditation was practiced we cannot know. In any case, insight meditation and the path of concentration and tranquillity were necessarily separated because, in the fixed concentration of the Visuddhimagga, insight could arise only upon leaving jhāna.

The basis for separating meditation into two paths and the controversy surrounding whether jhāna is necessary at all for the deepest levels of awakening, is the notion that jhāna is ancillary to insight meditation. Jhāna may be developed, or not, prior to insight meditation, according to one's own predispositions. In the Visuddhimagga, the entire reason for developing tranquillity is to attain jhāna in order to then turn to other practices for cultivating insight.

The suttas, however, do not make such a clear distinction. The suttas never clearly articulate a dry path of pure insight in which jhāna plays no role. One could separate insight meditation from samatha meditation, though both are part of the same path. The practice of right samādhi seems to integrate tranquillity and insight into a single meditative path. Mindfulness meditation is a concentration practice leading toward jhāna; insight meditation is not a separate practice. Although achieving tranquillity is not the ultimate goal of concentration meditation, the suttas regard tranquillity as important. Tranquillity is a supporting condition for insight to arise.

Tranquillity and insight are two inseparable facets of mental cultivation, mutually supportive and necessary. They can be cultivated independently, but ultimately must be brought together in a balanced way.

The two jhānas are equivalent in terms of the strength of concentration, but dissimilar in terms of the type of concentration. In both cases the mind has reached the peak of stillness. Jhāna in the suttas is a state of heightened mindfulness and awareness of an ever-changing stream of experiences, in which the mind is unmoving. Jhāna in the Visuddhimagga is a state of fixed concentration, where there is no experience of changing phenomena whatsoever, because the objects of the mind are unmoving.

The jhāna factors vitakka-vicāra, which can be understood in the suttas in at least two possible ways, as applying and maintaining the mind on the object of meditation or as other mental activity, such as volition, thought, and mental evaluation, are strictly confined in meaning in the Visuddhimagga to connecting and sustaining. Ekaggatā, most properly understood in the suttas as unification of mind inclusive of all changing experiences, is a one-pointed, fixed concentration in the Visuddhimagga. The prominent role of physical-body awareness in the sutta jhāna definition, which is underscored in the jhāna similes and the Mindfulness of the Body Sutta, is understood purely as the "mental" body in the Visuddhimagga.

The Visuddhimagga introduces several other concepts and terms that are not found in the suttas. Preparatory, access, and attainment concentration, as well as the signs (nimittas) accompanying these stages, are not found in the suttas. The word *nimitta* does appear in the suttas in connection with right concentration, but there it simply means "theme" or "basis" of concentration, and is equated with the four foundations of mindfulness.[44] The forty meditation subjects can be found in the suttas, but many are only mentioned peripherally, often with little or no explanatory detail. There are certainly not the extensive and meticulous descriptions found in the Visuddhimagga. In particular, kasiṇa practice, which is central to the Visuddhimagga understanding of jhāna, is never explained in detail in the suttas at all.

The suttas and the Visuddhimagga are in agreement that a state of strong concentration totally divorced from any awareness of the body is not necessary for awakening. They differ simply in that the suttas do not define such a state as constituting the four jhānas, whereas the Visuddhimagga does.

Table 3: Comparison of Jhāna in the
Pāli Suttas and the Visuddhimagga

	SUTTAS	VISUDDHIMAGGA
The 4 absorptions	Called the 4 jhānas	Called the rūpa jhānas
The 4 formless attainments	Called the āruppas	Usually called the āruppas; in a few cases called arūpa jhānas
Type of concentration	Unification of mind	One-pointed concentration fixed on a single object
Body awareness in jhāna	Seems to suggest heightened experience of and insight into the physical body and changing phenomena	No experience of the physical body and changing phenomena
Insight meditation practice	Suggests that insight practice can occur within jhāna	Insight must come while not in jhāna
Nimitta	General term used in a variety of contexts for "sign," "theme," or "basis," but not specifically as a visual concentration object to attain jhāna	A visual image that arises in access concentration, used as the meditation object to attain jhāna
Preparatory, access, and fixed concentration	Terms are not found	Terms are used

Jhāna is clearly not required for any of the stages of enlightenment in the Visuddhimagga. The suttas are ambiguous about the necessity of jhāna for stream-entry, and the case becomes increasingly strong with each successive stage of enlightenment. The controversies over what is the "real" jhāna resolve when we realize that there are two distinct jhānas in the Pāli literature, each one true and correct within its own system: "sutta jhāna" and "Visuddhimagga jhāna." These two jhāna systems are not the same. They comprise different meditative states, sharing some features in common, but with their own unique characteristics, potentials, and methods for realizing them. Each can be properly understood only within the overall context of the texts within which it appears.

PART TWO

INTERVIEWS WITH CONTEMPORARY MEDITATION TEACHERS

Living Dharma
Living Buddha masters

Interview with Jack Kornfield

Richard Shankman: What are your thoughts about the range of views regarding what is wise or skillful or right samādhi?

Jack Kornfield: I have two sets of thoughts and experiences to share.

The first begins with a question. Does "right samādhi" mean focusing on deep concentration the way U Ba Khin or Pa Auk Sayadaw advise, or is focusing on the natural concentration of mindfulness as Ajahn Chah and U Tejaniya teach the best way? Of course, the answer to both is yes.

What is true about Buddhist practices is that the Buddha's teachings are a great mandala of skillful means. In the early 1970s I collected teachings from twelve of the most highly regarded meditation masters in Thailand and Burma who were teaching variations of mindfulness or insight or vipassanā practice. This material became my first book, *Living Buddhist Masters*. Each of these teachers had different approaches to vipassanā practice, and some of them emphasized concentration more than others. All twelve styles were representative of fifty or a hundred ways that I know to do vipassanā.

In many cases they did not agree with one another on the best way to practice. Sometimes the styles were diametrically opposed to one another. In laying out *Living Buddhist Masters,* I deliberately contrasted the teachings, so that one great master who emphasized meditation on the body as the best way to attain enlightenment was next to another enlightened master who said the only way to get liberated is to meditate on the mind. I did this so people would understand that there are a number of different skillful means to cultivate the factors of enlightenment and come to liberation. Any practice that cultivates mindfulness and wise effort and investigation and joy and concentration and calm and equanimity and compassion will bring one to liberation, and there are many, many ways to do that.

This understanding of the mandala of skillful means is enormously helpful for us as we bring all the Buddhist traditions together in America. We are learning about Theravāda and Mahayana and Vajrayana understandings of samādhi, and comparable Hindu practices as well. And they are all being presented to the same greater community of practitioners in America. If we don't have the understanding of the mandala of skillful means, then we get fixated on our views, we believe we have the right way, and we lose wisdom. The maturity and wisdom of a human being comes when it is possible to see multiplicity, paradox, and complementary differences with a spacious mind and an open heart.

Throughout Buddhist Asia, people are very opinionated about their views on jhāna and on vipassanā and what makes insight.

RS: In Buddhist America, also.

JK: In Buddhist America, also, but it is not as bad here. There are a few very opinionated people, whose names I will not mention, but they make their opinions very clear. And I find that amusing. I don't see something wrong with holding a Dharma perspective strongly; it is the "I have the true way and the others are wrong" part that is added. In the Sutta Nipāta the Buddha explained that those who cling to views annoy other people. And suffer themselves. In fact, there is a much more open-minded and less dogmatic approach, in general, in the U.S. and in the West than I found between students and teachers in Buddhist Asia. This has come about because we have access to the Dharma in this entire mandala.

RS: We get to see so many great teachers and masters who clearly have profound wisdom and different perspectives and different sets of skillful means.

JK: We are so fortunate to have different sets of skillful means. Anyone who doesn't understand this yet will see it if they pay attention, and if they don't understand it, they will suffer.

I needed to learn this lesson very early on because my two root meditation masters were Ajahn Chah and Mahasi Sayadaw, and they had very different approaches to meditation practice, and very different approaches to enlightenment. They fundamentally disagreed on what brought one to enlightenment and on the nature of enlightenment, even though they would agree that enlightenment meant the freeing of oneself from greed, hatred, and delusion. But how you attained it was different. For Mahasi Sayadaw the way to enlightenment was through the progress of insight and very deep, sustained, profound mindfulness and concentration. For Ajahn Chah, enlightenment was attained by letting go. With Ajahn Chah, meditation was most simply a way to get quiet enough to see clinging in the mind and to learn how to release it. This is in the same spirit U Tejaniya Sayadaw teaches. But for Ajahn Chah, any attainment in meditation, jhāna, or any deep insight alone was not the source of enlightenment. Enlightenment came from letting go. I learned a great deal from each of these perspectives.

RS: That goes back to what you were saying earlier, that it is all just a range of skillful means.

JK: Exactly. From the moment the Buddha died, according to the stories in the texts, there were those who wanted to conserve things exactly as they were when the Buddha lived, and then there were those who wanted to adapt them and change them in different ways. This disagreement started at the death of the Buddha and continues to this day. We need those who conserve tradition, both the Visuddhimagga tradition and the sutta tradition, and the classical lineages within Theravāda or Mahayana. And we also need those who can adapt the language and the skillful means to a new culture. While the Buddha consistently kept to his core teachings, he also added new skillful means as his life went on. One skillful means isn't right and the other wrong. They're part of the mandala, in which every element complements the others. When we understand this, then we can appreciate the people who are very deeply tied to a particular historical tradition. They carry the wisdom of that perspective for all the rest of us. And those who are willing to expand that with new ways and bring that new language and skillful means into the mandala also contribute to the whole.

RS: Of course, there are those who say that's well and good, but there really is a "right way" that we do need to understand. That other paths might be good in certain ways, but they might actually not be leading to what the Buddha was talking about.

JK: That's the conservative position. But, in fact, if you go back to the old countries of Thailand and Burma and Sri Lanka, you can't get the Theravāda masters themselves to agree! I have heard so many masters say, "I teach the true way, right from the suttas, from the original. This is the real way the Buddha taught." I've heard a whole bunch of masters say that, and yet they contradicted one another when they said it. So I don't buy it. That's called "ignorance." The real freedom is what Ajahn Chah understood: the real freedom is the freedom of letting go. It's not the freedom of clinging to what one believes is historically true, because what is historically true is this mandala, and it's not one way.

This leads to the second part of the answer to your question. When Joseph [Goldstein] and Sharon [Salzberg] and I were teaching retreats in the first years, we used the practice of mental noting in the style of Mahasi Sayadaw. Sharon observed that people were not getting anywhere near as deep, on the whole, as they did when they sat with Goenka doing three days of ānāpānasati and then seven days of sweeping practice. Goenka offers a wonderful form of vipassanā practice that includes profound concentration, and the concentration was accentuated in those days by people doing long vow sittings and not moving.

Then the conversation went to the quality of wisdom. We acknowledged that people could get more deeply concentrated doing sweeping, but they weren't necessarily wiser. Some had very deep insights into anicca, dukkha, and anattā, and letting go and great wisdom came. But many other people had deep wisdom arise through the Mahasi practice without that deeper level of concentration building up in the course of ten days. And because they practiced all four foundations of mindfulness, they could see their own mental states and the clinging to them, their emotions and the clinging to them, and released them more directly with mindfulness than if they had focused for those days more primarily on concentration and body sensation.

So, there is a spectrum of concentration and mindfulness, and at each end there is a trade-off. If you focus a great deal on concentration, then often wisdom doesn't grow as quickly, quite honestly. It can grow deep later on, when concentration is turned toward wisdom. But first it brings the states of concentration, which have their own great benefit. On the other hand, if you are looking for understanding to grow quickly, such as on a three- or four-day retreat, then you might want to emphasize mindfulness more.

On a more mature level, for anyone who is a dedicated practitioner over a number of years, it is skillful to practice at both ends of that spectrum. If you can, it is valuable to train yourself in concentration to learn skillful means and ways of deepening your concentration. This concentration can be used for the dissolution of the self, the illumination of emptiness, and the understanding of selflessness and impermanence.

At the same time it is equally important to develop a steady, balanced mindfulness. You need to be able to be mindful as you move about, to let go of changing conditions and rest in unconditioned awareness, to notice the states of mind, notice the reactivity, notice the clinging, and be able to release it all. Otherwise, any attainments of concentration won't really serve you to live as a liberated being in the world. So both of these are important, during retreat practice and afterward. And, of course, people will have to respect their different propensities and temperaments, which make concentration more or less accessible.

RS: How much emphasis do you put on samādhi when you teach?

JK: I'm a Middle Path kind of guy. I emphasize mindfulness in the very beginning, because many people have so much difficulty and hindrances when they try to concentrate that without also practicing mindfulness they suffer a lot. Being mindful makes space to hold the difficulties and understand them with some wisdom. But I also teach concentration and make its practice a part of every retreat. As students settle down and their concentration deepens, I encourage them. I work quite individually with people, especially on longer retreats. If someone has the propensity or capacity for concentration, I will direct them to use skillful means to deepen through the jhāna factors into jhāna practice. Other students may not have the ability to concentrate very easily, or they may be dealing with trauma and difficulties. When trauma is present, to skip over it would either be impossible or would do them a disservice in their practice.

RS: It sounds like what you're saying is that you do not emphasize a single approach or technique or method, but try to find what is most useful in each individual case.

JK: No, the basic instruction I give is a combination of some concentration and lots of mindfulness. Then later, especially on long retreats, I work to adapt the instructions individually with people. But my instructions include both perspectives. If U Tejaniya is the all-mindfulness end of the spectrum, and the beginning of a Goenka retreat or Pa Auk Sayadaw is the all-concentration end, I'm somewhere in the middle.

RS: Would you say there is a place where both the mindfulness and the concentration are emphasized and come together and support each other?

JK: Yes, if by that you also mean momentary, or khaṇika, samādhi. If you read the suttas, there are many, many examples of liberation happening to students while listening to a Dharma talk. Now, we cannot know the state of their minds, but clearly they did not do this through a lot of concentration practice. They were listening in a deep way, and their minds became still and illuminated and there was a shift of identity, from a sense of self to a freedom from self. Of course, if you were attached to concentration being the way, you could say, in theory, "Oh, they were deeply concentrated in that moment listening to the Buddha."

RS: But we don't really know.

JK: We don't know that. And in fact, what I do know is that sometimes people are ready to let go and it doesn't involve concentration at all. It involves letting go. And letting go brings freedom.

RS: You have practiced with and taught wisdom resolutions. When you work with wisdom resolutions, do you use them for people who are at the level of absorption or jhāna in meditation?

JK: Yes. When people come on retreat, especially the longer retreats, and their concentration develops and they have some capacity to concentrate well, I will lead them to cultivate and deepen the jhāna factors and then enter jhāna. I like them to learn to dwell in these factors and states.

The language of dwelling is terribly important. Because originally, when I learned jhāna, I learned in systems where there was a great deal of effort and striving. And I found in the long term that that didn't help me so much.

RS: Is that coming out of the Mahasi tradition?

JK: It was the flavor of a number of Thai and Burmese traditions, quite honestly. There was a great deal of striving in a number of monasteries I practiced in. But I found that, while I could do that and make a great effort and get quite concentrated, it was an exhausting way to get concentrated. This kind of striving is not a very good path for most people in the West, unless they are young men looking for initiation, looking to go through the hardest thing they can find.

What I found instead is that wise effort is better cultivated through relaxed dedication and sustained focus, and this leads to learning to dwell in the jhāna factors as they begin to arise. Dwelling and relaxing allows you to embody and feel and deepen the jhāna factors with pleasure and delight and happiness, and all the things that they represent. Dwelling naturally deepens concentration. So wise effort brings a shift of consciousness from an effort to get somewhere, to dwelling in well-being.

RS: Also, once that happens, it seems to take on its own momentum.

JK: Exactly. You start to enter a stream of concentration quite naturally. Then, when I work with people, if the jhāna factors become strong, I teach them to use resolutions. First they learn to resolve for jhāna factors to arise, and then when the jhāna factors are quite strong and somewhat balanced, they make resolutions to enter first, second, third jhāna, and so forth. Initially they resolve for short periods of time and then longer, and then learn to move easily between jhānas.

Once people have some stable capacity to enter and rest in jhāna samādhi, I like to use wisdom resolutions. Instead of simply directing people to come out of the jhānas and notice the impermanence of the states, which is one traditional way to allow wisdom to arise, or to come out of the jhānas and notice the anicca, dukkha, anattā of whatever experience follows the jhāna, which is simply shifting from jhāna to a deep mindfulness practice, I find wisdom resolutions to be strikingly helpful.

RS: Did this come out of your own practice and experience?

JK: It came out of my own experience, although I know that other people are using them. They fit with the other kind of resolutions that U Pandita and Mahasi Sayadaw taught. My understanding has grown from making resolutions for the jhāna factors and jhānas. And these can be traced to the root source of resolutions, which are the kind of determinations that one finds in the suttas, where a monk turns their mind toward, or determines that they will enter, this jhāna or that jhāna. Those determinations are resolutions. They work with wisdom as well.

And so the kind of wisdom resolutions I use are ways to deepen understanding of the key Dharma teachings, key elements of wisdom. I will instruct someone like this: "When you come out of jhāna, whether second, third, or fourth, make the resolution 'May a deep insight into anicca arise.'"

RS: Do you make that resolution before you go into jhāna?

JK: Generally, as you are coming out of jhāna. In the same way, you can resolve, "May a deep insight into anattā arise" or "May a deep insight into emptiness arise." "May a deep insight into compassion arise." It can be any of the key Dharma qualities.

And then sometimes, but not always, just as with all resolutions, depending on the depth of that person's practice and the particular karmic conditions, wonderful displays of wisdom will arise. For example, I made the resolution for myself coming out of jhāna "May a deep understanding of emptiness arise" and all of a sudden felt myself, as if falling backward into the galaxies of space, body and mind dropping away, different than in the jhānas, and there arose a sense that intergalactic space and I are exactly the same thing, and the stars and the luminosity of form shines out of it. And I had no idea that was going to happen. I had no idea what would come of it.

Or I made a resolution to myself "May a deep understanding of anicca arise." And all of a sudden my attention went to the top of my head. I thought, "This is odd." Then what came into consciousness is all the hair that I'm losing. I thought this is a funny thing to happen. And spontaneously my attention slowly scanned down and went to my ears, where I'm losing hearing somewhat, and then it went to my nose, it started sweeping down through my body.

RS: On its own?

JK: On its own. As it went to my nose, I could feel my history of years of allergies and nasal surgery. And then it went to the fillings in my teeth, and then it went to a bad vertebra in my neck, and then down to my lungs, where I've had pneumonia, then it went to where I had an appendectomy and some lower-back problems, and it scanned down through my old runner's knees, and by the time it was done, I could feel the palpable falling apart throughout this body. I had no idea this insight was going to come. Wisdom resolutions allow for a profound intelligence of wisdom to simply display itself.

Setting the intention of a wisdom resolution opens a doorway for deep wisdom, just as setting a concentration intention opens a doorway for jhāna. When the conditions are developed, we can resolve for jhāna factors, "May happiness arise." And we become flooded and filled with happiness.

Or later we can resolve for any of the jhānas themselves. With wisdom resolutions when the mind is concentrated, malleable, pliable, luminous, clear with deep concentration, and is directed toward understanding—and this is right out of the texts—a dimension of wisdom, prajñāpāramitā, the pāramitā of understanding, displays itself, in the same way that jhāna states arise and display themselves. It's a beautiful thing to experience.

So in the list of wisdom resolutions it might be anicca or dukkha or anattā, or emptiness or compassion. It might be a deep understanding into dependent origination or interdependence. You could make a resolution for a deep understanding of letting go or of selflessness. You can play with it a little.

RS: It points to the power of intention when supported by the power of a concentrated mind.

JK: That's right. The power of a luminous and malleable, concentrated mind.

RS: You are talking about working with resolutions on entering and coming out of jhāna. Does this mean you are talking about a jhāna in which the workings of the mind have dropped away?

JK: They have quieted down to a great extent.

RS: There are no thoughts?

JK: Not absolutely, not at the level of jhāna I've practiced. It is not that there are never any thoughts, but for the most part it becomes really silent. It is like going from the windswept, weather-filled atmosphere, getting to the surface of the ocean, and then dropping down below the level of the water, like a scuba diver, into a completely silent and different dimension. While there are some reflections that might go by, it is a completely different state of consciousness.

One of the Spirit Rock/Insight Meditation Society teachers tells this wonderful story about when he was a young student in practice and first being taught jhānas. He worked with Joseph and Sharon in U Pandita's system, which included resolution practice. After his concentration had gotten strong, he was given a resolution for a jhāna factor like pīti. But he didn't know the Pāli and he had the meaning of the word confused in his mind. Then the most magical thing happened. He thought he was making a resolution for one kind of experience, and yet when he said, "pīti," his body became filled with joy and rapture. He didn't know this Pāli word given by his teacher, he thought it meant something else, but the real thing arose.

Whatever you call it, there is something in the psyche, in the greater consciousness, that knows these states and this terrain. And when the mind is deeply concentrated and open, and resolutions are made, magic happens. And of course, this can lead to the highest magic of all, as the Buddha said, the magic of the wisdom that liberates the heart.

JACK KORNFIELD trained as a Buddhist monk in the monasteries of Thailand, India, and Burma. He has taught meditation internationally since 1974 and is one of the key teachers to introduce Buddhist mindfulness practice to the West. He began his training after graduating from Dartmouth College in Asian Studies in 1967. Then he joined the Peace Corps and was assigned to the Public Health Service in northeast Thailand, which is home to several of the world's oldest Buddhist forest monasteries. He met and studied under the Buddhist master Venerable Ajahn Chah, as well as the Venerable Mahasi Sayadaw of Burma. After returning to the United States, Jack cofounded the Insight Meditation Society in Barre, Massachusetts, with fellow meditation teachers Sharon Salzberg and Joseph Goldstein, and is a founding teacher of the Spirit Rock Center in Woodacre, California, where he currently lives and teaches.

Interview with Ajaan Ṭhānissaro

Richard Shankman: Why do you think there's so much disagreement and controversy around samādhi?

Ajaan Ṭhānissaro: There are two basic considerations. First, the tradition talks about samādhi in so many different ways—and particularly if you take the Canon on one side and the commentaries on the other, they are really talking about two very different things. When you read the descriptions of nimitta and of jhāna in the Canon, they're very different from the nimitta and the jhāna you find in the commentaries. The Visuddhimagga uses a very different paradigm for concentration from what you find in the Canon. That begs the question, why do the commentaries differ so radically? Nobody knows.

Second, there's a much larger issue, which is—given that we're talking about purely mental states—each person's sense of the map inside the mind is going to be different. When I use a term and you use a term, there's no guarantee that we're actually talking about the same thing.

Once, when I was camping in Utah, we went to Powell Point. We had a guidebook and thought we were following the road to Powell Point, but we made a wrong turn somewhere and came out at Henderson Canyon instead. We walked out to the end of the point there and tried to identify the landmarks the guidebook said you could see from the end of Powell Point: the Henry Mountains and so forth. The one problem was that there was a very large cliff off to the east, which wasn't mentioned in the book.

After about fifteen minutes we realized that the cliff was Powell Point; we had made a wrong turn. So the next day we went up to Powell Point, and the hills we had originally thought were the Henry Mountains were something else entirely. The Henry Mountains were much farther east. The problem was that we had been standing at the wrong place, so our sense of the landscape was all skewed. You've got the same issue with people meditating—or even worse. When you talk about meditative experiences, who knows if we're standing on the same point? There are so many different points you can stand on, and so many states that are radically different but fit the same verbal description. What makes it worse is that even if the Powell Point of the mind were right to your east, you wouldn't be able to see it.

RS: There are teachers who say the only way to correctly understand the suttas is as interpreted by the commentaries.

AT: Where do the commentaries get their seal of approval? They're just one scholastic tradition that you can take into consideration, but there's no guarantee that the scholars got it right. The only real authority you have in cases like this is the honesty of the individual practitioner. You have to be honest with yourself as to what results you're getting out of your practice, where there's still suffering, and what further work still needs to be done.

RS: Do you think you can find substantiation in the suttas for the commentarial interpretations?

AT: The main paradigm for concentration practice in the commentaries comes from kasiṇa practice. The Canon does contain references to kasiṇa practice—experiences of nonduality where everything is a oneness of blue or of awareness or whatever—but in the Canon these practices are marginal. They're in the corners of a few suttas, but they're not the main paradigm.

RS: What would you say right samādhi is in the context of the eightfold path?

AT: Jhāna. That begs the question, how do you define jhāna?

RS: What is it about jhāna that makes it right samādhi? Why are the jhānas called right concentration? What's their use? Why are they there?

AT: Why do you have right mindfulness or right effort? They're parts of the path because they work. In right concentration, the mind needs to be clearly and strongly focused for two reasons. One is to see what's going on in the mind itself. If the mind is muddied or stirred up, it's like water in a puddle that's been stirred up. You can't see clearly what's there in the water. Second, when the mind is at ease around its object with a sense of equanimity, the mind is more malleable, more receptive to the insights that are needed to abandon its unskillful habits. You're more likely to be aware of—and to admit—what you've been doing that's been causing suffering.

RS: How much emphasis do you place on samādhi when you're teaching meditation?

AT: I make it the center of the practice. I don't see any clear distinction between mindfulness practice and concentration practice. When you look at the texts, there's no clear line drawn between them.

There are sutta passages that talk about the concentration that develops by following the four frames of reference (satipaṭṭhāna), starting with the body in and of itself. You focus on that, with directed thought and evaluation, then with directed thought and a modicum of evaluation, and then with neither directed thought nor evaluation. These passages are talking about developing jhāna around that frame of reference, and then with the other three frames of reference.

RS: I noticed that you interpret vitakka-vicāra as directed thought and evaluation.

AT: It's an essential part of getting the mind to settle down, especially if you're trying to get a sense of ease around the object. You need to get a sense of how well you're relating to the object. Are there ways that the relationship could be more comfortable? Once you get a sense of comfort, how do you spread it around the body? This is how you embody the canonical analogies for jhāna, which refer to permeating the body with a sense of comfort and ease. A certain amount of evaluation is needed to do this well: Could you spread it more effectively? Are you pushing it too hard so that it's actually making it an unpleasant experience? You've got to learn how to adjust your relationship with the object, and that's why you start out with directed thought and evaluation as part of the first jhāna. Once you've got a good relationship going, then in the second jhāna there's the state of unification with the object, a sense of oneness, that you carry all the way through the higher jhānas up to the infinitude of consciousness. I usually don't like to use sexual metaphors here, but you can't really unite into oneness until you're on good terms with each other.

RS: There are examples in the suttas of people attaining at least some level of deep insight or awakening apparently without jhāna or deep meditation practices.

AT: These are the cases where people gain awakening while listening to teachings. But we don't know what their minds were doing as they sat there listening. Usually the teaching was pointing directly to something going on in their minds, so they started observing their minds, entered concentration, and gained release.

RS: There are teachers who tend to shy you away from jhāna as being not necessary at all and even a potential trap.

AT: The Buddha wasn't one of them. There are some people who tend to be psychologically unstable and have to be very careful about how they handle states of concentration, but in general, if you have right view about jhāna, it's not dangerous at all.

Now there are some people who say jhāna isn't necessary, that it can be a hindrance because you can become attached to the experiences and mistake the āruppas for Nibbāna. But there are lots of things you can mistake for Nibbāna. If you're doing what you think is vipassanā and you hit, say, a state of nonperception—you may think that's cessation, the end of suffering. But the danger doesn't lie in the state. It's in how you interpret it. No matter what your technique, if you're the sort of person who tends to overinterpret your attainment, you're going to head in that direction no matter what. Some people tend to be very good at denial, they're good at not seeing their own defilements, and they can use the one-pointed kind of jhāna to exacerbate the problem. But they can also do that with any of the vipassanā techniques.

RS: How do you work with students when strong experiences come up, such as energies flowing in the body, seeing lights, and so on?

AT: It really depends on the individual. Some people can handle these things pretty maturely and others can't. When you see a light, try to make it disappear. If it does disappear, make it reappear. You want to learn to have control over these experiences before you really get involved with *ask more about* ✗

them, so they don't take control over you. That's the important principle. ✗
As for excess energy in the body, have it flow out the hands, out the feet,
so that it doesn't get too oppressive.

RS: You're describing two approaches. One is dissipating, letting the energy come out so that it brings the intensity down. And, secondly, not
necessarily having to adjust the intensity but developing the ability not to
get thrown off center by the experiences.

AT: Right. The best way not to get thrown off is to realize that you can
exert some control over it, that when it comes on, you can turn it off, because for most people a sense of lack of control is the scariest part of the
concentration practice.

RS: Could it be that someone might be in the first jhāna and have liberating insight there, but not identify for themselves that they're in the
first jhāna?

AT: Jhāna doesn't come with signposts saying, "Now Entering the First
Jhāna. Population: One. Elevation: Eight Miles High." You can enter
jhāna without knowing it, especially if you're not expecting your meditation method to lead to jhāna. You can also overinterpret your attainment
if that's what you're looking for. And you can overinterpret your insights.
This is why I tell my students that if something interesting happens, you try
to master it. Then you put a Post-it note on it. If something else happens,
you put a Post-it note on that, too. After you get a better sense of the full
terrain of your mind, you can rearrange the notes into a coherent map.

RS: You seem to have a very open-minded view of all the different ways
and things that can be defined as jhāna, recognizing that there is a range of
intensity, but that some forms are useful and some are not. For example,
some people would feel that when you block out sensations or experience,
it's not actually useful. And some people say if you don't block these out,
it's not real jhāna.

AT: There are some states of concentration where you can block out all
sensory input. You can sit for a couple hours and it feels like a minute.
There's just enough awareness to know when to come out when you want
to stop. You weren't unconscious, but the mind otherwise had no awareness of what was going on. There are also intense states of concentration,

lots of light, lots of bliss, lots of joy, but no input from outside. The only way you're going to gain any insight from these states is when you come out of them and reflect on where you were and how you got where you are now.

There are also states of jhāna where sensory input is not totally cut off, but it doesn't intrude on the mind. With these states there's more of an ability to observe what's going on in the jhāna while you're still in it. It's a little like the first jhāna piggybacking on the other jhānas, because you can evaluate what's going on and you can see where there's stress, what you're doing that's causing the stress, and you can see how you can drop that particular activity.

When you're fully into even this sort of jhāna, particularly from the second one up, you're not going to be doing any thinking or evaluating at all, but you can pull back a little bit without destroying that state, because it's not totally dependent on blocking off all outside input. The jhāna actually creates physiological changes in the body—changes in the breath, changes in the blood flow—and those remain even as you pull the mind slightly up from its object. You can then apply the Four Noble Truths to your experience of the jhāna—comprehending even the most subtle levels of stress and abandoning their cause. This is how you get from one jhāna to the next, but there will also come a point where you finally drop the last remaining bit of intention in the jhāna. When it's not replaced by any new intention, that's when the mind opens up into the deathless.

RS: The way you're describing it, insight arises while in jhāna, rather than the Visuddhimagga style, where you have to come out of the jhāna in order to reflect back on its inherently unsatisfying qualities.

AT: The Canon contains lots of passages describing people who can analyze a particular state of jhāna while they're in it. A couple of these include Aṅguttara 4:126 and 9:36, along with Majjhima 52 and 121. The most explicit example is Majjhima 111, which describes how Sāriputta analyzed the many mental factors present in jhāna while he was experiencing each level. Only when he reached the āruppas of nothingness and neither-perception-nor-nonperception did he have to withdraw from those states before reflecting on them.

You can use any of the jhānas as a basis for awakening, from the first on up. In each case you analyze the jhāna in terms of the five aggregates, which you come to see as stressful, not-self, impermanent, a dart, a cancer, an emptiness, and on down the line. In this way you develop a sense of dispassion and disenchantment for even the ease of jhāna. That's how you let go.

For the purpose of getting into jhāna, though, the most interesting passages in the Canon about jhāna are the analogies: the bath man, the lotuses in the lake, the man covered with white cloth.

RS: They're very beautiful.

AT: And very precise. Kneading the moisture through the bath powder is like working comfort and rapture through the body in the first jhāna. In the second, you don't have to work things through anymore; they spread automatically, like the spring water in the lake. In the third jhāna, the movement stops as the rapture gives way simply to a fully saturated sense of stillness and pleasure. And then in the fourth, even the coolness of the water subsides, and you're left with the brightness of your awareness. The Buddha chose his analogies well.

RS: It seems clear that you don't separate the path of practice into two paths of samatha and vipassanā.

AT: The Buddha never told people to "do" vipassanā. He said do jhāna, and he described vipassanā and samatha not as two separate techniques but as two qualities of mind that you bring to the practice so you can get into jhāna. Once you've mastered jhāna, the jhāna will make your samatha and vipassanā stronger, more precise. There's no clear line between a mindfulness practice, a concentration practice, and an insight practice. Some people go more naturally toward samatha or vipassanā, but you need both.

RS: In the Satipaṭṭhāna Sutta, the Ānāpānasati Sutta, and the Kāyagatāsati Sutta, one is instructed to breathe in and out, experiencing the whole body. Some interpret that it is talking about experiencing the whole physical body breathing, while others say it means staying with the whole duration of the breath but the focus can be at one point.

AT: It's the whole body.

RS: Does it matter?

AT: One of the drawbacks of concentration that's too one-pointed is that you're blocking out many areas of your experience, which means that a lot of things can hide away in the areas you're blocking out. If, however, you develop more of a 360-degree awareness of the body, you're more likely to be conscious of the more peripheral events in the mind. Also, if the awareness is a whole-body awareness, it's a lot easier to maintain the state of concentration as you open your eyes and move around. Whether the concentration while moving around would be termed jhāna, I really don't know, but there's a continuity of mindfulness. If you have only one point that you're totally focused on, then as soon as you move from that one point, your concentration is destroyed. But if you've got the whole body as your framework and you're constantly mindful of this framework, events can come through and go out, leaving the framework undisturbed.

RS: In the opening paragraphs of the Satipaṭṭhāna Sutta, one of the instructions for beginning practice is a phrase typically translated as "having put aside covetousness and grief of the world." How would you interpret that phrase?

AT: The phrase can also mean "putting aside covetousness and grief with reference to the world." In other words, the practice doesn't begin after you've put aside covetousness for the world. The beginning steps include the process of putting it aside.

As I said earlier, I don't see any clear distinction between mindfulness practice and jhāna practice. There are several passages in the Canon where the Buddha talks about developing satipaṭṭhāna in a way that sounds like working toward and getting into the first jhāna. One is the case of the monk who's like an elephant who's been trapped and tied to a post, going through all the torments of being tamed. In the same way the monk has to use the body in and of itself as his frame of reference. That's the post that he's tied to, and his mind is going to rebel. When it rebels, he's told to think of an inspiring theme, something uplifting to the mind. According to the commentary, this might be the recollection of the Buddha, the Dhamma, or the Sangha. Then when the mind calms down, he can stop using directed thought and evaluation with that uplifting theme and go straight into the second jhāna. So it would seem that everything up to that point is referring to issues in mastering the first jhāna.

RS: In the fourth foundation of mindfulness, one of the categories is knowing when the hindrances are there. And in the third foundation, we are instructed to know a contracted mind, and so on. So, clearly hindrances can arise and be known. It would seem to suggest that while satipaṭṭhāna practice is leading toward jhāna, putting aside covetousness for the world is not a prerequisite for beginning the practice.

AT: This is related to how you're defining your frame of reference. The grief can be there, but instead of looking at it in reference to the world, you see it just as an event of grief in and of itself. That's a very different state of mind: looking at these mental states as events arising and passing away, as opposed to viewing them in the context of any outside reference. You're changing your frame of reference in the course of doing this practice.

You could relate to the body in terms of how other people look at your body, whether it's strong enough to do the work you've got to do today, whether it's getting too old or whatever. That's looking at the body in terms of the world, whereas in satipaṭṭhāna practice you're looking at the body just in and of itself, with no reference to the world at all. There still may be grief and distress, but you're cutting away any reference they may have to the world so that you can maintain your focus on events in and of themselves.

RS: Do you think jhāna is attainable only in the context of long intensive retreats as opposed to shorter retreats? Can it be attained in daily practice?

AT: It really varies for the person.

RS: Do you think everyone has potential to attain jhāna?

AT: I don't see why not. But there's the question of whether everyone will be interested, or will put in the necessary effort. We all have the potential for following the path, but even the Buddha himself never answered the question of whether everyone is going to follow it.

RS: Since some people are more naturally adept at getting concentrated, and some less, do you teach the same way about working with the breath in both cases or do you tailor your teaching for those who aren't naturally going to get that concentrated?

AT: Ajaan Maha Boowa makes a useful distinction between people who naturally find it very easy to get the mind into concentration, and others who have to analyze their way in. With this latter group, if they don't really understand what's going on in their minds, they're not able to let go. And for those sorts of people I would encourage analyzing the breath, looking at how they're conceiving the breath, their perceptions of the breath, and how their perceptions shape the process of breathing. That may sound like a lot of mental activity, but it connects them with the breath because it makes them curious about the breath and the breathing process. They're not going to connect with anything unless they understand it and it captures their imagination. But then there are people who are happy just to sit with the breath and be very quiet. So you have to tailor your instructions to the individual.

For those who find it easy to get very concentrated, the danger is that they haven't had to work for it, and so it's not really a skill. They'll have days when, seemingly for no reason at all, they can't do it. If they haven't figured out the ins and outs of their minds, they can feel totally lost on those days. These are also the people who tend not to analyze things very much, and they have to be pushed—sometimes against their will—to ask the questions that will give them more insight into what they're doing.

RS: In the first jhāna are there body sensations?

AT: Oh yes, yes. In fact, there are body sensations in all four rūpa jhānas. As it says in Majjhima 44, the four frames of reference (satipaṭṭhānas) are the nimitta, or theme, of right concentration. One of those frames is the body in and of itself. If there weren't body sensations in jhāna, how could the body be a theme of right concentration?

RS: So the breath has not disappeared in jhāna.

AT: The in-and-out breath disappears at the fourth jhāna.

RS: Sounds?

AT: Yes, there can be sounds in the background. But as I said, this point varies with some people.

RS: There is a story in the Mahāparinibbāna Sutta of the Buddha sitting in meditation while five hundred carts go by and he has no experience of it.

AT: He was in a very pure form of an āruppa—a state of formlessness. There's a story in the Vibhaṅga to the fourth Pārājika rule, where Moggallāna states that he can hear sounds while in the imperturbable states—which isn't defined in that context, but in other contexts means either the āruppas or the āruppas plus the fourth jhāna. Other monks get upset when he says this, feeling that he's making a false claim—which is why the story falls under that rule—and so they take the matter to the Buddha. He states that Moggallāna's attainment is impure. Now, notice he didn't say that Moggallāna hadn't attained those states, simply that his attainment wasn't as pure as it could have been. And as we all know, Moggallāna was an arahant, so whatever his jhāna attainment, it was good enough for full awakening. And if it was good enough for him . . .

RS: Are there thoughts in the first jhāna?

AT: There's the directed thought and evaluation connected with the breath itself—evaluating how comfortable it is, and how to spread whatever sense of comfort is there—but these thoughts aren't very wordy or discursive.

RS: In relation to jhāna, when the suttas use the term *kāya* ("body"), are they referring to a mental body as opposed to a physical body?

AT: In the Kāyagatāsati Sutta, the Buddha first talks about focusing on the body in and of itself as a frame of reference, and he's obviously talking about the physical body: the breath, the thirty-two body parts, and so forth. When he then moves into instructions on jhāna, he talks about spreading the rapture, the ease through this very body. If he had meant a different body, he would have said so clearly. If you follow the people who insist that there's no experience of the physical body in jhāna, you have to assume that the Buddha was a very sloppy teacher, talking about body again and again in his jhāna instructions when he actually meant "no physical body." Either that, or you have to assume that he was devious. It's like when a crafty lawyer keeps saying, "The body is too big for my client to have killed it," the jury is going to think one thing: the client is innocent. If they later catch on that he's talking about the body of evidence, they're going to think something else: the lawyer can't be trusted. I doubt that the Buddha was sloppy or devious in his meditation instructions.

RS: Some people talk about skipping jhānas. Do people do that? Do you teach that?

AT: It is possible for people to go straight down to the fourth jhāna, but it may be that they're going very quickly through one, two, and three first—as in Ajaan Chah's image of a person falling out of a tree. You go past each branch, but too quickly for any one branch to stand out in your awareness. Being able to zero in on a particular jhāna like that is a great talent if you can develop it. You can tap into that whenever you need it. But I don't put my students through jhāna hoops.

RS: As people progress through the jhānas, do the grosser levels drop away on their own or does the meditator have to do something specific to move to the next stage?

AT: It can happen either way. By pulling slightly out of where you are, you can survey what's going on. You can't do this analysis at all unless you pull out a little bit, and it's a very basic, almost preverbal level of surveillance. You see where there's disturbance and where there's not, and if you see that the way you're relating to your object is causing the disturbance, you change that. That's how you can go intentionally to another level. In other cases, all you have to do is focus in, and the extraneous factors simply fall away.

RS: In the West now, there are a variety of jhāna systems being taught.

AT: I always found the most useful way of avoiding the jhāna wars is that, when you get into a state of concentration, whatever it is, you master it and then you analyze it. Is there any disturbance here? Then you look to see what the mind is doing around its object. If you see any kind of disturbance, in terms either of the state of concentration itself or of the defilements surrounding that state, then, if you're an honest person, you have to admit to yourself, "Okay, there's still more work to be done." And regardless of whether you're in jhāna or out of jhāna, if you approach every state of concentration this way, in full honesty, then you're going to get through it and eventually arrive at awakening. But honesty is the important part of the equation.

People like to compare their jhānas, which is not healthy for their practice: "My jhāna is better than your jhāna." "I'm in the third jhāna now. How about you?" As the Buddha said, this is the sign of a person of no integrity. So it doesn't really matter which jhāna you're in. You have to know what to *do* with whatever state of concentration you've got. If you're using it for the purpose of understanding stress and abandoning the cause of stress, then you're using it for the right purpose.

ṬHĀNISSARO BHIKKHU (Ajaan Geoff) was ordained in Thailand in 1976, and studied under Ajaan Fuang Jotiko, a master of the Thai forest tradition, until the latter's death in 1986. In 1991, he returned to the U.S. to help found Metta Forest Monastery in northern San Diego County, where he is currently abbot. He has translated many meditation guides from the teachings of the forest tradition, and is the author of several books, including *The Wings to Awakening, The Mind Like Fire Unbound, The Paradox of Becoming, Meditations, Meditations2,* and *Meditations3.*

Interview with Sharon Salzberg

Richard Shankman: How much importance do you put on samādhi in your own teaching?

Sharon Salzberg: I think it shifts. My training with Munindraji was very much around moment-to-moment mindfulness, which is a more continuous mindfulness that will give you the degree of samādhi that you need. You don't need to devote yourself specifically to samādhi training. And there are aspects of it that I think are really useful for people who live in the world, where you aren't going to devote the kind of sequestered time that intensive samādhi training might need. But then, my first teacher was Goenka, and his technique of sweeping the attention through the body is very concentrating, so that aspect of training is very important for me, too. So some of how I teach does depend on the context of the teaching, but by and large it would be the emphasis of a moment-to-moment continuity of mindfulness. A momentary concentration.

RS: It sounds like you are not diminishing the importance of samādhi, in general, but just emphasizing the cultivation of mindfulness as a style of practice, and letting the concentration strengthen along with it naturally on its own.

SS: It depends on what you mean by "samādhi."

If you are referring to having some degree of a concentrated mind, then, yes, it is important. If you mean the experiences of samādhi themselves, the rapture, bliss, the jhāna factors, then I am de-emphasizing them very consciously.

RS: How do you work with students when they have some of those experiences you are talking about—rapture, bliss, and other experiences that can come as a side effect of samādhi?

SS: I think it's just the ordinary way of saying these are experiences of strong concentration. You must have strong concentration to have that. They're wonderful, they open our minds to a sense of possibility, and, like anything else we get attached to, they can be the source of a lot of suffering. And so the next time that you're sitting and you're not in bliss, but you have knee pain, don't think that your meditation is falling apart or you cannot be mindful, because, in fact, you can be as mindful of the knee pain as of the bliss. We've all gotten attached to different states. It's very painful to be attached.

RS: Would you separate concentration practice from insight practice, or do you see them as integrated into one practice?

SS: I think it can be either. The way I teach, I don't know if you would call it "dry insight" or call it "integrated."

If you're talking specifically about jhāna, I tend to see it as its own dedicated adventure in consciousness, of exploring the realms of consciousness and seeing what the mind can do, what the boundaries of the mind are. So I sort of separate them in that way.

RS: You are clearly stressing the importance of some level of stability in the mind, and once you've gained a certain level of stability, to be able to be present and work with what's happening?

SS: Yes. What we need is, from that point of view, a lot of the moments in a row.

I love samādhi practice. I see it as an art form. Before I was writing, for example, I would say I didn't have a creative medium in my life. I don't paint or write poetry or play music or anything like that, and playing with consciousness was my art form. I love that one can explore the dimensions of consciousness in those ways. But its role in liberation is the question.

RS: Do you think you can have liberation without having strong samādhi in your daily practice?

SS: Again, it depends on what you mean by samādhi. I know that the texts emphasize jhāna, and the Buddha himself did that path.

If by samādhi you mean moment-to-moment awareness that is not distorted by grasping, aversion, or delusion, that's a moment of liberation, in a certain way. Deep insights also come from that moment-to-moment mindfulness, which is not that easy. It's not like, "Oh, if you're not going to attain jhāna, here's the lazy way." It's not that easy. But if it's true, and I know it's true from experience and from seeing others, that momentary concentration and continuous mindfulness provides a platform for a deep insight into anicca, dukkha, and anattā, then you don't need that sort of specific devotion to jhāna.

And you string enough of those moments in a row and it's impactful. It is not just a vague, ephemeral, passing thing. So I think yes. Maybe another way of reframing the question is, Can you be perfectly mindful of the state of restlessness? Theoretically, anyway, we can be very mindful in a continuous fashion of a state that would never be said to characterize samādhi—restlessness, sleepiness, agitation, dread—but yes, in the preliminary sense in which I was using it, the presence and the steadiness, aiming and sustaining attention, that needs to be there. If that's not there, then you are just restless and sleepy and full of dread, and caught in it.

RS: How would you define right samādhi?

SS: Some steadiness or steadfastness of attention, enough so that there is a connection with the meditation object. You don't need jhāna, you need access concentration or momentary concentration. But access concentration can be developed through shifting attention on different objects, depending on what's predominant.

Or if you think in terms of the jhāna factors, it's aiming and sustaining attention, or initial application and sustained application of mind, that I often talk about. Sometimes people get so hung up on the degree of rapture, delight, or light. It becomes an object of clinging.

So it is a very conscious thing in my mind, especially when I'm teaching and people are about to leave a retreat situation and going to something much more harried, that that degree of delightful experience is usually the first thing to go. And then we can have all the regret and sadness and angst that can happen when we lose those meditative states, not realizing that we can actually be mindful throughout the restless, sleepy, disturbed, noisy times.

RS: You're saying that there is not some meditative state that we need to get to in order to deeply penetrate the nature of reality, but it's more how we work moment to moment? Emphasizing the nonclinging moment to moment more than anything.

SS: There is this tremendous power when we can strengthen the quality of concentration. But how many people can actually sustain that successfully outside of retreat? For most people concentration is somewhat dependent on conditions being supportive, quiet rather than noisy.

RS: You're being realistic about whom you're teaching.

SS: Yes, but also aware of how touching into some of these meditative states can increase longing. If you get into a deep state of concentration, I think of it more as a blessing. It's also faith-producing and it's a tremendous experience that is different from ordinary consciousness. And you know, then, that there is more to life than this ordinary consciousness.

But then you go home and it's noisy and your kids are running around or your phone is ringing, or you live in New York City with all those sirens, and there is a way in which clinging to jhāna can make us more afraid. We can worry, thinking, "I can't have that experience. I can't get it back. I've got to leave New York. I've got to move into my closet" or, "I've got to put those earphones on that they use at airport tarmacs." Anything to get that experience back. And the Dharma is so much more than any particular kind of experience. We need to be careful about clinging or striving after any state of samādhi that is in any way vulnerable to changing conditions.

There is the difference between a state and a trait, the "state" being a temporary confluence of conditions coming together and a "trait" being a new way of being. From that point of view, I think the state of concentration is not so vitally important, but to be less fractured and scattered in order to support a real in-depth, continued exploration of the causes of suffering is what really matters. One of the implications of what Mahasi Sayadaw taught was the prospect of liberation in this very life through removing it from the need for very rarified states of consciousness. That really returned it to laypeople, and it had that kind of sociological effect. He was, as you know, very controversial.

If the concentration is developing to the point where thoughts are not entering so much, and you are feeling like you are really getting somewhere, and you are identified or clinging to that state in some way, then it might be useful to do something else, such as walking practice. Something to help you get out of holding on to that experience.

RS: In addition to being a vipassanā teacher, you are also associated particularly with mettā (loving-kindness) practice. Mettā has a number of different levels. It can be practiced just as a purification of the mind and the heart. And then there are people who do mettā practice as a samādhi or specifically as a jhāna practice.

SS: I don't really emphasize the jhāna aspect because I don't teach long retreats at the moment. Mettā, as a jhāna practice, would be more likely in longer retreats. If I teach an eight-day mettā course, there may be some people in that who will have previous practice or just natural ability to do jhāna practice. But most people in an eight-day are not going to have the conditions come together in such a way that that's there.

It's not that jhāna is unattainable, but that it's not so readily available. It can take a lot of time and dedication. It wouldn't be very likely that most people in an eight-day retreat would come to that level. And that doesn't mean that mettā is not extraordinarily important for them. It often is extraordinarily important for them. It's just not in the sense of cultivating jhāna.

RS: What you're saying is that samādhi practice really ends up happening in a monastery.

SS: I don't really know, but my impression is that a sustained and comprehensive practice of it, by and large, is in a quieter, more controlled environment.

RS: Can anyone attain jhāna?

SS: I don't know. I actually don't know how to define jhāna. If you think about it as the strongly arising and balancing of those five jhāna factors, then I'd say yes, that I know many people have an experience like that. When I read about Sāriputta being hit over the head with a rock and not feeling it when he was in the first jhāna, I'm not sure I know anyone who has accomplished a level like that. So, in those terms then, I think it's not that common.

RS: In the Satipaṭṭhāna Sutta, there is the opening phrase of beginning meditation "ardent, mindful, clearly knowing, and having put aside covetousness and grief for the world." There is a question of how much concentration is really needed.

SS: It seems clear that samādhi alone is not enough. I can almost see the nonaversive, nongreedy aspect of mindfulness that is putting away the covetousness and grief for the world.

RS: And not referring to samādhi at all?

SS: Mindfulness is a quality of relationship to the object of awareness. Just having an experience, say hearing a sound, is not really being mindful. Knowing a sound without grasping, aversion, or delusion is being mindful. So it is about a certain way of relating to our experience. And concentration is ethically neutral. You could be concentrating with tremendous grief and aversion and so on.

The liberating nature of mindfulness is not just in the noticing. It's in the particular way of relating. And so right there, you put away covetousness and grief for the world.

RS: There is the experience where the mind becomes very fixed on the meditation object, and the type of concentration where the mind becomes still but all the flow of experiences are still happening.

SS: That makes more sense to me. In the end, outside of the retreat context, generally speaking we cannot impede the flow of experience. We just don't have that kind of control.

SHARON SALZBERG is one of America's leading spiritual teachers and authors, and has played a crucial role in bringing Buddhist meditation practices to the West. She has been a student of Buddhism since 1971 and has led meditation retreats worldwide since 1974. She teaches both intensive insight meditation and the profound cultivation of loving-kindness and compassion. She is a cofounder of both the Insight Meditation Society in Barre, Massachusetts, and the Barre Center for Buddhist Studies.

Interview with Bhante Gunaratana

Richard Shankman: Why do you think there is so much disagreement among various teachers around the topic of samādhi and jhāna?

Bhante Gunaratana: One reason is that some talk from their experience and others talk from their scholarly understanding. The scholars depend mostly on commentaries, such as the Visuddhimagga, though others simply stay with the suttas.

What the suttas say is not the same as what the Visuddhimagga says, and therefore those who have practiced and talk about jhāna or samādhi from their experience might teach differently from what the Visuddhimagga explains. I think this is one reason why they have these sentiments.

RS: You're saying that the suttas and Visuddhimagga are not always saying the same thing?

BG: That's right. They're actually different.

RS: The Visuddhimagga divides meditation into two paths: samatha, calm; and vipassanā, insight. And there's also the distinction made between dry insight, without jhāna, and insight supported by jhāna. It seems that in your teaching you do not make these distinctions.

BG: Dry insight, without the support of mental calm, is a commentarial idea. You can never find any reference to dry insight in the Sutta Piṭaka. Even the word is not there.

The Venerable Buddhaghosa (who wrote the Visuddhimagga) invented these terms. Parikamma samādhi (preparatory concentration), upacāra samādhi (access concentration), appanā samādhi (absorption concentration)—even these are his own words. You don't find these terms in the suttas, either. So therefore we don't see any evidence for supporting dry insight in the suttas. If you read the suttas, anybody can see this.

I don't want to separate this. Even in a single sitting, at one moment one time you may feel that your concentration is very good, and another moment you experience the concentration is not very good, but your mindfulness is good. So you practice that.

With concentration, you can never practice straight away without any problem. You have sleepiness, restlessness, worry, and all these hindrances. They keep bombarding your mind all the time. In those times you use mindfulness to deal with these hindrances and then to proceed with concentration. And therefore anytime you practice concentration, you have to use mindfulness to deal with problems. You cannot simply focus your mind to get you through problems. You can't do that.

Meditation always needs the support of mindfulness, and therefore, when you practice concentration, you naturally bring the sources, information, and support from mindfulness. When you practice mindfulness, you gain concentration, and because your mindfulness is very strong, you learn how to deal with the hindrances to gain concentration. So if you start with mindfulness, you gain concentration. If you start with concentration, you use mindfulness.

The Buddha used a simile, likening samatha and vipassanā to two swift messengers delivering the message of liberation. They work together to bring the message of liberation.

Right concentration is really mindfulness and concentration together.

RS: How would you define right samādhi?

BG: Right samādhi is invariably defined in the Noble Eightfold Path in terms of the four jhānas.

RS: Would you call the Visuddhimagga path of samatha right samādhi?

BG: The Visuddhimagga does not emphasize the practice of mindfulness in order to practice samatha. The Buddha was always citing mindfulness, emphasizing its relationship with concentration.

The Visuddhimagga uses kasiṇas as objects for gaining concentration and deep states of calm. In the suttas the Buddha mentions all forty of the objects of meditation discussed in the Visuddhimagga, including kasiṇas, but he has not elaborated on them. He just casually mentions the list, but you don't get any detail at all. But the Visuddhimagga goes into very great detail explaining how to develop kasiṇas.

RS: As you know, different teachers define jhāna in different ways. How would you distinguish between strong states of concentration, such as access concentration of the Visuddhimagga, and jhāna?

BG: Although I don't find the term "access concentration" in the suttas, borrowing the Visuddhimagga word, I must say that access concentration is not strong enough to penetrate nonself. The purpose of gaining concentration is to see impermanence, unsatisfactoriness, and nonself at the deepest level. Access concentration cannot do this. Vipassanā practice makes us understand these three characteristics to some extent. Only deep concentration can do this penetration with deep and sharp concentration. That is why the Buddha said that a concentrated mind can see things as they really are. The Buddha has not said anywhere that deep mindfulness can see things as they really are. For this very reason concentration is placed as the last factor of the Noble Eightfold Path.

RS: Is that the reason jhāna is right samādhi?

BG: That is correct. Consolidating all the wholesome mental factors is called "samādhi." When you consolidate all the wholesome mental factors, that is the stage where you gain jhāna. Access concentration is just getting ready for that consolidation, but not being consolidated as yet. And therefore at that level, your attainment of any stage of enlightenment is questionable.

RS: When you teach meditation to your students, how much emphasis do you place on the cultivation of samādhi versus emphasizing the mindfulness and just letting the samādhi naturally strengthen on its own?

BG: I want to emphasize the necessity of developing both concentration and mindfulness. Because these two must go hand in hand when you practice mind concentration, mindfulness naturally comes in. For example, you have to overcome hindrances when you try to attain jhāna concentration.

The techniques and methods the Buddha has recommended to overcome the hindrances are always based in mindfulness and also concentration. The first step for all of this is restraint.

"To restrain" means morality and practicing mettā. And then mindfulness and clear comprehension. These are mentioned everywhere the Buddha has talked about practicing right concentration. Samādhi is the crown of meditation. Restraint is a supporting factor, a stepping-stone, so to speak, to gaining concentration, especially for right samādhi.

If you talk about samādhi without it being right samādhi, then you can talk about concentration without talking about mindfulness. Right concentration always has mindfulness; otherwise, it is not right concentration.

RS: Teachers do not all agree that jhāna is necessary to attain enlightenment, regardless of the style of practice you engage in.

BG: When you attain enlightenment, you have to attain jhānic concentration at the attainment of stream entry. You may not have practiced jhāna, per se, separately. But when you attain stream-entry, that attainment is always attained at the jhānic concentration level.

So that is what is called "supramundane jhāna." You don't need mundane jhānas. You may have practiced mundane jhānas, but later on you may not have used them.

RS: Mundane jhānas are those experienced before entering one of the stages of enlightenment?

BG: Yes. Mundane jhāna is the meditative state of jhāna before you have attained one of the four stages of enlightenment. The mundane jhānas have their own purpose, such as to be reborn in the brahma realms and so forth. The specific purpose of supramundane jhāna is to liberate oneself from fetters.

So when you practice, say, mindfulness, you just practice mindfulness. You'll gain some concentration and you'll use the concentration to practice mindfulness. And if you keep practicing mindfulness, when the mind is ready to destroy the first three fetters, you will see reality clearly. Your doubt about the Buddha, Dhamma, Sangha, rebirth, kamma (Pāli; Sanskrit: *karma*), and so forth will completely vanish. At that moment the mind is so clear, you gain concentration and at the same time you enter the stream and the path. And that is attained with supramundane jhāna concentration.

RS: Are you saying you always start with mundane jhāna, and it changes into supramundane jhāna with the attainment of stream-entry?

BG: You start with mindfulness. As many meditation teachers say, you don't need jhānas, assuming it is only mundane jhāna. You simply practice mindfulness. When mindfulness is very clear, the mind becomes concentrated. With that concentration, doubt will vanish and supramundane jhāna concentration arises. You attain stream-entry.

When the fetters are destroyed, hindrances are naturally destroyed, because hindrances arise from fetters. So long as fetters are there, hindrances arise. So in order to remove hindrances completely you have to destroy the fetters, because they are the roots.

One enters the stream with supramundane jhāna concentration. And therefore jhāna concentration is absolutely necessary to penetrate the hindrances and destroy the fetters, as long as you are talking about supramundane jhāna. No other concentration can destroy fetters. And therefore to say that jhānas are not necessary is confusing, unless we clarify and define what kind of jhāna you don't need.

RS: There are examples in the suttas of people who attained some degree of deep insight without jhāna, from just hearing a Dharma talk.

BG: There are five ways of attaining that state. In each case your mind has to be calm, relaxed, and peaceful in order for joy to arise. By listening to a Dhamma talk you can be really filled with joy and you are so serene that you completely, totally focus your attention on the teaching. And you become filled with joy. Full of joy you become happy, and happiness leads to concentration.

So by listening to a Dhamma sermon, by giving a Dhamma sermon, by devotion in reciting suttas, by investigating very deeply into the Dhamma, and by focusing the mind on one object in meditation, in these five ways you gain the same result.

Therefore, what you said is true, you can gain deep insight by listening to a Dhamma talk. In those days, when people listened to Dhamma talks, their minds were completely focused on the teacher. They didn't have complicated minds like we have today, confused minds. Today so many things are happening to us every moment, from so many directions.

So these days when we're trying to focus our mind on something, especially Dhamma, we cannot do that. Also, in those days people's minds were so pure and clean. And also the Buddha and his enlightened disciples were very supreme individuals, and when they delivered Dhamma talks, they were crystal clear.

RS: In addition to the five jhāna factors, the suttas list about eleven additional factors present in jhāna, including mindfulness, feeling, and sense contact.

BG: Yes. Mindfulness is there. Feeling is there. Contact is there. Then consciousness is there, in addition to the five factors. There are so many factors. These are all consolidated in that particular state.

RS: Is there awareness of the body in jhāna?

BG: Only when you are in jhāna, not out of jhāna, can you see the most subtle reality in the body and mind. And so that is why the Buddha emphasized many times that through the concentrated mind you can see things as they really are, not when the mind is unconcentrated. In that concentrated mind mindfulness is pure. Now you have two powerful factors: powerful concentration and powerful mindfulness. And to support them, you also have equanimity. Equanimity is the balancing factor. Concentration is the sharpening factor. Mindfulness is the seeing factor.

When these three come together, you see reality exactly as it is. The Visuddhimagga does not emphasize this, but you can see it in the suttas.

RS: Do you think everyone can attain jhāna?

BG: Everyone can attain jhāna, but some people are very slow. Some people are fast.

RS: Do you think it's possible to attain jhāna in the daily-life context?

BG: In the daily-life context it cannot happen unless you take some time off from daily activities. That is why the Buddha emphasized the necessity of being secluded from sense pleasures, secluded from unwholesome states of mind, and so forth. You've got to cut off at least temporarily from them. These two situations are ideal, because you have temporarily left them behind.

So laypeople can attain jhāna provided they follow the steps, spending time quietly in a solitary place. It's just like going to the Olympics. Even a monk can compete in the Olympics if he practices diligently in the proper way. All they have to do is practice and practice and practice and follow the same rules.

RS: One of the factors of jhāna is sometimes translated as "one-pointedness," whereas sometimes a different term, "unification of mind," is used.

BG: I don't agree with the mind uniting with the external object to gain concentration and become one. It can never happen. When you use any external object to gain concentration, you use it only temporarily in order to collect the mind. Once you get that, even according to the Visuddhimagga, you have a preparatory nimitta and access nimitta as signs to learn external objects.

Once you learn it, you memorize it. That is paṭibhāga nimitta. Once you memorize it, you no longer have the external object. What you have is the memory. It is totally internal. Then you focus the mind on that. Then even that object can disappear and the mind itself will gather around one point. It is like a whirlpool. A whirlpool creates a vortex. Water does not come from outside. Because of the power of the water's turning, a center is created in one point, called a vortex, but it needs external things to make it go in a circle. The water goes into one place and then it turns around. It keeps turning, turning, turning, turning, turning, turning to create a vortex.

Similarly, you use one object, an external object, in-breath and out-breath or a kasiṇa or something else, for the scattered mind to focus upon. And then once you focus on it, you'll remember it and then you'll forget the external object and it will stay with your memory. Then you focus the mind there. The mind unifies within itself.

Once you gain that concentration, you have nothing more to do with that external object. It is this concentration that you use to see your own experience of impermanence, which is going on at a very subatomic level in your body and mind. And external objects have nothing to do with that.

RS: In the beginning section of the Satipaṭṭhāna Sutta one is instructed to practice "having put aside covetousness and grief for the world," which is generally understood as attaining enough concentration to suppress the hindrances, at least temporarily.

BG: You cannot destroy covetousness until you attain the state of non-returner. Only when we attain this state are greed, covetousness, and hatred completely destroyed. Before that, you cannot destroy them at all. Even in the attainment in the second stage of sainthood (once-returner), you merely weaken them.

Until the roots of the hindrances have been destroyed, the hindrances are merely suppressed. Greed and aversion or resentment will be suppressed. By suppressing these two, you don't suppress all of the hindrances, because doubt is still there, restlessness and worry are still there, and sleepiness and drowsiness are still there, so only two of the hindrances are suppressed. You do this by discipline and restraining your mind.

RS: Not necessarily through high concentration, you're saying?

BG: No, no, not through high concentration, restraint. If you can gain high concentration before you begin mindfulness meditation, you have already done a lot of work before that. But in the very beginning you cannot do all this. So you have to at least have discipline and restraint. By restraining your senses you can suppress your greed and aversion without requiring strong concentration.

RS: You're saying that in the beginning the hindrances must be suppressed through restraint, but later, when you've strengthened concentration, they may be suppressed through strong samādhi? It just depends on where you are in your practice?

BG: That's right.

RS: Some teachers teach that the stages in the Ānāpānasati Sutta correspond to jhāna, while others teach that they don't.

BG: Some people say the Ānāpānasati Sutta is a very deep sutta, even though it appears to be very simple. And they say that it corresponds to jhāna when you come to the second tetrad, which begins with two of the jhāna factors, pīti and sukha. Based only on these two factors—pīti and sukha—they say, when you finish the first tetrad, you will attain jhāna. In other words, you've got to spend a lot of time practicing the first tetrad to gain jhāna. A lot of time.

But attaining pīti and sukha doesn't necessarily mean that you are in jhāna. You can have ordinary pīti and sukha, ordinary joy and happiness. And that is how I understand it. The sutta is referring to just ordinary joy and happiness.

I have my own interpretation of the explanation of the sutta. In the Ānāpānasati Sutta each tetrad is complete in itself. That is why the Buddha mentions four times that you can practice the seven factors of enlightenment. It is mentioned four times. That means at the end of the first tetrad you have completed mindfulness of the body. When you complete mindfulness of the body, you have already completed mindfulness of feeling, mindfulness of consciousness, and mindfulness of dhammas.

All of them are there. That is why you will be able to practice the seven factors of enlightenment at the end of the first tetrad. And if you don't attain the seven factors of enlightenment at the end of the first tetrad, then you try in the second. Then, at the end of the second practice with the second tetrad you can develop the seven factors of enlightenment, and so on. Four times you can practice the seven factors of enlightenment.

That is, each section is complete in itself. So therefore I don't agree that you've got to finish all sixteen steps in order to practice the seven factors of enlightenment, because the sutta itself says four times, at each tetrad, that you fulfill the seven factors of enlightenment.

But that is not how many people look at the sutta.

RS: The Satipaṭṭhāna, Ānāpānasati, and Kāyagatāsati suttas all talk about experiencing the "whole body" of breath. Some interpret this to mean one should be mindful of the entire breath from beginning to end, but could still focus on the breath at one particular location, maybe at the nose, for example. Others teach that it means being mindful of the entire body breathing.

BG: The Buddha has said that the breath alone is one of the bodies. What do we have in a body? We have four elements: earth, air, water, fire. This is what we find in the breath. We find four elements in the breath. And therefore the breath alone is fully qualified to be called a body, the breath body.

Therefore, if one practices the first tetrad, that individual has practiced mindfulness of the body just by practicing mindfulness of the breath. Some people ignore this particular sentence where the Buddha says the breath is a body, and they give their own interpretation.

Born in rural Sri Lanka, BHANTE HENEPOLA GUNARATANA has been a monk since the age of twelve, and took full ordination at twenty in 1947. He came to the United States in 1968. Prior to coming to the United

States, "Bhante G," as he is fondly called by his students, spent five years doing missionary work with the Harijanas (Untouchables) of India and ten years in Malaysia. In 1985 Bhante G cofounded the Bhāvanā Society in West Virginia and became its abbot. Bhante G is known for his emphasis both on samādhi and on mettā as part of spiritual training, and teaches in a style that emphasizes loving-kindness as a basis for right concentration.

Interview with Christina Feldman

Richard Shankman: What is "right samādhi" of the Buddhist eightfold path?

Christina Feldman: I would probably look at that question from two angles. One angle would be from the angle of practice, of the path of right samādhi, and the other angle would be from the perspective of the fruition of that path as right samādhi. Right samādhi as a path is the cultivation of a collected mind, the cultivation of one-pointedness. This is the samatha, tranquillity, training, and it is a process of concentrating and secluding the mind. So it is practicing a very, very bare-bones attentiveness. I would distinguish it from vipassanā, or the insight path, simply by the intentions that are set. Insight practice by nature is an inclusive practice that embraces all the foundations of mindfulness. Samādhi, or samatha, practice has a more singular intention—which is solely to attend to the chosen object of meditation. It is the factor of investigation that is let go of so as to be primarily engaged with bare attention and the cultivation of a secluded mind. That means resting very wholeheartedly, very single-pointedly, upon a primary object of attention, whatever chosen object that is. The refinement of that, of course, is a massive discussion. But the fruition of right samādhi, I would say, is the jhānas, or the absorption states.

There is a wider way of describing right samādhi, which is not so much the one-pointedness with a single object but with a one-pointedness with whatever object arises.

RS: A momentary concentration.

CF: Yes. It is the kind of samādhi that is very important to the development of insight. It is part of the path of learning to calm and steady the mind, releasing the tendency to proliferate and be lost in thought. The path that would be directed toward the fruition in terms of absorption states and deeper levels of concentration is simply a deepening of that same capacity to calm and steady the mind, but using a more limited focus, such as the breath or an image. It is a release of the investigation factor and a primary emphasis upon the concentration factor.

RS: Some teachers will start people with a formal samatha practice and then they will switch to vipassanā, while other teachers develop them both together. They are doing vipassanā practice, but the intention is that the samādhi and the sati are developing together. How would you tend to teach with most students?

CF: That is true. On a short retreat, such as a ten-day retreat, I would certainly place an emphasis on the combination of samatha and vipassanā, because for most people samādhi is the Achilles' heel in their practice. They just don't have enough concentration, and the tendency to be lost in thought and be distracted is powerful for many people. For most people there is not a sufficient foundation of stillness that allows insight to really penetrate. It makes insight practice much harder if there is no samādhi developed. So, on a group retreat, even when it is advertised as an insight meditation retreat, I tend to develop the samatha and the vipassanā together.

If a person wanted to develop right samādhi, the absorptions, I would respect that wish and offer some guidance about how to deepen the samatha. My experience is that even when people are primarily focused upon developing deeper levels of samatha, there is inevitably a world of insight that arises around that practice. I do find that it is often people with some maturity in practice and experience in insight meditation who are most able to undertake a samatha training without becoming lost in ambition or frustration.

I do find that samatha and vipassanā are too often presented as being entirely different paths, something I do not feel to be true. It is true that in the deeper states of absorption there is no insight developing, because within the absorption the mind is so still and the activities of the mind and sense impressions upon consciousness have been calmed. To develop insight, you must be in touch with changing experiences so you can see deeply, have insight into, the characteristics of those experiences, the impermanence, the selfless nature, and the suffering. So there is not the grist for insight within the calmest and stillest meditative states. Bear in mind, for samatha to develop, there also needs to develop a great skillfulness in understanding and calming the obstacles to samatha, which appear in the form of the hindrances—dullness, agitation, craving, aversion, and doubt. For most people who are doing a very dedicated samatha practice, there is plenty of insight that arises quite naturally and quite spontaneously outside of the formal practice periods. But again, for someone focusing on samatha practice I would not encourage them to turn toward and further cultivate and deepen insight, but just to acknowledge the insights that arise and appreciate the ways in which a mind of stillness is inclined toward understanding and depth.

In the higher jhānas there are such strong parallels between the nature of the jhāna and some of the understandings of emptiness and dissolution that sometimes it is hard to find the distinction.

RS: In samatha practice is your primary object ānāpāna (breathing)?

CF: Yes.

RS: Are there certain types of people who incline more toward—and should be doing—samatha practice, and certain other types who should be doing vipassanā without focusing on formal samatha practice?

CF: There is a question of temperament here. And I have never been able to specifically say how to define that, whether it is temperament, whether it is pāramīs, whether it is karma, or what it is, but some people are much more inclined to be able to develop the jhānas. I think everybody is temperamentally inclined to be able to reach access concentration, the stage of concentration just before attaining jhāna. But I have worked with students who are all working within the same time frame, the same context, putting in the same amount of effort, the same amount of right motivation—everything is pretty much the same—and one person would go into jhānas and another person would not. So I'm very careful about not prescribing the jhānas as a practice suited for everyone. And there are certain temperaments that actually do not do well with the jhānas.

RS: Do not do well in the jhāna states or do not do well as far as attaining jhāna?

CF: Attaining jhāna. To develop the jhānas requires such a level of deep ease of mind that people who are more prone to striving or pressing do not do well in the practice because they undermine the very foundations of ease.

RS: Are you saying there are some people who are not going to attain jhāna?

CF: I think that is so. Usually when I teach people samatha practice, I recommend that they sit for a month, because it almost takes me that long to actually see if they are going to have the temperament to develop jhānas. It takes a little time, and you don't want to set this up as either-a-success-or-failure type of venture.

RS: It sounds like you are saying there is a lot of variation in how long it takes for those who can develop jhāna to do so.

CF: Some people know they can. For many people it is not unusual to have a brush with the first jhāna on a short group retreat. And then you know those people have the temperament. If they can do that on a short retreat, then certainly they have the temperament.

RS: Do you think jhāna is only attainable in the retreat setting, or can the dedicated practitioner do it in daily practice?

CF: I have never seen anybody do that as their first practice. I have seen people who have done extensive samatha training, and then in daily practice they don't just lose it. If they have really matured that practice, I really do think in daily practice they can, pretty much, have access to the first jhāna at will if they have an ongoing practice. For some of the deeper jhānas, probably not.

RS: As samādhi develops, all kinds of experiences can arise, such as energies moving in the body, seeing lights, opening of various energy centers, and all sorts of phenomena. How do you work with people when those kinds of experiences arise?

CF: You don't pay attention to those experiences. That's the basic answer. There may be very many ways that you have to learn not to pay attention to them and not get hooked by them. But, of course, there are many phenomena that arise with absorption practice. There seems to be a relationship between the intensity of cultivating a technique and the level of the sometimes more esoteric experiences that arise. But the jhāna practice requires, in my understanding, such a sustained simple focus, not diverted by anything. And I see no reason to be more diverted by interesting phenomena than by other things, like the hindrances.

RS: A distinction is sometimes made between dry insight and insight "wetted" by the jhānas. There are examples in the suttas of people who do not have a practice background and just hear a discourse of the Buddha or another monk and they have a stream-entry experience. Do you think liberating insight can come without strong samādhi?

CF: Oh, yes. Yes.

RS: There is a wide range of what is being taught as jhāna. Why do you think there is so much disagreement about what the jhānas are?

CF: I think it has to do with depth, actually. You see, I think, among those threads of disagreement you will find there are many places that people agree in terms of characteristics of the jhānas. But I think the difference is more in the definition of depth. Plenty of people in practice, for example, might have a moment of rapture, or some of the jhāna factors arise, and some people will describe that as a jhāna. Some people will describe it as a jhāna factor. My first teacher, who taught about absorption states, suggested leaving clothes outside the monastery door because in jhāna you would not notice if the monastery burned down. My first teacher defined the first jhāna as sustaining that state for three days and three nights without moving. That was his definition of the first jhāna. I think it has to do with depth. It has to do with the breadth of the absorption. I don't think there is a lot of disagreement about presenting the characteristics of the jhāna. My understanding is that the suttas are fairly repetitive and fairly clear about the characteristics of the different jhānas.

RS: The suttas do define jhānas in terms of jhāna factors. The jhāna factors are present throughout a wide range of depth or strengths of samādhi. What some people teach as jhāna is what other teachers would call access concentration. How do you describe access concentration?

CF: Access concentration, to me, is when the attention sustains itself effortlessly upon the object, and the background phenomena of body and mind are posing no distraction. So the attention is more effortless and it is sustained and it has some of the factors of being very pleasant, slightly rapturous, very easy. And it is sustained, it doesn't want to go anywhere else. It is happy resting upon the object. That's what I would describe access as.

RS: How would you distinguish between strong access concentration and jhāna?

CF: There is a click of the mind, there is a shift of consciousness in which the jhāna factor is what actually becomes predominant, and the mind is absorbed in the object so that there is no longer any separation between the breather and the breath, and the mind is absorbed into the object. And in my experience and the way I've experienced it with students, it is quite a clear shift in consciousness. It is certainly recognizable as a very altered state of experience. And it is pervasive. It is very different from anything experienced before it.

RS: Not just defined in terms of jhāna factors, but there is a unification of the mind.

CF: There is the unification into the object, the absorption into the object.

RS: Not everybody defines *jhāna* in this way.

CF: No.

RS: Are there any body sensations or sounds in jhāna?

CF: In which jhāna?

RS: The first jhāna.

CF: In the first jhāna I'd say yes.

RS: At what point would you say body sensations and sounds completely disappear?

CF: The third jhāna.

RS: It sounds like you are saying that at that point there is no experience of the meditation object, but only of the absorption itself and the remaining jhāna factors.

CF: Yes.

RS: What about thoughts?

CF: In the first jhāna, background thoughts. But more like cartoon bubbles. Intermittent, spaces between, no continuity, and no distracting factors. Just very much in the background. In the second jhāna, even lighter. Again, I would not want to offer an absolute definition, there is such a range of views of what characterizes a jhāna.

RS: Once in the first jhāna, can the person direct the attention?

CF: The first jhāna is a prime condition for doing this. But I also think there are more ways, throughout the jhānas, in which the mind can be directed. Not within the jhāna, but prior to going in. There are many ways in which the Buddha talks about turning the jhānas toward the development of insight, and my understanding of that is that it primarily happens through your intention before going into the jhāna. But your intention goes in with you as a kind of guide, direction, or inclination. It's not that there is any activity from the intention within the jhāna, but the intention is there. For me this is one of the parameters of the jhāna, being able to go in and access at will. Being able to sustain and being able to access at will. So the intention clearly is a factor that you take into the jhāna with you, otherwise you would not be able to sustain and to access it at will.

RS: Sometimes people are taught to skip jhānas as part of gaining mastery. For example, to go directly from the first jhāna to the third.

CF: Absolutely. I encourage people to do that. Absolutely, once they are established. I'm teaching people initially how to go through sequentially and then how to deepen and master the capacity to do that, but then, especially the first and second jhānas, I will encourage them to skip. Because I don't think they need to keep building up, rebuild the foundations every time. For example, the rapture that is predominant within the first jhāna is incredibly useful for the energy and motivation it can offer. After a time it is seen to be comparatively gross and not necessary for establishing the concentration.

RS: As you progress through the jhānas, do the grosser levels drop away on their own as you continue to practice, naturally opening to the next stages, or at each stage do you have to do something specific to go to the next jhāna?

CF: I think that it happens pretty much on its own through continuing the practice. When I teach, I encourage students to stay with the jhāna long enough until they can make that shift into the next jhāna easily, which usually means that the grosser hindrance factors have dropped away for them to do that. When a jhāna has stabilized, it is the right time to reset the intention to refine it, focusing upon the more subtle characteristics of the mind and bringing it into the forefront of the consciousness. For example, if rapture becomes fairly readily accessible, it is the right moment to look for the quieter, more stable happiness that lies underneath the rapture and to bring that into the forefront as the new focus.

RS: Do you want people to master arūpa jhānas or, in your system, are the first four jhānas enough?

CF: I think the first four are plenty. If the person has the capacity to do the arūpa jhānas, I would certainly not discourage them from doing so.

RS: If someone can enter any jhānas, will they have the capacity to develop arūpa jhānas?

CF: I believe so.

RS: Once students have developed jhāna, and have then directed their practice to insight practice, what would you call the level of samādhi when they are doing insight practice?

CF: Access or first jhāna.

RS: Is jhāna necessary for stream-entry?

CF: I would not say so at all. It's the same answer as the one to the question, is samatha necessary for liberating insight?

RS: The suttas do not seem to make a hard, clear distinction between the paths of samatha and vipassanā. They seem to present a much more synthesized or integrated view of them.

CF: There is not much mention of jhāna in the Satipaṭṭhāna Sutta.

RS: In the Satipaṭṭhāna Sutta, before beginning the formal mindfulness practices, one begins by "having put aside covetousness and grief for the world," which is clearly talking about suppressing the hindrances, at least temporarily. So there is a certain level of samādhi there. What level of samādhi would you say that is talking about?

CF: It is actually very hard to discern that. Because there are so many places in the suttas where the Buddha talks about going into this jhāna and this jhāna and this jhāna and then turning the attention toward insight. You often get the impression that jhānas are almost prescribed as being the foundation of insight and something a person should accomplish first. There is a certain speculativeness about that. I would find it hard to adopt that as a hard-and-fast rule. It could be interpreted in so many ways. It could be interpreted as just saying that now we are actually shifting the locus of our attention; we've surrendered aversion and greed and are actually committing ourselves to practice. There is such a variety of ways that that could be translated.

RS: In the Ānāpānasati Sutta, some of the sixteen stages seem to correspond to jhāna factors. Would you say that sutta is talking more clearly about absorption states?

CF: Again, I think that would be a subject for a great debate. If you listen to someone like Larry Rosenberg and how he teaches ānāpāna, it is very much taught as an insight practice. But clearly it could also be taught as a samatha practice, and perhaps it is purely a question of intention here.

RS: There are sutta passages that, after giving the stock passage defining the jhāna, say that one pervades the body with that jhāna factor. That seems to say that body awareness is staying quite connected to the experience in the jhāna. It seems that it is in the Visuddhimagga model where there is no more body awareness in jhāna. Would you comment on that?

CF: It really can be quite subtle, because even in access concentration the body definition starts to very much fade away. And I would say that is almost one of the characteristics of access, because how a person knows that access concentration is being achieved is that it's difficult to find the limbs, we might say. Certainly, in the first jhāna, body consciousness has very much faded and it's very much in the background. So the energy of the jhāna, you could say, yes, it is pervading the body. I think it is the same with the following three jhānas, too. The energy of the jhāna or the quality of the jhāna is pervading everything. When I teach people to cultivate the jhānas, I get them to build up a cellular memory of the quality of the jhāna so that they can always recall that into consciousness. This is often how I get people to learn how to skip the jhānas, too, because they have learned to recognize each jhāna almost as a cellular memory, almost built into the body as a cellular memory. And being able to recall that and pervade the body with that can be a shortcut into the jhāna. And the body then disappears.

When I teach this building the cellular memory, it is a very important part of being able to access at will. When you evoke that, you do evoke the rapture, you do evoke the peace, you do evoke the equanimity, you know what it feels like. And you are knowing what it feels like first, almost as a cellular memory within the body. Then you build on that and then the body disappears.

CHRISTINA FELDMAN has been training in the Tibetan, Mahayana, and Theravāda Buddhist traditions since 1970, and has been teaching meditation internationally since 1974. She is the cofounder and a guiding teacher of Gaia House, a Buddhist meditation center in Devon, England, and is a guiding senior dharma teacher at the Insight Meditation Society in Barre, Massachusetts. In addition to teaching retreats worldwide, she is committed to the Personal Retreat Program at Gaia House.

Interview with Leigh Brasington

Richard Shankman: You seem to teach a form of jhāna that is much more readily accessed than that taught by many other teachers.

Leigh Brasington: We don't really know for certain what the Buddha was teaching as jhānas, although I strongly suspect that the Buddha was teaching deeper concentration than I do. Over time I have learned that there are a number of different methods. The methods generally have two things you can optimize—but only one at a time. The first is the ease of accessibility and the other is the depth of concentration. So if the question is, why am I teaching what I am teaching as the jhānas, I would say that the level at which I teach them seems to be the level at which laypeople can learn them and use them effectively. In other words, I'm giving up some of the depth of concentration for ease of learning. Given that laypeople are going on ten-day, two-week, maybe month-long retreats, what can be taught in that period of time that can enhance students' practice by enhancing their concentration?

RS: It sounds as though you are saying that there can be a range of depth of samādhi associated with any given jhāna state. That what constitutes jhāna is only partially the strength of concentration, but more the other associated factors.

LB: That's right. Although it would be good if students were learning the jhānas at a deeper level, I'm not going to say, "Well, since you can't do it at value 100, we're going to dismiss anything you do at value 50 or 25."

It turns out that any amount of concentration as a warm-up to insight is helpful. And given that students are stumbling into states that have the jhāna factors and that they are generally stumbling in at approximately the level of concentration at which I'm teaching, it seems like it's a natural level to teach to laypeople. If someone wants to learn the jhānas at a deeper level, then they are going to need to dedicate more time to working with the jhānas, such as finding a long-term intensive retreat environment.

My hunch is that the level of concentration that the Buddha was teaching cannot be achieved on a retreat of less than a month and, furthermore, cannot be achieved in forty-five-minute sitting periods. My own experience has shown me depths of concentration that do more closely match the experiences described in the suttas, but these can only be attained with long sitting periods of three or four hours, and on a long retreat of a month or more.

RS: Why do you think there's so much disagreement about what the jhānas are and how they are taught?

LB: Partially, it's because there are three major sources of jhāna material, all of which are incomplete. There are the suttas in which the descriptions of the jhānas are very simple. There is no how-to in the suttas, thus leaving them open for quite a broad range of interpretation. Since Pāli is not even a currently spoken language, many questions cannot be definitively answered. For example, what does "vitakka" really mean in the context of the jhānas? This leads to people interpreting this sparse material in different, yet internally consistent ways.

A second source is the Abhidhamma, which interprets the jhānas differently from what you find in the suttas. There you find a scheme of five jhānas covering the same territory as covered by four jhānas in the suttas. Finally, you have the Visuddhimagga, which gives quite a different interpretation from what you find in the suttas; a much deeper level of concentration is being taught.

So we have different schemes in the literature, and it depends to some extent on where someone is learning the jhānas, whom they're learning them from, and what literature is being used in that tradition. This material has been preserved for up to 2,500 years, with people making little tweaks along the way and not necessarily communicating with one another, and that has also led to different interpretations.

RS: Could you outline basically how you understand what those differences are?

LB: In the suttas, the jhānas are described most of the time using a standard formula. The standard formula for the first jhāna has four factors—one-pointedness is not mentioned. There are just the four factors of vitakka, vicāra, pīti, and sukha.

The formula for the second jhāna indicates that the vitakka and vicāra fall away, and they're replaced with inner tranquillity and oneness of mind; so now the concentration comes in and the pīti and sukha continue. Thus the suttas describe four factors for the second jhāna as well.

The third jhāna says one remains imperturbable, mindful, and clearly aware. Imperturbability, mindfulness, and clear awareness have come into play, although what is not specifically mentioned is when they arrived. They're just there. The formula indicates that the pīti goes away and the sukha remains; there is no specific mention of the tranquillity or the oneness of mind, so since they aren't said to go away, one assumes that they remain. So you actually have many more factors for the third jhāna.

The shift to the fourth jhāna is to a place beyond pleasure and pain, beyond gladness and sadness; so one arrives at a neutral mind-state. The sukha is obviously gone, since the pleasure has gone away.

When you look at this description, it's not really a factor-based description. The whole idea of a factor-based description probably comes from the Abhidhamma, where they started breaking things into pieces and analyzing them in a great deal of detail.

Now, there are a few suttas, perhaps three, where you can find five factors for the first jhāna, where one-pointedness is introduced as a fifth factor. But these are in the minority, for sure, and tend to be what is referred to as "later suttas." On the whole, the jhānas are described quite differently in the suttas than in the later literature.

The word *jhāna* means "to meditate," so when the Buddha tells his monks, "There are empty huts, roots of trees, go meditate," he's saying "go jhāna." Everybody was doing jhāna. If you look at the Visuddhimagga, the description of the states has reached a point of extreme concentration. In fact, it gives the odds that only one in one hundred million, at best, can reach absorption. But in the suttas, you find large numbers of people becoming absorbed.

What's being talked about in the Visuddhimagga are very deep states of concentration. The definition of what constitutes a jhāna has, in a thousand-year period, progressed to a much deeper state.

We might ask how this happened. Think about who was preserving the Buddha's teaching during these thousand years. It's a bunch of guys hanging out in the woods—no TV, no women. They've got just their minds to work with. And so they start working on the jhānas. And if somebody can take it a little bit deeper, obviously he's doing it "better." The natural human tendency is, "Well, if I can do it better than you are doing it, I'm doing it the right way, and I'll teach you to do it my way."

So I would guess that over time jhāna evolved from pretty serious states of concentration to the extreme states that we find preserved in the Visuddhimagga. The Abhidhamma seems to be somewhere in between, but obviously getting very, very deep during that period, since people were able to see their mind-moments and so forth.

RS: There is also disagreement among teachers about whether or not attainment of jhāna is necessary before practicing vipassanā.

LB: It's quite rare to find any teaching in the suttas that goes all the way to enlightenment that doesn't include the jhānas, with the exception of ānāpānasati. The middle eight steps of ānāpānasati, steps 5 through 12, mention pīti and sukha, but it certainly is possible to interpret these not at the level of jhāna.

So there appears to be a path that is outlined that doesn't include the jhānas: working with the breath. Other than that, the predominant path is the graduated training, with the jhānas an essential part of it. So perhaps the dry-insight path—the path without the jhānas and with minimal concentration—comes from the ānāpānasati teachings. However, it seems likely to me that the graduated training—with the jhānas—was more widely taught in the time of Buddha.

RS: Some interpret the middle tetrads in the Ānāpānasati Sutta as referring to strong concentration.

LB: I would agree with that. However, I'm not willing to say that those middle eight are the first four jhānas, as is sometimes taught. I would say that the middle eight serve the same purpose as the jhānas—to generate a deeply concentrated mind—and then the last four steps are the insight practices. Although I'm not willing to say they're identical, I will say that if you practice the jhānas, you are covering much the same material as those middle eight steps.

Pretty much all the various interpretations of ānāpānasati agree that the first four steps lead to access concentration. The middle eight are a deepening of concentration, with one camp saying they are the jhānas—this being pretty much a minority camp—and the other camp saying these are a non-jhānic deepening of concentration. And then the last four steps, everyone agrees, are insight practice.

RS: What level of samādhi is required in order to suppress the hindrances?

LB: Access concentration will do it. But a deeper level of samādhi will make the various insight practices, such as the twenty-one practices of the Satipaṭṭhāna Sutta, much more efficient. This is what you see in the graduated training. The Buddha first teaches the morality section and abandoning the hindrances, then he teaches the jhānas, and finally the directing of the mind to knowledge and vision.

The purpose of the jhānas is to generate the concentrated mind that can most effectively investigate the nature of the mind and body. In the Satipaṭṭhāna Sutta you are to have a mind that has put aside hankering and fretting for the world—or "covetousness and grief for the world"—and then you are to investigate both mind and body. So I would say that actually the relationship between the jhānas and satipaṭṭhāna is that as you read the graduated training, for example from the Dīgha Nikāya 2, and you come to that part about directing the mind to knowledge and vision, you insert the Satipaṭṭhāna Sutta practices at that point.

This is what I teach on retreats: step through the jhānas and then do the practices from the Satipaṭṭhāna Sutta. And on a retreat, I systematically go through all twenty-one of these practices. There is such a wealth there that is seldom fully addressed.

RS: Some teachers are concerned about people becoming attached to jhāna states.

LB: It's not an uncommon thing, and it is the responsibility of teachers to keep tabs on their students and not let them get stuck there. In fact, it is irresponsible for teachers to have students who are falling into these states and to not recognize what's going on and let the students wander off and get addicted. This seems to be a serious failing in some meditation communities; people are falling into these states and getting addicted because they are not getting instructions on working with these states. And simply telling somebody not to be attached is absurd. It's like "just say no"; whether it's drugs or sex or whatever you're just saying no to, it doesn't work. And it doesn't work in meditation, because someone has found something that enlivens their practice and makes them want to meditate and you're telling them, "Don't be attached, just say no."

However, once a student starts doing insight practice with the mind concentrated to the level of jhāna, the whole problem of attachment disappears, because the level of wisdom that arises, the depth of insight that shows up when your mind is very concentrated, is so much more interesting than just getting high.

RS: Can jhāna be attained only in a long-term, intensive-retreat format, or in daily practice, too?

LB: It's difficult to learn the jhānas outside of a retreat setting. But I have met people who have learned them in daily life. They tend be people who practice sitting meditation more than two hours a day. So I would say if you're going to learn the jhānas in daily life, you need a daily sitting practice of four to five hours.

After learning these states on an intensive retreat, it is possible to access them afterward if the student has a dedicated daily practice. But as you know, you go away from a retreat, and unless you're sitting at least a couple of hours a day, your level of samādhi and every other retreat state just fades away over time. A student's ability to access jhānas in daily life is dependent on how well they know the states and how dedicated their daily practice is.

RS: Since the jhāna factors can be present in a wide range of levels of samādhi, what distinguishes strong access concentration from jhāna?

LB: Access concentration means that you are continuously with the object of meditation, and if there are thoughts, they are wispy and in the background and not pulling you away from your object of meditation.

RS: It's unbroken mindfulness?

LB: Yes, unbroken mindfulness of the meditation object. When you're pulled away, you've fallen out of access.

RS: You're saying you could be in access concentration and still have times when you're pulled away where you're popping in and out in the course of a sitting?

LB: Yes, if the access concentration is weak. You could be in access for a minute and fall out for twenty seconds, and get back in for five minutes and fall out for three seconds. If it's access concentration, you're not being pulled away, but it is possible to fall out of access and then return fairly quickly.

RS: Then what distinguishes access concentration from jhāna?

LB: Well, the jhānas have specific factors. The jhānas basically are the mind coming to rest on these specific objects, rather than on something like the breath or a feeling of loving-kindness or a mantra.

Now, this doesn't necessarily mean that you're locked in and totally undistractable. That depends on the level of your concentration. Thus, you could be only lightly in the third jhāna and fall off and wind up planning your vacation to Hawaii. But you might not be there very long and you might be able to pop right back into the feeling of contentment that is the third jhāna. So technically you are in the third jhāna, you became distracted and fell out, and then you reentered the third jhāna without having to go through one and two.

RS: Are you saying that when you are in a particular jhāna during a sitting period, you can still get distracted, going in and out, in and out, in and out?

LB: You could. This is better than sitting there and spending forty-five minutes planning your trip to Hawaii. This, of course, is not as good as if you're fully there and not going in and out and in and out. But what you want is the best that you can do given your life in this crazy twenty-first-century world. So, for most laypeople it means that you get some degree of ability to absorb into the object of the jhāna, but you don't necessarily become totally undistracted, although that certainly would be optimal.

Now, as you progress through the jhānas, the objects become more and more subtle. Staying focused on these increasingly subtle objects definitely deepens your concentration beyond what you were experiencing at the level of access concentration. And as you get into these deeper levels, the likelihood of falling into distraction certainly diminishes substantially.

RS: As people progress through jhāna practice, do the grosser levels drop away on their own as they continue the practice, opening to the next level on their own, or does the meditator actually have to do something for that to happen?

LB: It seems that the mind will naturally move from one level to another if you're concentrated enough. This means that if you go on retreat, once you get into the first jhāna, you can just sit back and watch it move to two and three and perhaps even into four without having to do anything. The problem is that when you go home, it's not likely to happen because you're not going to be as concentrated, and also since it takes a while, you don't leave yourself enough time to do any insight practice. So although it will move on its own, it is very important, in my opinion, that people learn to intentionally move between the jhānas. In fact, what I recommend is that people learn to go up through the numbers and back down through the numbers, intentionally moving back and forth. This helps you learn how to move into them and also gives you two views of the jhāna. Its essence is not so much confused with the method of entering it, and so you really know what the essence is because you come at the jhāna from two different directions.

RS: So when you're in these jhāna states, you can direct the mind, you can have some intention and make something happen?

LB: Right—more or less. When you are directing the mind, you have let go of being in the jhāna but you have not fallen into distraction. The intentional moving is a letting-go process to move from one to two to three to four. There's a letting go of the grosser aspects of the first jhāna to move to the second. There's a letting go of the pīti entirely by jhāna three. It's a letting go of the pleasure to move to jhāna four. So there is some minor doing—letting go—in order to intentionally move yourself on.

RS: So you can contemplate, know the experience, investigate it?

LB: When you're in a jhāna, not really. Some teachers say that you do insight practice in the jhāna. However, I can't even remember to try it then. The mind can be directed to move to the next jhāna or even to jump to some other jhāna if you're quite skilled, or to stop and come out and do insight practice. But these are brief flickerings out of the jhāna state and quickly into whatever comes next. I can't really maintain the jhāna and do anything else. That unification of mind that appears in the second jhāna, by definition, I would think, precludes doing any sort of investigation.

RS: In the first jhāna do thoughts arise?

LB: In the first jhāna, because there's not a unification of mind, I would say that by definition it's possible for thoughts to arise. But the thoughts are not pulling you away.

RS: What about sounds or body sensations?

LB: There are things that can override your samādhi at any jhāna level. The pain in your knee can become so strong that even in the fourth jhāna it just starts overriding the depth of your concentration.

RS: If that hasn't happened, though, do you lose the body sensation?

LB: As you get deeper in, the body sensations tend to go further and further away. The noticing of sounds drops off based on the depth of your concentration. If you are concentrated enough, even in the first jhāna, you wouldn't notice any sounds. If you're not particularly concentrated in the fourth jhāna, you would notice sounds. So it's a function of concentration or depth of jhāna rather than any individual jhāna itself. But for most people sounds tend to have a receding sense as they get deeper in, until on a retreat some people do report that by the fourth jhāna sounds just aren't being heard. However, by the time you have arrived at the formless jhānas, there are no more body sensations. To enter these states, the concentration required does block it out.

RS: On retreats, how do you work with people for whom it seems they are not going to get into jhāna? Do you have them continue with practices aiming toward jhāna or have them switch to some other kind of practice?

LB: When I teach a retreat, I give just three talks on the jhānas, and maybe a fourth talk where the jhānas are an essential ingredient, out of eighteen talks in a ten-day retreat. There's one talk on sīla, and the rest of the teaching is on insight. So I'm putting out a huge amount of material on insight practices for students to work with. And I try to describe this as "get as concentrated as you can and then do insight work." My primary goal is to teach the jhānas without making them seem like a big deal, so that those for whom they are not available don't feel like they're missing out, but they get the idea that concentration to the best of their ability is an integral ingredient, is actually a warm-up exercise for insight. All of jhāna practice as well as access concentration is a warm-up exercise to the main event, which is the insight practice.

LEIGH BRASINGTON began practicing meditation in 1985 and is the senior American student of the late Venerable Ayya Khema, who requested that he begin teaching. Leigh assisted Venerable Ayya Khema's teaching on retreat beginning in 1994, and began teaching his own retreats in 1997. He completed a four-year teacher-training program at Spirit Rock Meditation Center with Jack Kornfield in 2006. Leigh is also a student of Venerable Tsoknyi Rinpoche. When not teaching in North America and Europe, he lives in Alameda, California, where he continues to work part-time as a software engineer.

Interview with Ajahn Brahmavaṃso

Richard Shankman: Why do you think there is so much disagreement and controversy surrounding samādhi and jhāna?

Ajahn Brahmavaṃso: One of the main reasons is that people in the West do not have much experience of jhāna, and because of their lack of experience they are taking what is ordinary samādhi to be something much deeper than it is. At the same time, in the West we are finally getting access to very good translations of Buddhist teachings, from the Chinese and the Pāli sources. People are reading these sutras for themselves and they see that jhāna is essential to the path. Thus, there is an interest in the deeper forms of samādhi called jhānas and, at last, they are coming into the picture. As samādhi and jhāna are starting to become relevant, of course, there will be some controversy regarding what they really are. But later on, as people start to experience these things, the controversy will be resolved.

RS: There is some disagreement among teachers as to whether or not attainment of jhāna is necessary. There are even concerns that the meditator will get attached to the pleasant meditative states and that this will increase craving rather than help alleviate it.

AB: That makes no sense. The Buddha said, very clearly, that you should not be afraid of the jhānas, that you should develop them, make much of them, and cultivate them. He also said that the jhānas are the only meditation that he praises and recommends. And these are very, very strong statements, which are not just in the Theravāda suttas, but also in the

Chinese Āgamas, so they are accepted as legitimate sayings of the Buddha. So to say that you should not do jhānas because you will get attached to jhānas, or that they are not necessary, is actually flying in the face of what the Buddha said.

RS: So you would say it is a wrong view?

AB: Yes, absolutely. Yes, I would say that. I would be that strong. People would only say that jhānas were unnecessary if they had never experienced them. When you have experienced a jhāna, it is obvious that the only way you can attain those states is by letting go of craving. These are called "stages of letting go," not "stages of attachment." The idea that you can get attached to a stage of letting go is ridiculous.

It is the other sensory desires and the other material things in the world that we should be afraid of. Those are the things we should let go of. And that is why the Buddha said you should distinguish between the two types of pleasure: the pleasure depending on the world, on the five senses, especially, of seeing, hearing, smelling, tasting, and touching; and the pleasure of the jhānas. He said that the first should be restrained, and the other one followed.

Against that we have what the later teachers started talking about, what we might call "commentarial Buddhism." The commentarial Buddhism of Theravāda, which arose a long time after the Buddha passed away, started to change things. There is confusion these days between what the Buddha actually taught and commentarial Buddhism. They express different positions, in particular on the need for jhāna. That is one of the reasons why Westerners are not really quite sure about the necessity of jhānas. If we make that distinction between original Buddhism and commentarial Buddhism, I think much of the confusion will be resolved.

RS: Do you think the Visuddhimagga presents a view of samādhi and the path of meditation that is consistent with the Pāli suttas?

AB: No, the Visuddhimagga is inconsistent with the Pāli suttas. There are many areas that are very useful, so one should not throw out the baby with the bathwater, as they say, and just reject it offhand. There are many useful tips in there, but it is not an authority. It is not something one can rely upon without any discrimination. There is much in there that does not make sense at all to anyone who has been a meditator.

RS: Are you referring to the way that the Visuddhimagga emphasizes nimitta, for example?

AB: Actually, that is one part that I think is accurate. I use nimitta in my teachings. Where I disagree with the Visuddhimagga is on what you do when you have a nimitta arrive. I seem to remember that, in the Visuddhimagga, you are encouraged to expand the nimitta, to contract it, and to play around with it. I found that to be a very unhelpful teaching.

RS: Are you saying nimitta is important, but it may not necessarily have to be specifically a visual image as given in the Visuddhimagga?

AB: Nimittas are important, and the visual-like nimitta is the best one. It is not seen with the physical eye. It is purely a mental phenomenon. It appears as if it is a light, like a moon or a flashlight or a headlight in front of you. This is a pure mind object, but the only way you can interpret that to make sense of it is to compare it to your known data bank of experiences from your five senses.

The experience that is the most similar for most meditators is that of a strong light. So sometimes that nimitta can seem incredibly brilliant, so much so that you think you cannot stare at it any longer, until you realize that this is not a visual thing at all. It is a purely mental phenomenon, and it doesn't matter how brilliant it gets. It is like looking into the sun, but it is quite safe, because it is a pure mental image.

Some people can use an equivalent nimitta, which is a feeling nimitta that is experienced similar to the sense of physical touch. But I have to emphasize that the sense of physical touch is gone already. This is just a way it is interpreted. However, of these two, the visual nimitta is by far the most useful. It is stronger and easier to work with. It is the one that I encourage. But you do not develop it by expanding and contracting and moving it around.

RS: What is it about jhāna, in particular, that makes it "right samādhi" as opposed to some other meditative state?

AB: What is meant by "right" or "wholesome" or "skillful"? It all depends on the goal. If your goal is to be a wealthy person, then the right practice is to work hard and be competitive rather than cooperative, because it is right in the context of that particular goal. And in the context of the eightfold path, the word *sammā* is contingent on the goal that is to end rebirth, to stop saṃsāra, to eradicate the defilements that are the cause for rebirth. In the context of ending rebirth, each of the factors of the eightfold path is important. Anything less than sammā samādhi, "right samādhi," and you do not have enough power of mind to achieve this goal.

Consider the simile of a tadpole that was born in a lake, grew up in the lake, and lived all its time in the lake. How can the tadpole know what water is? It may read books on water, including the commentaries and Abhidhamma, but will never understand what water is. But as soon as that tadpole grows into a frog and leaps outside of that water, only then can it know what water is.

That simile works like this: The first jhāna is the first time when the body and the five senses have disappeared. So when one gets into the first jhāna, that is the first occasion when one has completely let go of the body and the five senses, just like the first time that tadpole, transformed into a frog, has gone out of the lake. Only when you have leaped out from the world of the five senses and body are you able to know what a body is and what the five senses are. You cannot know what these five senses truly are when you are swimming around in them. You cannot know what a body is when it is always there for you.

But much more profoundly, in the second jhāṇa your will has disappeared. It is not just that you do not want to do anything. You cannot do anything. The potential to involve yourself with affairs has been completely removed. It is like you have leaped out from another lake that you had been immersed in as long as you can remember, the lake called "will." In the second jhāna, from that standpoint, you can understand what "will" truly is. Thus, jhāna not only gives you a powerful mind, free of the hindrances, but it also gives you the raw data, the means by which you know what this nonself business is.

RS: As people progress through the jhānas, do the grosser levels drop away on their own as one continues to practice, or does the meditator have to do something?

AB: At that point it progresses on its own. If you can do anything, you are not in jhāna.

"Concentration" was never a very good translation for *samādhi,* and I have moved from that to "attentive stillness." If you can understand that samādhi is stillness, you can understand how all will actually disturbs the process of stilling the mind.

I hold a cup of water in my hand and I ask people who are sitting in the front to say when the water is still. And because the water in the cup is still moving around, I try harder to hold that cup of water still. No matter how hard I try, I cannot hold a cup of water still in my hand. There is always some agitation. Trying to hold a cup of water still is like trying to hold your mind still. There is no way in the world anyone can hold their mind still.

But then I just place that cup of water on the ground. The water in the cup moves less and less until, after a few seconds, it comes to a stage of stillness that I can never achieve when I hold it in my hand. The same method applies to stilling your mind in meditation. If you would only let go of will, choice, controlling, directing, then your mind would get very, very still. You do not actually say, "Mind get more still, get more still." It is just a natural process, which happens when you let things go. When the cause of agitation has been removed, the mind gets more and more still. As it gets more and more still, you proceed naturally through the jhānas like a passenger, not as a driver.

RS: The term "attentive stillness" seems to have a strong mindfulness connotation. Is that what you mean?

AB: Yes. I put it in there because sometimes people have a weird understanding that a jhāna is some sort of trance state, a state of low mindfulness. In fact, in jhāna, the mindfulness increases enormously, really waking up and being fully alert, fully aware. Even the texts say that awareness reaches its purity, its peak of purity, in the fourth jhāna.

RS: Do you separate meditation practice into two paths, a samatha and a vipassanā, or do you see them as one integrated path?

AB: I see them as one integrated path. I practiced nine years with Ajahn Chah, and many, many times Ajahn Chah would say the same thing. He would hold up his hand and say, "Can you see the front of my hand?" and I would say, "Yeah." "But you can't see the back, can you?" I would say, "No." "The back of my hand is still there," he would say, and he would turn the back of his hand around. "See, you can see the back of my hand now, but you can't see the front of my hand, can you?" I said, "No, I can only see the back of your hand." "The front of my hand is still there," he would say. That is just like samatha and vipassanā. They are like the front and the back of the hand. You cannot split them up. Sometimes you think that you are just doing samatha, but vipassanā is right behind, inseparable. Or at other times you think that you are practicing only vipassanā, but samatha is right behind, indivisible. There is no such thing as pure vipassanā and there is no such thing as pure samatha.

RS: There are teachers who put the emphasis on the moment-to-moment mindfulness and will tend not to emphasize samādhi, letting it naturally strengthen on its own. It is a momentary concentration.

AB: Indeed. That is why I prefer translating *samādhi* as "stillness" rather than "concentration." "Momentary samādhi" then becomes "momentary stillness." What does the term "momentary stillness" sound like to you? It is an oxymoron, two words put together that mean completely opposite things. If you are still, you will remain still longer than a mere moment. If it is samādhi, it is never momentary. The idea of "momentary concentration" was imposed by the methodology of the Abhidhamma. And because the Burmese tradition is so heavily influenced by that Abhidhamma, they have bent their meditation instructions to fit their Abhidhamma, rather than just following the suttas and following experience.

We pay far too much attention to the Abhidhamma, which was not the word of the Buddha. It was not taught by the Buddha. It came after the time of the Buddha. And that particular methodology distorted the teachings on meditation, and it has been a great hindrance to the attainment of jhāna, and realization based on jhāna.

RS: There are certainly examples in the suttas of people who have had some deep awakening or insight, maybe stream-entry, on just hearing a talk of the Buddha or from one of the monks. And there is certainly no mention of any samādhi there. So do you think that liberating insights can come at all without strong samādhi?

AB: Without perfecting sammā samādhi, which means "jhāna," you cannot perfect wisdom. So said the Buddha! Let me give you a simile, which I have used many times effectively. If you have a degree from college, perhaps your parents have a picture of you receiving your degree. They do not have any pictures of you attending lectures, or tutorials, or doing the examinations. The only thing they have is a picture of you receiving a final degree, the last moments of the attainment. That is very similar to what is recorded in the suttas. Instead of recording the hard work, such as the keeping of precepts, the giving up of the world, the practice of jhānas, and so on, the suttas only record the inspiring last moment, the graduation ceremony, as it were. The enlightened ones in the texts just hear that one last teaching, which is the straw that breaks the camel's back. If you put a straw on a camel, it never breaks its back. It is because of all the other stuff that was there as well.

RS: Do you use the term "access concentration"?

AB: That is one of the terms that I do use, *upacāra samādhi*. Again, it is not in the suttas, but comes from the Visuddhimagga. But I think it is a useful addition, because it does describe the real state just prior to the jhānas and just after the jhānas. However, I prefer the term "neighborhood" or "threshold" to "access."

In the case of a house, you cross the threshold on the way in and on the way out. In the case of jhāna, the threshold that you cross on the way out is the important one. On the way into jhāna, threshold samādhi is very unstable, so it is not all that useful. In any case, if you are that close, you would be a fool not to go farther into the jhāna.

When you come out from jhāna, that is the access samādhi that is very stable and lasts a long time. This threshold samādhi is where the deep insights happen, on the way out of jhāna, not on the way in.

The only way you can understand whether it is threshold samādhi or not is to see what is just beyond there. Once you know what jhāna is, you know what is just before and what is afterward, and that is neighborhood samādhi. If you have not gotten into a jhāna, then you will never really know what threshold samādhi is.

RS: Are you rendering the term *vitakka-vicāra* more as the sense of "connecting and sustaining," rather than as "applied and sustained thought"?

AB: Yes. Vitakka-vicāra is a movement of the mind, which is not verbal, it is automatic. It is not something deliberately willed. Nor is it any part of the thinking process. It is what I call in experiential terms "the wobble in the first jhāna." A wobble means there is a lack of absolute stillness, but it is still pretty still.

The reason it is happening is because there is still a residual amount of involuntary control, a lot of holding on to the bliss, the pīti-sukha. And because of that involuntary holding on to that bliss, the mind is not totally stable. The holding on to it is called "vicāra." It is a type of attachment, a very subtle form of attachment. And the vitakka is the automatic mental process of moving toward the bliss. But this is not thinking. It is completely subverbal. Once vitakka-vicāra is completely abandoned, then you are absolutely still. It is the trademark feature of the second jhāna.

RS: In the beautiful similes that are used in describing jhāna, the jhāna factors are pervaded throughout the whole body. If all feelings of the body disappear, it is not clear how to interpret that.

AB: The word *kāya* in Pāli is well translated by the English word "body." We have a physical body, but also have a body of evidence, a body of experience, and these are all immaterial "bodies." We use the word "physical body" just to make sure we know what body we are talking about. *Kāya,* just like the word "body," means an accumulation of things, a conglomerate, a group of things.

Pervading the "kāya" with the jhāna factors means that the experience of bliss pervades the whole "mental body" throughout the jhāna. It does not mean experiencing the jhāna with the physical body. That is a misunderstanding of the use of the word *kāya* in Pāli. It is quite clear that in jhānas you cannot feel anything to do with the body.

VENERABLE AJAHN BRAHMAVAṂSO was born in 1951 and ordained at twenty-three. He subsequently spent nine years studying and training in the Thai forest meditation tradition under Venerable Ajahn Chah. In 1983 he assisted in establishing a forest monastery near Perth, Western Australia, and is now the abbot of Bodhinyana Monastery and the Spiritual Director of the Buddhist Society of Western Australia (BSWA). Together with BSWA, Ajahn Brahmavaṃso was instrumental in setting up the first independent training monastery for women in the Theravāda tradition, Dhammasara Nun's Monastery at Gidgegannup, east of Perth. He is the spiritual advisor to the Buddhist Society of Victoria and the Buddhist Society of South Australia, and Spiritual Patron of the Buddhist Fellowship in Singapore and several other centers.

Interview with Pa Auk Sayadaw

Richard Shankman: Many Western students are interested in samatha practice and jhāna. Why do you think there is so much disagreement about what the jhānas are?

Pa Auk: One reason there is disagreement about jhāna and samādhi is because people do not understand the Pāli texts well. According to our Theravāda tradition, jhāna practice is explained clearly in the Visuddhimagga, the Path of Purification. People should trace back to the original suttas, the original commentaries and subcommentaries, and then to the Visuddhimagga, and only then will they understand the meanings.

Although jhāna practice is described clearly in the Visuddhimagga, it is very brief and concise on some points. Because of this there are certain points they may not understand well, especially the signs of concentration, nimitta, and how to do jhāna practice. This is why they should study the suttas and the commentaries, too.

There are forty samatha meditation subjects. Of these forty, nearly thirty can produce jhāna. These practices are the ten kasiṇas, ten foulness meditations, thirty-two parts of the body meditation, the four divine abidings, the four types of immaterial jhānas, and ānāpānasati, mindfulness of breathing. Any of these meditation subjects can lead to jhāna. But when they are practicing these, it is important that they practice systematically according to the method in the Visuddhimagga.

RS: Of these samatha meditation subjects, is there one you particularly emphasize?

PA: All of these practices can be useful, but I emphasize mindfulness of breathing, ānāpānasati. If they practice ānāpāna, they should train systematically. The Buddha taught four stages—number one, long breath; number two, short breath; number three, the whole breath-body; and number four, subtle breath or cessation of breath. The awareness should stay at the "touching point" of the breath, which is either the tip of the nose or the upper lip. The awareness should stay with the breath at this one point, and should not follow the breath inside or outside.

When one practices these four stages, an ānāpāna nimitta is necessary. A nimitta is a sign of concentration. For breath meditation, at any of these four stages, when concentration develops, a nimitta naturally appears. For beginners the nimitta is usually a gray smoky color appearing in front of them. When the nimitta appears, they should continue to concentrate on the natural breath, and slowly, as their concentration develops further, they will see that the breath and the nimitta will become one. At that stage, their mind usually or automatically stays focused on the sign, the nimitta, and at that point they should concentrate on the nimitta only.

As their concentration develops further, the gray smoky nimitta will change in color to white. The white color nimitta is called "the learning sign," *uggaha nimitta*. Continue to concentrate on the learning sign, the white form nimitta, and with continued practice that white one will change into a transparent nimitta, which is called the *paṭibhāga nimitta,* "the counterpart sign." Now you must concentrate wholly on that transparent nimitta. When you concentrate well on that transparent nimitta, it will become transparent like a morning star. Slowly your concentration will go deeper and deeper until you reach the stage of full absorption.

Unless you see the counterpart sign, your samādhi may be superficial, not real jhāna. In any case, this is only the beginning stage of jhāna, and jhāna for beginners is not very stable. It is important to practice again and again, systematically, and then you will be able to maintain full absorption concentration for one, two, or three hours. Only after fully mastering the first jhāna can you go on to jhāna two, then jhāna three, then jhāna four.

So if they practice systematically in this way, they may attain true jhāna, fine-material (rūpa) jhāna.

If the meditator wants to practice the immaterial jhānas, they should begin with the ten kasiṇas rather than ānāpāna. They must practice the ten kasiṇas systematically. In each kasiṇa they should train to attain all four fine-material jhānas, and only then can they go to the four immaterial jhānas, stage by stage.

RS: Is there always a nimitta in order to obtain jhāna?

PA: Yes. In some jhānas, especially ānāpāna, a nimitta is necessary to attain access concentration as well as full absorption jhāna concentration. Access concentration of ānāpāna and full ānāpāna absorption jhāna both take the same nimitta counterpart sign, ānāpāna paṭibhāga nimitta. The object is the same. The difference between them is that in the access-concentration stage the jhāna factors are not yet so strong. But when they reach full absorption stage, appanā jhāna, their jhāna factors are very strong and powerful. Because of this they can maintain their full absorption jhāna for a long time—one, two, or three hours—without interruption.

The Visuddhimagga mentions nimitta for some samatha meditation subjects, such as loving-kindness, mettā jhāna, that is not a real jhāna, but an "as if" jhāna. What is a real nimitta and an "as if" nimitta?

If you want to practice loving-kindness meditation to attain mettā jhāna, you should first focus on one person, who must be the same sex. You should choose one of these formulas, whichever you prefer: "May this good person be free from danger." "May this good person be free from mental suffering." "May this good person be free from physical suffering." "May this good person be well and happy."

For example, if you choose "May this good person be free from mental suffering," you should try to focus on that person's image, especially on their smiling face. Then you should send mettā: "May this good person be free from mental suffering." The person's image must always be in your mind. When you are sending mettā subsequently to each person, a dear one, neutral one, or hated one, you should try to attain first, second, and third jhāna. You must try again and again in this way until there is no difference between any of these types of people and yourself, until all four kinds of persons are very easy to send mettā to, until they are equal.

At that time, when there is no difference between them, we can say the meditator has broken down the barrier or boundary. If it is very easy to send mettā to the dear one to attain jhāna, and the neutral one is also easy, but the hostile one is not easy, if there is any difference, then you have not yet broken down the barrier. When everyone is the same, then you have broken down the barrier.

This breaking down the barrier is the sign of concentration, also called a "nimitta." It is not a real nimitta, but rather an "as if" nimitta only, because there is no real image. If you send mettā at that time to all beings, you can easily attain mettā jhāna, which is a very strong and powerful jhāna. So this breaking down the barrier is called the nimitta. But at that time there is no light counterpart sign, no ānāpāna counterpart sign.

RS: I have heard that even for your monks and nuns who practiced with you for a long time, not everyone can attain jhāna, that some people do and some do not. Is that true?

PA: Yes. If they practice diligently, if they can control their mind, they can attain jhāna. Some people cannot control their mind because their mind is always wandering. That is one reason it is not easy to attain jhāna. Another reason is their sīla is not so strong, their effort is not so strong, and their wisdom faculty is not so sharp. And because of this the four accomplishments—desire, consciousness or mind, vigor, and discrimination or the wisdom faculty—are not strong enough to enable them to maintain their concentration. Another reason is their pāramīs. If they do not accumulate pāramīs for the attainment of jhāna, it also may be difficult.

RS: For people who do not attain jhāna, should they continue to practice samatha or should they switch to vipassanā?

PA: We teach four-elements meditation, both for those who attain jhāna and for those who do not. For those practicing samatha, only after they have attained jhāna, especially up through the fourth jhāna, or even all eight attainments, do they switch to vipassanā, and their practice is very clear. They practice four-elements meditation systematically, and one day they will see small particles, called "kalāpas." When they see kalāpas, if they can see four elements for each kalāpa, or in some kalāpas, then this is the last stage of samatha, as well as the beginning stage of vipassanā. In this beginning stage of vipassanā they can understand ultimate materiality in the small particles.

Their discernment of ultimate materiality, of the four elements in each kalāpa, is very clear. Their understanding is much clearer than for those who did not attain jhāna. This is because their jhāna concentration can produce a strong, powerful light, which is called the "light of wisdom." With the assistance of the light of wisdom, if they discern ultimate materiality, as well as ultimate mentality, their understanding is very clear. This is why we teach samatha first, before undertaking vipassanā meditation.

For those who do not attain jhāna, we also teach four-elements meditation. And if they practice diligently, they, too, can see small particles, and when they see small particles, they can discern in the small particles the four elements. Then, if they continue, they can understand their essence, color, odor, flavor, nutritive essence, and so on. It will take longer for them to discern ultimate materiality, because their wisdom faculty is not sharp enough to see clearly. So they must practice again and again, and they will be able to see ultimate materiality and mentality. But their wisdom and their understanding of ultimate materiality are not as clear as for those who have attained jhāna.

RS: When the meditator has attained jhāna and then switches away from samatha to vipassanā, is he or she then in access concentration?

PA: No, not access concentration. I mentioned earlier that if you practice ānāpāna up to the fourth jhāna, that fourth jhāna produces a strong, powerful light called "the light of wisdom." The light of wisdom is still there when you emerge from the fourth jhāna. Upon emerging from the fourth jhāna, you shift to four elements systematically, and at that time there is no jhāna and no access concentration. But there still is light. If you quickly switch your attention to the four elements as the meditation object, you will clearly see the four elements, and very certainly will see kalāpas, because of the subtlety of the fourth jhāna. The fourth jhāna is the foundation for vipassanā.

When you practice four elements systematically and when you see small particles, and if you can see in the kalāpas four elements again, this is also called access concentration. But it is not real access concentration. Why? The real access concentration is close to jhāna. In four-elements meditation, however hard you try, you cannot attain jhāna. So this is not a real access concentration. In ānāpāna, if you practice systematically, one day the nimitta appears, and if you concentrate well on that nimitta, you can enter access concentration. If you continue to train hard and if you continue your concentration, then you may attain full absorption. This access concentration is real access concentration. But that access concentration and four-elements access concentration is not the same.

Because of this similarity, when your samādhi is strong enough to discern four elements in each kalāpa, the commentary says that is access concentration. Such a level of access concentration occurs throughout the vipassanā. At that time their samādhi is vipassanā samādhi, vipassanā concentration, which is nearly the same as access concentration.

RS: Can a person attain stream-entry without jhāna?

PA: Yes, it is possible. They must first practice four-elements meditation. In the Visuddhimagga, for those who are bare-insight meditators, suddha-vipassanā-yānikas, they must begin with four-elements meditation. These days many meditators do not follow this rule, and for this reason they do not see small particles, or kalāpas. Because they do not start four-elements meditation systematically when they are practicing vipassanā directly, they cannot analyze, when they see kalāpas, four elements in each kalāpa.

RS: Is jhāna only attainable in long-term intensive retreat practice, or if someone is very diligent in daily practice, can they also attain jhāna?

PA: It is definitely possible to attain jhāna in daily practice. But it depends on the person's environment and their practice. There are some meditators who meditate two or three sittings within one day, with each sitting being one or two hours. If they practice diligently in this way, they can develop the nimitta. At that point, when they sit, very soon they can see the nimitta, the ānāpāna nimitta, and for those people, within one or two weeks they can attain jhāna if they practice diligently. It is possible if they can maintain their concentration on that nimitta sign of concentration. But if they cannot maintain it, it will take a long time.

RS: Do you want your students to master the immaterial attainments, or are the first four jhānas enough?

PA: It depends on their own desire. It is not necessary, but if they want to practice four immaterial jhānas, it is okay. If they practice using the ten kasiṇas and realize the eight attainments, their concentration is very powerful. Some meditators like immaterial jhānas. They are very comfortable for them.

Sometimes they may become tired when practicing vipassanā meditation, and because of tiredness their mental powers are weak. At that time if they rest in one or more of the immaterial jhānas, when they emerge from that jhāna, their mind will be fresh. So this is a dwelling place for meditators.

Practicing vipassanā is like attacking on the battlefield. The armies do not attack each other in the village or in the town. If they want to attack, they must go outside the town to a battlefield, and behind that battlefield there is a fort. When they get tired from shooting arrows and attacking each other with swords, they enter their fort, where they can eat and rest. The fort is very safe. Afterward, when they are fresh, they come back to the battlefield.

In the same way, when you are practicing vipassanā, you can get very tired. Vipassanā is like attacking on the battlefield. When tired, you go back to rest in samatha, the eight attainments. After resting in the eight attainments your mind is very fresh and you can go back to the vipassanā battlefield.

In vipassanā, when you penetrate again and again into ultimate materiality, your mental body begins to get tired and you cannot easily see clearly. At that time you should go back to rest in one of the jhāna attainments. One of the four immaterial jhānas is especially good to dwell in; the immaterial jhāna of the base of neither-perception-nor-nonperception is the best. If you rest in that jhāna for one or two hours, when you emerge from that jhāna, your mind will be fresh. At that time you should go back to practicing vipassanā again.

But if students do not want to develop the immaterial jhānas, if they want to go directly to vipassanā, when they reach the fourth jhāna stage, we usually teach them vipassanā, having them begin practicing four-elements meditation systematically.

The VENERABLE ACINNA, commonly referred to as the VENERABLE PA-AUK TAWYA SAYADAW (and, in less formal circumstances, as "Pa-Auk Sayadaw"), is the current abbot and principal teacher at Pa-Auk Forest Monastery in Burma. In 1944, at age ten, he ordained as a novice monk, and during the following decade he pursued the life of a typical scholar-novice, studying the Pāli Texts. In 1954, at age twenty, the Sayadaw received the higher ordination as a bhikkhu, continuing his studies of the Pāli Texts. In 1964, he turned his attention to intensifying his meditation practice and for the next sixteen years he made forest dwelling his primary practice, living a very simple life devoting his time to meditation and study of the Pāli Texts. In 1981, he was asked to take over abbot responsibilities of Pa-Auk Forest Monastery. Although he oversees the running of the monastery, the Sayadaw spends most of his time meditating in seclusion. Since 1983, both monastics and laypeople have been traveling to Burma to study meditation with the Sayadaw.

APPENDIX 1

Does It Matter Where You Watch the Breath?

MEDITATION USING THE BREATH IS AMONG THE MOST COMMON meditation practices. A wide range of systems and techniques exists for meditation practice, incorporating mindfulness of breathing to varying degrees, from being the entirety of the practice to having no place in it at all.

Three of the most important and detailed discourses on meditation practice are the Satipaṭṭhāna (Foundations of Mindfulness), the Ānāpānasati (Mindfulness of Breathing), and the Kāyagatāsati (Mindfulness of the Body) suttas. The Satipaṭṭhāna Sutta comprises a detailed instruction on mindfulness of every conceivable situation. The Kāyagatāsati Sutta narrows the focus to just the first section of the Satipaṭṭhāna Sutta, mindfulness of the body, and includes a section emphasizing the connection between jhāna and body awareness. The Ānāpānasati Sutta narrows the focus further, to just the breath, expanding the instructions and adding much detail.

All three of these important discourses include two terms in the opening sections, the interpretations of which contribute to the various views and disagreements on the nature of jhāna and the proper course of meditation practice. Some of the disagreements about the "correct" method of breath meditation stem from various interpretations of these two terms:

"Here a bhikkhu, gone to the forest or to the root of a tree or to an empty hut, sits down; having folded his legs crosswise, set his body erect, and established mindfulness **in front of (parimukhaṃ) him,** ever mindful he breathes in, mindful he breathes out. Breathing in long, he understands: 'I breathe in long'; or breathing out long he understands: 'I breathe out long'. Breathing in short, he understands: 'I breathe in short'; or breathing out short he understands: 'I breathe out short'. He trains thus: 'I shall breathe in experiencing **the whole body (sabbakāya)**'; he trains thus: 'I shall breathe out experiencing **the whole body**'; he trains thus: 'I shall breathe in tranquillizing the bodily formation (kāyasankhāra)'; he trains thus: 'I shall breathe out tranquillizing the bodily formation.'"

The Pāli term *parimukha* means "in front," derived from *pari,* meaning "around" or "all around," and *mukha,* meaning "the face, the mouth, an entrance or opening," or "in front of." This term can be taken literally to mean that mindfulness should be established at the area in front of the face, at the nose, or around the mouth. And although the suttas themselves are not explicit about this meaning, that is how this instruction is understood in the Visuddhimagga:

"The navel is the beginning of the wind issuing out, the heart is its middle and the nose-tip is its end. The nose-tip is the beginning of the wind entering in, the heart is its middle and the navel its end. And if he follows after that, his mind is distracted by disquiet and perturbation."[1]

"Suppose there were a tree trunk placed on a level piece of ground, and a man cut it with a saw. The man's mindfulness is established by the saw's teeth where they touch the tree trunk, without his giving attention to the saw's teeth as they approach and recede . . . so too [one] sits, having established mindfulness at the nose tip or on the upper lip, without giving attention to the in-breaths and out-breaths as they approach and recede."[2]

The term "in front" can also be taken symbolically to indicate that mindfulness should be at the forefront of one's attention, rather than as referring to a single anatomical location. According to this interpretation, it is the act of being mindful that is of primary importance, more so than the object of mindfulness or where the attention is focused. This interpretation makes particular sense in relation to the mindfulness practices other than mindfulness of breathing.

In the Mahārāhulovāda (Greater Discourse of Advice to Rāhula) Sutta, Rāhula sits in meditation and establishes mindfulness in front of him in order to contemplate the five aggregates of material form, feelings, perception, mental formations, and consciousness as not-self, after being admonished to do so by the Buddha, his father.[3] Only later, when advised by Sāriputta to develop mindfulness of breathing, does Rāhula ask for instructions in mindfulness-of-breathing meditation.

This suggests that Rāhula was not doing breath meditation when he initially established mindfulness in front of him, since he had not been instructed in the practice until he sought help later on. In this case, "in front" connotes establishing mindfulness foremost in one's mind while directing the attention to the five aggregates. However, the fact that Sāriputta advises Rāhula to develop mindfulness of breathing after the Buddha told him to contemplate the five aggregates suggests that the contemplation is fulfilled through breath meditation. This argument is strengthened by the Ānāpānasati Sutta, which declares that mindfulness of breathing fulfills the four foundations of mindfulness and the seven factors of enlightenment. This could imply that Rāhula was initially attempting to focus his mindfulness on the breath at the nose in order to contemplate the five aggregates, and only asked for guidance when Sāriputta encouraged him to continue the practice he was already engaged in.

The second term open to interpretation is "whole body." Again, the suttas do not provide us with explanatory detail. If we take the term at face value, then in this third step of the meditation instructions the awareness should open and widen to encompass the experience of the entire body while breathing. On the other hand, the Visuddhimagga understands "whole body" to mean the "whole body of the breath," meaning awareness of the entire breath from the beginning, through the middle, and to the end:

"He trains thus *'I shall breathe in . . . I shall breathe out, experiencing the whole body'*: he trains thus, I shall breathe in . . . I shall breathe out making known, making plain, the beginning, middle and end of the entire in-breath body . . . the entire out-breath body. Making them known, making them plain, in this way he both breathes in and breathes out with consciousness associated with knowledge. That is why it is said 'He trains thus "I shall breathe in . . . shall breathe out"'.[4]

This interpretation finds substantiation in the Ānāpānasati Sutta, where the breath is called "the body of breath": "I say that this is a certain body among the bodies, namely, in-breathing and out-breathing."[5] The suttas define the "bodily formation" that is tranquillized in the fourth step in the mindful-breathing sequence to be in-breathing and out-breathing,[6] further supporting the idea that when the term *body* is used, it is meant to entail mindfulness of the breath rather than of the entire body. However, in the first two steps the meditator has already developed mindfulness of the full in- and out-breath from beginning to end, so interpreting "whole body" to mean "whole body of breath" would seem to make this third step in the breathing-meditation sequence superfluous. Also, in the jhāna similes one is encouraged to knead the pleasure and rapture through the whole body. That also could be taken as an indication that one has to be aware of the whole body in order for breath meditation to lead to jhāna.

The precise meaning of these terms was surely clear at the time the suttas were composed. Although we may never be able to arrive at the original intended meaning with complete certainty, it may not matter from a practical standpoint. Mindfulness of breathing at the nose can be used either to develop one-pointed awareness or as a doorway into an all-encompassing awareness. Focusing awareness on a single point, such as the breath at the nose, can produce fixed, single-pointed concentration to the exclusion of all other experiences. The same practice can lead naturally to a spacious, inclusive awareness. If practiced with proper intention and guidance, many meditators discover that through mindfulness of the breath at one place, such as the nose, the awareness naturally opens up to include all the experiences of the body, as well as the mind and heart.

We have many examples of meditation masters attaining profound degrees of insight and liberation through a variety of practices and techniques, and instructions regarding attending to the breath vary from the nose, to the abdomen, to the chest, to whole-body breathing.

APPENDIX 2

The Four Stages of Enlightenment

ENLIGHTENMENT IN THE PĀLI TRADITION IS MEASURED IN FOUR stages. These four stages of enlightenment do not entail attaining special, transcendent states of being. Enlightenment is not measured in terms of acquiring anything at all, but in terms of gaining freedom from fetters, forces in the mind that bind beings to the cycle of births and deaths. Meditative attainments and specialized states of mind are not valued for their own sake, but only in service of eradicating the fetters. Any of the four stages may be attained in a single lifetime.

The ten fetters are as follows: (1) personality belief, (2) skeptical doubt, (3) clinging to rites and rituals, (4) sensuous craving, (5) ill will, (6) craving for fine-material existence, (7) craving for immaterial existence, (8) conceit, (9) restlessness, and (10) ignorance. The first five are known as "lower fetters" because they bind individuals to the material world. The remaining five are "higher fetters" because they bind to the deva fine-material and immaterial realms.

The first stage of enlightenment is called "stream-entry," so named because once this stage has been reached, a person is considered to have so deeply entered the stream of the Dharma that he or she is no longer liable to being reborn in an unfortunate destination, and is certain to realize Nibbāna in no more than seven more lifetimes. The stream-enterer is one who has eradicated the first three of the lower fetters.

By weakening the fourth and fifth lower fetters, in addition to having previously eliminated the first three, the Dharma practitioner reaches the second stage of enlightenment called "once-returner." The once-returner will be reborn in the sensual realm only one more time before attaining one of the final two stages of enlightenment.

With the complete destruction of the lower five fetters, the meditator is known as a "non-returner," one who will attain final Nibbāna directly after rebirth in the Pure Abodes, the highest of the deva realms. The arahant, or "worthy one," has reached the fourth and highest stage of enlightenment through the destruction of all ten fetters, is fully enlightened, and has ended the cycle of birth and death.

APPENDIX 3

Organization of the Pāli Canon

THE THERAVĀDA PĀLI CANON IS ORGANIZED INTO THREE GROUPS, known as "the three baskets": the monastic code (Pāli: Vinaya Piṭaka), the discourses (Pāli: Sutta Piṭaka), and analysis (Pāli: Abhidhamma Piṭaka). The discourses, which are of primary interest in this discussion, are teachings ascribed to the Buddha or his disciples, presented in the form of dialogues, Dhamma talks, and poems. They are organized into five nikāyas, or "collections," comprising more than ten thousand suttas. The five collections are:

1. Long Collection (Dīgha Nikāya), consisting of 34 of the longest discourses in the Sutta Piṭaka.
2. Middle Length Collection (Majjhima Nikāya), consisting of 152 medium-length discourses.
3. Grouped or Connected Collection (Saṃyutta Nikāya) consisting of several thousand relatively short suttas, which are grouped together in 56 saṃyuttas, or groups, according to theme.
4. Numerical Collection (Aṅguttara Nikāya, meaning literally "increasing by a factor": *uttara,* "progressive or further," and *anga,* "part or factor") also consisting of several thousand short suttas organized into eleven nipātas, or chapters, the book of ones, the book of twos, and so on, up through the book of elevens. Each nipāta is numbered according to the number of factors dealt with in its suttas.

5. Collection of Shorter Works (Khuddaka Nikāya) consisting of between fifteen and eighteen books (depending on the edition), including the Dhammapada, Sutta Nipāta, Jātaka, Udāna, Itivuttaka, and other lesser-known works.

APPENDIX 4

Samatha Meditation Practices of the Visuddhimagga

CHAPTER 3 BRIEFLY MENTIONED THAT FORTY PRACTICES ARE GIVEN in the Visuddhimagga for samatha meditation. These forty meditation practices are explained in more detail here.

Ten Kasiṇa Meditations

The kasiṇas are visual objects used for meditation contemplation. The Pāli term *kasiṇa* means "entire or whole." The ten kasiṇas used as meditation subjects are the four elements of earth, water, fire, and air; the four colors blue, yellow, red, and white; light; and limited space. In kasiṇa meditation, the meditator selects and prepares the appropriate contemplation object, focusing the attention on it exclusively as the preliminary sign of concentration.

An experienced meditator can directly observe the elements earth, fire, or water, as well as any of the colors as found in nature. The air kasiṇa can be apprehended by noticing the tops of trees or plants moving in the wind or the touch of it on the body. Light and limited space can be apprehended as they appear through a hole in a wall, a keyhole, or a window opening.

For all but very experienced meditators, a kasiṇa should be constructed. The constructed earth and the color kasiṇas consist of a disk about one foot in diameter with a very smooth and uniform surface. The earth kasiṇa is made of clay the color of dawn, and color kasiṇas are colored blue, yellow, red, or white, as desired. For a water kasiṇa, a bowl is filled with clear water; a fire is lit and viewed through a hole about a foot wide in a piece of leather or cloth to create a fire kasiṇa; the constructed air kasiṇa is identical for both the beginner and the experienced meditator, focusing on air in the movement of plants or as felt on the body. A light kasiṇa can be made by projecting a circle of sunlight, moonlight, or light from a lamp on a wall, and the space kasiṇa is constructed by cutting a hole in a wall or piece of material.

With the exception of the air kasiṇa, once a kasiṇa has been created, the meditator "should seat himself on a well-covered chair with legs a span and four fingers high, prepared in a place that is two and a half cubits, [that is, two and a half times elbow to fingertip] from the kasiṇa disk. For the kasiṇa does not appear plainly to him if he sits further off than that; and if he sits nearer than that, faults in the kasiṇa appear. If he sits higher up, he has to look at it with his neck bent; and if he sits lower down, his knees ache."[1]

The meditator should then gaze intently at the kasiṇa, focusing solely on the perception of the kasiṇa's fundamental quality, ignoring any other perceived attributes. For example, for a color kasiṇa, one should concentrate on the color itself, paying no heed to its size, shape, or texture. As an aid the name of the color may be repeated mentally, such as "blue, blue," "yellow, yellow," "red, red," and so on. Similarly, with the earth kasiṇa there should only be the perception of earth, ignoring its color or any irregularities in the clay, and repeating mentally "earth, earth."

Practicing in this way the kasiṇa "should be adverted to now with eyes open, now with eyes shut. And he should go on developing it in this way a hundred times, a thousand times, and even more than that, until the learning sign arises. When, while he is developing it in this way, it comes into focus as he adverts with his eyes shut exactly as it does with his eyes open, then the learning sign is said to have been produced."[2] At this point the meditator ceases gazing at the kasiṇa and continues meditation upon the purely mental learning-sign visual image.

Each of the ten kasiṇas has its own learning and counterpart signs.

The signs for the earth kasiṇa have already been given in the definition distinguishing between the learning and counterpart signs. "In the learning sign any fault in the kasiṇa is apparent. But the counterpart sign appears as if breaking out from the learning sign, and a hundred times, a thousand times, more purified, like a looking-glass disk drawn from its case, like a mother-of-pearl dish well washed, like the moon's disk coming out from behind a cloud, like cranes against a thunder cloud."[3]

For the water kasiṇa "the learning sign has the appearance of moving. If the water has bubbles of froth mixed with it, the learning sign has the same appearance, and it is evident as a fault in the kasiṇa. But the counterpart sign appears inactive, like a crystal fan set in space, like the disk of a looking-glass made of crystal."[4]

The learning sign of the fire kasiṇa "appears like [the fire to keep] sinking down as the flame keeps detaching itself. But when someone apprehends it in a kasiṇa that is not made up, any fault in the kasiṇa is evident, and any firebrand, or pile of embers or ashes, or smoke appears in it. The counterpart sign appears motionless like a piece of red cloth set in space, like a gold fan, like a gold column."[5]

The learning sign of the air kasiṇa "appears to move like the swirl of hot [steam] on rice gruel just withdrawn from an oven. The counterpart sign is quiet and motionless."[6]

For all four color kasiṇas, "any fault in the kasiṇa is evident in the learning sign. The counterpart sign appears like a crystal fan in space, free from the kasiṇa disk."[7]

For the light kasiṇa the learning sign is "like the circle thrown on the wall or the ground. The counterpart sign is like a compact bright cluster of lights."[8]

Finally, the learning sign for the limited space kasiṇa "resembles the hole together with the wall, etc., that surrounds it . . . The counterpart sign appears only as a circle of space."[9]

Once the counterpart sign has arisen through any of the ten kasiṇa practices, it should be extended, meaning it should mentally be expanded in stages to ever-larger sizes until it extends to "the verandah, the surrounding space, the monastery, the boundaries of the village, the town, the district, the kingdom, and the ocean, making the extreme limit the world-sphere or even beyond."[10] Only counterpart signs achieved through the ten kasiṇa practices need to be extended in this way.

Ten Foulness Meditations

The ten foulness meditations consist of gazing upon and contemplating corpses in various stages of decay, such as bloated, festering, dismembered, gnawed, scattered bones, and so on. These practices obviously require access to a corpse.

The Visuddhimagga devotes much attention to working with and being supported by a qualified teacher and other community members in these contemplations, since the meditator is susceptible to all sorts of mental and emotional problems when undertaking such practices.

Through continued and sustained contemplation, learning and counterpart signs arise just as with kasiṇa practice, and these can be used as doorways into jhāna. These will not be discussed in detail here.

Ten Recollections

The ten recollections are mindfulness practices in which each subject's special qualities are taken as the object of contemplation. They are divided into two groups: eight reflective exercises involving thoughtful mental contemplation, and two involving direct, nonverbal observation similar to the style of practice in the preceding kasiṇa and foulness meditations. In the eight reflective meditations, the meditator brings to mind the various qualities associated with each recollection, contemplating its essential features and distinguishing characteristics using words and images.

Each practice begins by recollecting a specific phrase that encapsulates the essence of the subject. Each element of the phrase is then reviewed in detail, beginning with an abstract comprehension of the word's meaning and progressing to deeper levels of understanding beyond the conceptual level. Concentration strengthens along with intuitive understanding as the mind remains focused on the meditation subject.

The Visuddhimagga goes into great detail on how to practice each recollection. The full range of options and instructions is beyond the scope of this book, but we will outline the basic elements for each recollection.

The first three recollections, which are known as "the three refuges" and "the three jewels," are the Buddha, the Dhamma, and the Sangha.

Recollection of the Buddha

"The Blessed One is such since he is accomplished, fully enlightened, endowed with clear vision and virtuous conduct, sublime, the knower of the worlds, the incomparable leader of men to be tamed, the teacher of gods and men, enlightened and blessed."[11]

The Visuddhimagga devotes several pages to expanding upon the Buddha's attributes given in this expression, each of which should be contemplated in detail. For example, he is accomplished because he knew, saw, understood, and penetrated all aspects of dependent origination. He is fully enlightened because he discovered and penetrated the Four Noble Truths. He fully understood the truth of suffering, he abandoned the origin of suffering (clinging), he realized the cessation of suffering, and he developed the path leading to the cessation of suffering.[12] "Blessed is a term signifying the respect and veneration accorded to him as the highest of all beings and distinguished by his special qualities."[13]

Recollection of the Dhamma

"The Dhamma is well proclaimed by the Blessed One, visible here and now, with immediate fruit, inviting of inspection, onward-leading, and directly experienceable by the wise."[14]

The Dhamma is said to be well proclaimed because it depicts a life of purity, and is good in the beginning, the middle, and the end. The Dhamma is good in the beginning because it is the discovery first made by the Buddha, because it begins with virtuous conduct, and because it is the discovery of what can be attained by one entering the path of practice upon first hearing about it. In the middle it manifests as the attainment of serenity, insight, and other signs of progress. The Dhamma ends with full enlightenment.

Recollection of the Sangha

"The community of the Blessed One's disciples has entered on the good way, the straight way, the true way, the proper way, that is to say, the Four

Pairs of Persons, the Eight Individuals; this community of the Blessed One's disciples is worthy of gifts, worthy of hospitality, worthy of offerings, worthy of reverence, as an incomparable field of merit for the world."[15]

The community of the Blessed One's disciples is the community of those who have heard the Buddha's instructions and have entered on the good way, that is, the right way of living and practice, being irreversible, in conformity with the truth, and regulated by the teachings. The way is straight, following the Middle Path between the extremes of asceticism and indulgence in sense pleasures. It is true because it has Nibbāna as its aim, and it is proper because those who follow it act virtuously.

Each pair of the Four Persons comprises those on the path toward and those who have realized each of the four stages of enlightenment. They are called "the Eight Individuals" when listed separately.

Recollection of Virtue

Whether as a layperson or a monastic, one's own virtuous living should be recollected as "untorn, unrent, unblotched, unmottled, liberating, praised by the wise, not adhered to, and conducive to concentration."[16]

For monks and nuns, virtuous living entails living in accordance with the monastic code of conduct in the Pāli Canon. For a layperson, virtue is encapsulated in the five precepts mentioned in chapter 1. In either case, virtues are untorn, unrent, unblotched, and unmottled when they are maintained well without interruption and are not affected by sense desire and aversion. As such, they are liberating, since the mind is freed from the craving that leads to clinging.

Reflecting on one's own virtue should not lead to pride or self-satisfaction, and virtue is not adhered to when these corruptions of virtue are present.

Recollection of Generosity

"It is gain for me, it is great gain for me, that in a generation obsessed by the stain of avarice I abide with my heart free from stain by avarice, and am freely generous and openhanded, that I delight in relinquishing, expect to be asked, and rejoice in giving and sharing."[17]

This recollection is intended for one who is naturally devoted to constant giving and sharing. Or, if just starting, one begins with the actual practice of generosity. Once well established in various forms of generosity, the meditator takes up the recollection using the standard formula.

Recollection of Deities

"There are deities in various realms [numerous deities and their realms are listed]. These deities were possessed of faith, virtue, learning, generosity and understanding such that when they died here they were reborn there [in whatever realm they were reborn], and such faith, virtue, learning, generosity and understanding are present in me."[18]

According to Buddhist cosmology, beings live, die, and are reborn in various forms throughout numerous realms. The deities enjoy long-lived, blissful existences in heavenly realms, but are not immortal; they have remarkable powers, but are not to be worshipped. They may possess extraordinary qualities far beyond those of ordinary humans, but are subject to the same universal laws of karma and impermanence governing human life.

The deities are taken as examples of beings who have developed their virtuous qualities to a high degree and been reborn in the heavenly realms according to their wholesome karma. The purpose of this meditation is to gain inspiration from the exalted degree of these qualities in the devas and to reflect on those same qualities in ourselves. The meditator "should possess the special qualities of faith, etc., evoked by means of the noble (Eightfold) path, and he should go into solitary retreat and recollect his own special qualities of faith, etc., with deities standing as witness."[19]

Recollection of Death

The basic, and most direct, formula to be contemplated is "Death will take place; the life faculty will be interrupted" or "Death, death." For some, meditating on this simple formula will be sufficient to arouse mindfulness of death and a sense of urgency in Dharma practice. For those who do not easily make progress with these instructions, eight ways of recollecting death are prescribed:

Death as a murderer. From the moment of birth, death stalks us as a murderer stalks his victim, never turning back until it reaches and kills us.

Death as the ruin of success. No success, fortune, or gain lasts forever. All health ends in sickness, all youth ends in aging, all life ends in death.

Death by comparison. Everyone, including those with great fame, strength, and even enlightenment, has been overtaken by death. "Death will come to me even as it did to those distinguished beings."[20]

Sharing the body with many. The body is shared with many creatures living both inside and outside the body, who are born, grow old, and die within and on us.

The frailty of life. This life is delicate and frail. It is dependent upon air and food, and can only exist within a narrow range of heat and cold. Life cannot continue if just one of these is not present in the proper amount at the proper time.

Unpredictability. Death is a certainty, but we do not know when or how it will come.

The fleeting nature of life. We cannot know if we will live long enough to take the next breath. Life may be as short as a few moments, or at most a hundred years. It is not certain if we will live long enough to chew and swallow four or five mouthfuls of food.

The shortness of the moment. In the ultimate sense, life only occurs a single moment at a time. "Just as a chariot wheel, when it rolls, rolls only on one point [where it touches the ground], and when it rests, it rests on only one point, so too, the life of living beings lasts for only a single conscious moment. When that consciousness has ceased, the being is said to have ceased."[21]

Recollection of Peace

Recollection of Peace is the last of the ten recollections, coming after Mindfulness of the Body and of Breathing. It is presented here since it is the last of the reflective contemplations.

"In so far as there are dhammas [experiences, phenomena], whether conditioned or unconditioned, fading away is pronounced the best of them, that is to say, the disillusionment of vanity, the elimination of thirst, the abolition of reliance, the termination of the ground, the destruction of craving, fading away, cessation, Nibbāna."[22]

"Peace" refers not to feeling more peaceful but to the supreme peace of Nibbāna, which is the ultimate goal of Buddhist teaching and practice.

Mindfulness of the Body

Mindfulness of the body and of breathing are the two of the ten recollection practices entailing direct perception, rather than the thoughtful reflection of the previous eight meditations.

Mindfulness-of-the-body meditation consists of the six sets of body awareness exercises from the Satipaṭṭhāna (Foundations of Mindfulness) Sutta, discussed in chapter 1. Because of the great importance mindfulness of breathing holds as both an insight and a concentration subject, it is treated separately as the tenth recollection.

The remaining five practices are mindfulness of the four postures—sitting, standing, walking, and lying down—of clear comprehension and full awareness during all activities, of parts of the body, of the body's four constituent elements, and of the nine charnel-ground contemplations.

The Visuddhimagga considers mindfulness of the four postures and of full awareness to be pure insight practices, not suitable for concentration meditation. The charnel-ground contemplations on a corpse in various stages of decay have already been covered in the foulness meditations, and mindfulness of the four elements is treated separately as the last category of these forty meditation subjects, to be discussed below. Contemplation of the parts of the body is the only remaining practice considered in the Mindfulness of the Body recollection.

"What is intended here . . . is the thirty-two aspects . . . . In this body there are head hairs, body hairs, nails, teeth, skin, flesh, sinews, bones, bone-marrow, kidneys, heart, liver, diaphragm, spleen, lungs, large intestines, small intestines, contents of the stomach, feces, bile, phlegm, pus, blood, sweat, fat, tears, grease, spittle, snot, oil of the joints, and urine."[23] This list, which the Visuddhimagga takes from the Satipaṭṭhāna Sutta, contains thirty-one parts. The brain, which was added in later Pāli literature, is said to be included with the bone marrow here. Each of the parts is described in precise detail, according to their size, shape, color, and location.

The recollection begins by reciting each of the parts sequentially in a specific order, first aloud for many repetitions, and later on mentally. Throughout the exercise close attention is given to the color, shape, location, and defining boundaries of each part. Perception of each body part begins conceptually, but should surmount the mere conceptual to direct perception of the counterpart sign, which arises in each part as the appearance of repulsiveness. Jhāna may be attained at each of the thirty-two parts.

Mindfulness of Breathing

Mindfulness-of-breathing meditation entails observing the sensations of the breath at one of two places: the tip of the nose for a long-nosed person, and the upper lip for a short-nosed person. The attention should not rest at any other place in the body, and one should not follow the flow of air away from the nose through the throat, lungs, or to the movement of the belly.

The practice is structured according to the Ānāpānasati Sutta, discussed in chapter 1, proceeding through its sixteen steps, which are divided into four tetrads. In the Visuddhimagga scheme of dividing meditation into paths of calm and insight, the first three tetrads are considered to be both calm and insight practices, while the fourth tetrad deals with insight only. The first tetrad leads to jhāna, and the remaining three tetrads refer to practice once jhāna has been achieved.

A beginner should start by counting breaths up to ten, and continue practicing in this way until concentration strengthens somewhat and mindfulness remains settled on the in- and out-breaths. At this point meditation proceeds without counting as the attention is fixed on the touch of the breath at the nose.

As practice continues the counterpart sign arises, which can be either tactile or visual:

"When he does so in this way the sign soon appears to him. But it is not the same for all; on the contrary, some say that when it appears it does so to certain people producing a light touch like cotton or silk-cotton or a draught. But this is the exposition given in the commentaries: it appears to some like a star or a cluster of gems or a cluster of pearls, to others with a rough touch like that of silk-cotton seeds or a peg made of heartwood, to others like a long braid string or a wreath of flowers or a puff of smoke, to others like a stretched-out cobweb or a film of cloud or a lotus flower or a chariot wheel or the moon's disk or the sun's disk."[24]

With the appearance of the counterpart sign the mind has attained access concentration, the hindrances are suppressed, along with any defilements, and mindfulness is well established. The attention is now turned wholeheartedly onto the counterpart sign until reaching absorption into jhāna.

Four Divine Abidings

The divine-abiding (Pāli: Brahmavihāra) meditations are recollections for cultivating wholesome, virtuous qualities of the heart and mind, as well as concentration. Also known as the four sublime states, these exalted mental states are loving-kindness, compassion, sympathetic joy, and equanimity. Loving-kindness meditation promotes welfare for oneself and others, and wards off ill will. Compassion allays suffering and is an antidote to cruelty. Sympathetic joy gladdens the practitioner and prevents boredom, while equanimity promotes neutrality toward beings and counteracts greed and resentment.

Each of the divine abidings has near enemies, corruptions that can easily be misperceived as the sublime state itself, and far enemies, which act as hindrances in direct opposition to them. The near enemy of loving-kindness is greed, since it corrupts loving-kindness with attachment; of compassion is grief, which arouses pity; of sympathetic joy is happiness tinged with attachment; and of equanimity is delusion or unknowing. The far enemies of each are ill will, cruelty, boredom, and greed and resentment, respectively.

The first three practices can lead only as far as the first three jhānas. Beyond that, the meditator must turn to equanimity practice, which can only be taken up after the third jhāna has been attained through one of the first three divine abidings, and which can only produce the fourth jhāna.

Loving-kindness (Pāli: mettā)

The practitioner wishing to pursue loving-kindness meditation should begin by reviewing the danger in hate and the advantage in patience. Then, beginning with oneself, the meditator systematically cultivates loving-kindness toward all beings by working in a prescribed order with a person dear to oneself, then someone neutral, and finally to a hostile person. Someone who has died should not be used since it is said the meditator will not be able to attain jhāna that way. A person of the opposite sex should not be used either, in order to avoid inspiring lust.

The practice begins with pervading oneself with loving-kindness by continuously repeating the phrase, "May I be happy and free from suffering" or "May I keep myself free from enmity, affliction, and anxiety and live happily."

"Even if he developed loving-kindness for a hundred or a thousand years in this way, 'I am happy' and so on, absorption would never arise. But if he develops it in this way 'I am happy. Just as I want to be happy and dread pain, as I want to live and not die, so do other beings, too', making himself the example, then desire for other beings' welfare and happiness arises in him . . . So he should first, as an example, pervade himself with loving-kindness. Next after that . . . he can recollect . . . a teacher or a preceptor . . . With such a person, of course, he attains absorption."[25]

If resentment arises when developing loving-kindness toward a hostile person, an array of practices are given as antidotes, such as bringing to mind some purified state possessed by that person; reflecting that through the countless round of births all beings have been our mothers, brothers, and so on; admonishing yourself; and so on.

The practice is maintained for each category of people until one reaches the stage of "breaking down the barrier," which is marked by unshakable, impartial, and openhearted caring. The counterpart sign arises with "breaking down the barriers," marked by impartial, openhearted caring toward all classes of beings, whether dear to oneself, neutral, or hostile.

Compassion (Pāli: karuṇā)

The practice is similar to loving-kindness meditation, except that the phrases are different and the categories of people are worked through in a different order.

One begins by reviewing the danger in a lack of compassion and the advantage in its increase. The meditator then brings to mind someone who is clearly suffering, and arouses compassion by reflecting, "This being has indeed been reduced to misery; if only he or she could be freed from suffering." If a suffering person cannot be found, then practice can begin with someone who appears to be happy and prosperous but who acts in unskillful ways, creating suffering for others or future suffering for themselves, by reflecting that "Though this poor wretch is now happy, cheerful, enjoying wealth, still for want of even one good deed done now in any one of the three doors [of body, speech, and mind] he or she can come to experience untold suffering in the states of loss." Having aroused compassion for that person in this way, practice continues progressively with the dear person, the neutral person, and then to the hostile person.

As with loving-kindness meditation, the meditator should continue until the counterpart sign appears, that is, the breaking down of barriers to compassion toward all classes of individuals.

Sympathetic Joy (Pāli: muditā)

Sympathetic-joy meditation should begin with someone who is constantly glad or for whom it is easy to feel gladness, by reflecting, "This being is indeed glad. How good, how excellent." The practice proceeds with a dear, a neutral, and a hostile person, continuing until the counterpart sign arises with breaking down the barriers.

Equanimity (Pāli: upekkhā)

Equanimity practice can only be used to attain the fourth jhāna, and one who wishes to develop it must already have reached the third jhāna through one of the previous three divine-abiding practices. Other methods of attaining the third jhāna, such as kasiṇa meditation, are not suitable here since the meditation object is dissimilar. Equanimity meditation begins by the meditator's emerging from the third jhāna and reflecting on the danger of the other three divine abidings, in that they are dependent on other beings. Then, starting with equanimity toward a neutral person, the meditator progresses to a dear person, a good companion, a hostile person, and lastly oneself, breaking down the barriers in each case until the fourth jhāna has been attained.

Four Immaterial States

These meditative states are the āruppas discussed in chapter 3: the base of boundless space, the base of boundless consciousness, the base of nothingness, and the base of neither-perception-nor-nonperception. These meditation subjects can only be taken up after attaining the fourth jhāna using any of the kasiṇas, except the limited-space kasiṇa.

One Perception

Repulsiveness in Nutriment

This contemplation is similar to the ten meditations on foulness, except that it leads only to access concentration. The practitioner reflects in various ways on the repulsiveness of food, such as the difficulty in obtaining it, the fact that it is easily spoiled, the details involved in the processes of digestion and excretion, and so on.

"When one devotes himself to this perception of repulsiveness in nutriment, his mind retreats, retracts and recoils from craving for flavors. He nourishes himself with nutriment, without vanity and only for the purpose of crossing over suffering [attaining Nibbāna] ... development of mindfulness occupied with the body comes to perfection in him ..."[26]

One Defining

The Four Elements

Meditations on the four elements—earth, air, fire, and water—were discussed previously as part of the ten kasiṇa practices. Unlike the kasiṇa practices, where the four elements were contemplated in terms of their own distinct characteristics, such as the quality of hardness for the earth element or heat for the fire element, here each part of the body is reviewed in terms of how it is related to and composed of the four elements.

This meditation may be practiced in two ways, either in brief, for a person of quick understanding, or in detail, for a person of "not over-quick understanding." Numerous very detailed practices are outlined.

For example, to begin practice in brief, one should "advert to his own entire material body and discern the elements in brief this way: "In this body what is stiffness or harshness is the earth element, what is cohesion or fluidity is the water element, what is maturing (ripening) or heat is the fire element, what is distension or movement is the air element," and he should advert and give attention to it and review it again and again as "earth element, water element" that is to say, as mere elements, not a being, and soulless."[27]

Through sustained effort, access concentration, but not absorption, arises. If meditation does not progress to this stage, a series of further practices are given in increasingly complex succession, such as reviewing each part of the body in detail and how it is composed of the four elements, or grouping various body parts together according to which element they are associated with.

NOTES

Introduction

1. MN36.30
2. MN36.38–43

Chapter 1

1. DN33.1.11(5), AN4.41
2. MN4, 19, and 36
3. MN4.28–33
4. AN9.36
5. AN6.70
6. DN29.24
7. DN2.83
8. MN77.28
9. AN6.50
10. MN14.4
11. SN22.88
12. MN30.23
13. SN45.8
14. MN29.4
15. MN29.4
16. MN113.21–29
17. MN66.21
18. AN6.50
19. AN5.24, AN7.61, AN8.81, and others
20. AN10.2
21. DN2.64

22. DN2.67
23. SN46.33
24. DN2.68
25. MN125.21
26. SN35.99
27. SN12.23
28. MN26.15–16
29. DN2.75–81, DN11, DN12, DN22.21, MN141.31, AN3.88, SN45.8
30. MN117.3, SN45.28, AN7.42. See also DN18.27.
31. See *Satipaṭṭhāna: The Direct Path to Realization* by Anālayo (Cambridge, Eng.: Windhorse Publications, 2003), pp. 73–74.
32. MN117.14
33. DN16.1.17, DN28.2, SN47.12, AN10.95, AN6.57
34. SN46.7
35. SN46.27
36. MN118.43, SN46.6
37. SN46.1
38. SN46.29
39. The Pāli term translated here as "happiness" is *sukha,* which is translated as "pleasure" in the jhāna definition.
40. DN2.75
41. MN4.22–26
42. MN10
43. DN22
44. SN47
45. See *The Buddhist Path to Awakening* by R.M.L. Gethin (Oxford, Eng.: Oneworld Publications, 2001), pp. 29–36; and *Satipaṭṭhāna: The Direct Path to Realization* by Anālayo, pp. 29–30, for discussions of why satipaṭṭhāna should be considered as referring to the act of being mindful rather than to the objects of mindfulness.
46. SN47.8
47. MN44.14, SN41.6
48. MN44.12. The Pāli term translated here as "basis of concentration" is *samādhinimitta.* A nimitta is a distinguishing mark or sign, but in this context, the term means "basis for establishing concentration" rather than "mark of concentration."

49. MN125.22–25
50. MN117.34
51. MN125.22–25
52. SN47.10
53. MN10.34, DN22.12
54. MN10.42, DN22.16
55. DN22.17–21
56. MN27.18, MN38.38, DN2.68, and others.
57. MN125.21–22
58. SN47.4
59. See Anālayo, pp. 117–18, which makes reference to versions of the Satipaṭṭhāna Sutta transmitted in other early Buddhist schools. In these, mindfulness of breathing is not the first practice, but follows mindfulness of the four postures and of all activities.
60. MN 118.15
61. SN54.8
62. SN54.8
63. The Pāli term used here, *sabbakāya,* is sometimes interpreted as referring to the "entire body of breath" rather than the literal meaning of "entire body." See appendix 1 for a detailed discussion of the usage and various interpretations of the term.

Chapter 2

1. MN36.21
2. MN108.26
3. MN108.26–27
4. MN43.19
5. SN36.31
6. MN111.4
7. AN9.35
8. MN43.20
9. MN39, MN77, MN119
10. SN21.1
11. MN44.15
12. SN36.11
13. SN12.23

14. DN2.75
15. For example, MN44 and MN117
16. SN40.1
17. MN78.13
18. MN128.31, SN43.3&12, AN8.63, DN33.1.10(50)
19. MN128.31
20. MN111.4–10
21. MN77.28
22. MN8.8, MN25.16
23. MN140.21
24. AN3.58
25. DN2.87–97, DN34.1.7, AN9.35, SN16.9
26. DN33.1.10, MN2.6, MN9.70, AN6.63, and others
27. DN2.83–86, MN77.29–30

Chapter 3

1. MN24. This list of seven stages of purification occurs only one other place in the suttas, at DN34.2.2, as part of a nine-factored list.
2. The additional details of organization come from other works, especially the Paṭisambhidāmagga, and some methods might be original to the Vism.
3. Pm 278 (taken from the Ñāṇamoli translation of the Vism, chapter VIII, note 63).
4. Vism IV,31
5. Vism III,28
6. Vism III,30
7. *Vitakka-vicāra* has been translated here as "applied and sustained thought," reflecting how the term is understood in the Visuddhimagga, as opposed to the translation in the chapter on the suttas as "thought and examination."
8. Vism IV,88
9. Vism IV,108
10. Vism IV,94
11. Vism IV,99
12. Ibid.
13. Vism IV,100

14. Vism IV,109
15. Vism IV,83
16. Vism IV,106
17. Vism IV,124–25
18. Vism XXIII,27
19. Vism IV,137
20. Vism IV,148
21. Vism IV,151
22. Vism IV,171
23. Vism IV,173
24. Vism IV,175
25. Vism IV,180
26. Vism IV,185
27. Vism IV,195
28. Vism X,5
29. Vism X,6–8
30. Vism X,12
31. Vism X,25
32. Vism X,27
33. Vism X,35
34. Vism X,32–33
35. Vism X,49–50
36. Vism X,40
37. Vism X,40–41

Chapter 4

1. MN119
2. Vism IV,175
3. SN56.1
4. MN111. Refer to MN52 and MN64 for further examples.
5. AN9.36
6. MN36.34–43
7. For example, DN2, DN3, DN4, DN8, DN10
8. MN9
9. AN4.93
10. AN4.170

11. MN149.10
12. AN2.3.10
13. AN2.17.5
14. AN4.94
15. The Pāli term is *paññā,* translated variously as discernment, wisdom, and insight.
16. Vism XXIII,18
17. For example, MN56.18, DN3.2.21, DN5.29, AN8.22
18. MN48.8–15
19. SN46.38
20. AN6.64
21. The Pāli word *nissaya,* here translated "in dependence on," suggests the idea "on the basis of." Thus the passage is explaining how the attainment of the destruction of the āsavas occurs "on the basis of" each of the jhānas and āruppas; but it is not saying, "The first jhāna is a minimum requirement for attaining destruction of the āsavas."
22. AN9.36, MN52.4, MN64.9
23. AN3.88
24. AN9.36
25. MN52
26. AN4.123
27. MN64.7–15
28. MN10.46
29. AN4.169
30. AN3.85
31. SN55.5
32. SN55.2, DN33.1.11
33. SN55.40
34. SN55.33, 55.37; AN8.49, 8.54
35. SN55.3
36. AN3.85
37. Vim 412, p. 68 of Buddhist Publication Society translation
38. Vim 430, pp. 158–59.
39. Patis 3.170
40. Patis 3.171

41. Patis 3.182
42. The asuras are powerful beings said to live in a heaven realm and are continuously clashing with the devas. Rāhu, an asura king, from time to time abducts the sun and the moon, a mythological representation of the solar and lunar eclipses.
43. AN4.50
44. MN44.12

Appendix 1

1. Vism VIII,197
2. Vism VIII,202
3. MN62
4. Vism VIII,171
5. MN118.24
6. MN44.14, SN41.6

Appendix 4

1. Vism IV,26
2. Vism IV,29–30
3. Vism IV,31
4. Vism V,4
5. Vism V,8
6. Vism V,11
7. Vism V,14
8. Vism V,23
9. Vism V,26
10. Vism IV,127
11. Vism VII,3
12. Vism VII,22–26
13. Vism VII,53
14. Vism VII,68
15. Vism VII,89
16. Vism VII,101
17. Vism VII,107
18. Vism VII,115
19. Ibid.

20. Vism VIII,24
21. Vism VIII,39
22. Vism VIII,245
23. Vism VIII,44
24. Vism VIII,214–15
25. Vism IX,10–11
26. Vism XI,26
27. Vism XI,41

GLOSSARY

Abhidhamma: highly systematized analysis of the Buddhist teachings, as preserved in the Abhidhamma Piṭaka, the third division of the Pāli Canon

abhijjhā: covetousness

abhiññā: direct knowledge, higher knowledge, supernormal powers

ānāpānasati: mindfulness of in-breathing and out-breathing

anattā: not-self

anicca: impermanent

appanā samādhi: fixed or attainment concentration. In the Visuddhimagga (term does not appear in the suttas), the concentration present during jhāna.

arahant: worthy one, a fully liberated person

arūpa: immaterial, formless

āruppa: immaterial realm, formless

āsava: taint, corruption

asura: titan

aṭṭha samāpatti: eight attainments, the four jhānas plus the four immaterial attainments

bala: power, strength

bhikkhu: Buddhist monk

bhikkhunī: Buddhist nun

bodhisatta: a being destined to become a Buddha

bojjhanga: factor of enlightenment

brahmavihāra: divine abode

brahmin: a holy person

byāpāda: ill will

cetaso: mind, heart

citta: mind
deva: celestial or heavenly being, god
dhamma (Sanskrit: *dharma*): (1) the teachings of the Buddha, (2) phenomena, (3) mind-objects, (4) states of the mind and heart
dhamma-vicaya: investigation of dhamma (phenomena, states of the mind and heart)
domanassa: grief
dukkha: suffering, pain, unreliability, unsatisfactoriness
ekaggatā: unification of mind
ekodi-bhāva: singleness of mind
iddhi: psychic power, supernormal power, spiritual power
Iddhipāda: road to power, basis for spiritual power
Indriya: faculty, list of five spiritual faculties
jhāna: (1) state of meditative absorption, (2) meditation
kalāpa: bunch, group, group of qualities of things
kāmacchanda: sensual desire
kamma: karma, volitional action
karuṇā: compassion
kasiṇa: external device to aid developing concentration
kāya: body
khandha: aggregate, group; a human being is a collection of five aggregates—form, feeling, perception, mental formations, and consciousness
khaṇika samādhi: momentary concentration. In the Visuddhimagga (term does not appear in the suttas), the concentration attained by one who does not attain jhāna, but who begins directly with insight meditation.
mettā: loving-kindness
muditā: appreciative or sympathetic joy
Nibbāna: the highest goal of the Buddha's path, liberation from suffering
nimitta: sign, mark, appearance
paññа: wisdom, discernment
pāramī, pāramitā: perfection. Later Pāli literature lists ten perfections, qualities exemplified by the Buddha. These are generosity, morality,

renunciation, wisdom, energy, patience, truthfulness, resolution, loving-kindness, and equanimity.

parikamma nimitta: preliminary sign, meditation object experienced at the beginning stages of meditation (in the Visuddhimagga only)

parikamma samādhi: initial undeveloped concentration

parimukha: in front

passaddhi: tranquillity

passati: to see, to recognize, to realize, to know

paṭibhāga nimitta: counterpart sign, sign of access concentration (in the Visuddhimagga only)

pīti: rapture

rūpa jhāna: fine-material or formal jhānas

samādhi: concentration

samatha: serenity, calm, tranquillity

samatha-yānika: one who takes calm as his vehicle, i.e., one who practices insight based on attainment of jhāna

sambojjhanga: factor of enlightenment

sammā: right, thoroughly, properly

sampasādana: inner composure, tranquillity, self-confidence, internal assurance, serene purity

sangha: Buddhist monastic community

sankhāra: formation

sati: mindfulness

satipaṭṭhāna: foundation of mindfulness

sīla: virtue, morality

suddha-vipassanā-yānika: one whose vehicle is insight. In the Visuddhimagga, one who practices insight without first attaining jhāna.

sukha: happiness, pleasure, pleasant, joy, bliss

sukkha-vipassaka: bare-insight worker. Another term for suddha-vipassanā-yānika (see above).

sutta: discourse, the first division of the Pāli Canon

Theravāda: doctrine of the elders, the school of Buddhism whose scriptural writings are preserved as the Pāli Canon

Tipiṭaka: three baskets, the Pāli Canon

uggaha nimitta: learning sign, acquired image

upacāra samādhi: access concentration
upekkhā: equanimity
vicāra: examination, sustained thought
vinaya: discipline, monastic code of conduct
vipassanā: insight
viriya: energy
vitakka: thought, applied thought

SOURCES FOR THE PĀLI TEXTS

Bhikkhu, Ṭhānissaro, trans. *Handful of Leaves.* www.sati.org. Sati Center for Buddhist Studies. Five-volume anthology from the Pāli Suttas. Available on a donation basis from the Sati Center for Buddhist Studies.

Bodhi, Bhikkhu and Bhikkhu Ñāṇamoli, trans. and ed. *The Middle Length Discourses of the Buddha.* Boston: Wisdom Publications, 1995. A translation of the Majjhima Nikāya.

Bodhi, Bhikkhu, trans. and ed. *In the Buddha's Words: An Anthology of Discourses from the Pāli Canon.* Boston: Wisdom Publications, 2005.

Bodhi, Bhikkhu, trans. *The Connected Discourses of the Buddha.* 2 vols. Boston: Wisdom Publications, 2000. A translation of the Saṃyutta Nikāya.

Fronsdal, Gil , trans. *Dhammapada.* Boston: Shambhala Publications, 2005.

Ñāṇamoli, Bhikkhu. *The Path of Purification.* Kandi, Sri Lanka: Buddhist Publications Society, 1975. Onalaska, Wash.: Pariyatti Publishing, 2003. A translation of the Visuddhimagga.

Norman, K. R., trans. *The Rhinoceros Horn and Other Early Buddhist Poems.* London: Pāli Text Society, 1985. A translation of the Sutta Nipāta.

Thera, Nyanaponika and Bhikkhu Bodhi, trans. and ed. *Numerical Discourses of the Buddha.* Walnut Creek: Alta Mira Press, 1999. An anthology of suttas from the Aṅguttara Nikāya.

Walsh, Maurice. *The Long Discourses of the Buddha.* Boston: Wisdom Publications, 1995. A translation of the Dīgha Nikāya.

CREDITS

All translations by the author, except the following, which are reprinted with permission:

MN4.22-26, MN4.28, MN10.4, MN10.46, MN14.4, MN29.4, MN30.23, MN36.30, MN36.34-43, MN36.43, MN44.12, MN64.7-15, MN113.21-29, MN117.3, MN117.14, MN117.34, MN118.15, MN118.24, MN125.21, MN125.22-25, MN149.10: © Bhikkhu Ñāṇamoli, 1995. Reprinted from *The Middle Length Discourses of the Buddha,* with permission from Wisdom Publications, 199 Elm Street, Somerville, MA 02144 USA. www.wisdompubs.org

SN12.23, SN35.99, SN36.31, SN40.1, SN45.8, SN46.7, SN46.27, SN46.29, SN46.33, SN47.4, SN47.8, SN47.10, SN54.8, SN55.3, SN55.5, SN55.40, SN56.1: © Bhikku Bodhi, 2000. Reprinted from *The Connected Discourses of the Buddha: A Translation of the Saṃyutta Nikāya,* with permission from Wisdom Publications, 199 Elm Street, Somerville, MA 02144 USA. www.wisdompubs.org

AN4.170: © Bhikku Bodhi, 2005. Reprinted from *In the Buddha's Words: An Anthology of Discourses from the Pāli Canon,* with permission from Wisdom Publications, 199 Elm Street, Somerville, MA 02144 USA. www.wisdompubs.org

DN2.64, DN2.83, DN22.17-21, DN29.24: © Maurice Walshe, 1995. Reprinted from *The Long Discourses of the Buddha,* with permission from Wisdom Publications, 199 Elm Street, Somerville, MA 02144 USA. www.wisdompubs.org

MN10.42: © Anālayo, 2003. Reprinted from *Satipaṭṭhāna: The Direct Path to Realization,* with permission from Windhorse Publications, 38 Newmarket Road, Cambridge CB5 8DT, U.K.

INDEX